REAL WORLD
VIDEO
COMPRESSION

ANDY BEACH

PEACHPIT PRESS
BERKELEY, CALIFORNIA

REAL WORLD VIDEO COMPRESSION

Andy Beach

Peachpit Press
1249 Eighth Street
Berkeley, CA 94710
510/524-2178
Fax: 510/524-2221

Find us on the Web at: www.peachpit.com

To report errors, please send a note to errata@peachpit.com

Peachpit Press is a division of Pearson Education

Senior Editor: Karyn Johnson
Developmental Editor: Stephen Nathans-Kelly
Production Coordinator: Becky Winter
Copyeditor: Kimberly Wimpsett
Proofreader: Haig MacGregor
Composition: David Van Ness
Indexer: Jack Lewis
Cover Design: Charlene Charles-Will

ISBN-13: 978-0-321-51469-1
ISBN-10: 0-321-51469-6

9 8 7 6 5 4 3 2 1

Printed and bound in the United States of America

*This book is dedicated
to my loving wife,
Lisa Weisman*

CONTENTS AT A GLANCE

TABLE OF CONTENTS

PREFACE

We humans quite like our little moving images and have found ways to move them outside of the box in our living rooms and into a variety of new frontiers. The key to successfully migrating video to each of these new places is compression technology. Digital video, compressed or otherwise, is all about bits. It seems like it should be easy to move those bits from one place to another, and yet it isn't. A myriad of little settings, tweaks, steps, and reasons make the process of moving video from one medium to another a frustrating pain in the neck. If you mess it up, the results are unwatchable at best and unplayable at worst. With so many possibilities as to what went wrong, troubleshooting becomes a prolonged guessing game, punctuated by panic-inducing checks of deadlines.

Sorry, I didn't mean to make you hyperventilate.

It's truly amazing how much video compression is going on right now. Kids with iPods are converting their DVD libraries to portable media, broadcasters are putting their prime-time episodes online for free, and telecoms are experimenting with HD video over broadband. Throw in the cell phones we carry that can easily handle video and the enormous video billboards we regularly see at sports stadiums and Times Square, and suddenly we find that there is an awful lot of video that needs compressing.

Now I'm the one hyperventilating.

WHAT THIS BOOK IS NOT

This book is decidedly not a technical tome on the nature of video compression and streaming media. I will not get into the science of encoding (well, maybe just a tiny bit), and I won't explain how committees of smart people came up with the standards we use to make this all work. Yes, I will discuss some fairly complex topics, but believe me, this is just the beginning. There is a world of math and science associated with this technology, but for the most part it doesn't mean a lick if you're in the last hour of your production, trying to figure out why your encodes are failing.

Though I'll discuss some aspects of video production, this book is not about shooting the best video possible. I have been on my fair share of shoots, but I don't feel qualified to try to tell you the best way to shoot video. Plenty of other books do that. I also will not explain how to do special effects, how to edit video better, or how to troubleshoot hardware and software.

SO, WHAT IS THE BOOK ABOUT, THEN?

This book focuses on the essential information you need to get your video online, on disc, or onto some other device. Sometimes discussions in compression get bogged down in all the options available. What I'll try to do in this book is present you with some fundamentals and some best practices.

I'll start by covering the fundamentals of video and video compression, giving you the most essential background information you'll want to know. Next we'll explore the current applications you'll most likely run across while encoding your video. I'll discuss their merits and explain the most common workflows for each. Finally, I'll discuss the most common delivery media for your compressed video and use those same applications to create some specific content for various delivery media.

My hope is that by combining the fundamental information, practical knowledge about the tools of the trade, and insight into the delivery platforms, I'll leave you well armed to tackle the variety of content that's thrown your way.

But I didn't want you to hear this just from me, so I asked a variety of friends and co-workers to contribute their own insight into the world of video compression. Their profiles are intermingled with the chapters, and although they all are involved in video compression, their professions are incredibly varied.

WHO SHOULD READ THIS

If you have ever suddenly had to add video compression to your regular work responsibilities, willingly or otherwise, then this book is for you.

Video compression, encoding, and transcoding (they are all more or less the same) used to be the exclusive province of engineers who specialized in these tasks and were worried about meeting transmission specs or addressing other technical issues. Nowadays, pretty much anyone involved in the Web, traditional film and video production, and other interactive media realms will need to know at least a little bit about compression. On top of that, the Web has created a new wave of individual publishers (you know, bloggers), some of whom are getting into the video production and distribution game.

So if you were ever disappointed (or perhaps even shocked) by the results of your video compression, then read on, and I hope you find some help.

That's not to say this book is just for newbies. Although this book lays out the fundamentals of video and video encoding, it contains a variety of work-flow suggestions and deliverable-specific information that can help even the most seasoned compressionists improve their games. If there is one thing I believe about this profession, it's that there is always something else to learn.

COMPANION WEB SITE

The exciting part about this industry is that the ways we use video keep changing. Of course, that's the problem with it, too. As soon as this book is published, some new whiz-bang cool thing will come out, and I won't have had a chance to include it. And like I mentioned, there is a wealth of specific information that I have intentionally left out of this book in the hopes of focusing on the basics.

Fortunately, we have the ever-dynamic Internet to keep us up-to-date, and this book has a companion Web site that will serve as both information spillover and a point of reference for breaking news. Visit *www.peachpit.com/ rwvideocompression/* for additional information about specific codecs, updates on the compression applications discussed in the book, and new recipes that might help you with your work. Don't just wait for the answers to come either—use the site to send in questions and comments.

About the Author

I'm no scientist or engineer. I'm just a video geek who got into compression in a big way. My perspective on the whole topic generally comes from the point of view of actually using the medium (which I think is a good thing). This means I may not have the most thorough explanation of a given issue, but I will give you the right amount of information to get your project back on track.

I got into video compression because I graduated from college and became a video editor and producer. Because I was also geeky, I was good at doing stuff other than just going to tape with the edits. When I first started, that wasn't such a big deal, but by '97 or '98, it had become a very handy talent. I've learned everything I know about compression by screwing up repeatedly and learning from my mistakes. This, like so many professions, is all about doing it and doing it again until you get it right.

Acknowledgments

I've had the privilege of meeting and working with a number of talented people in both the production and software development worlds since I decided that doing what interested me was better than finding a real job.

After 12 years on the production and interactive side of the business, I took a job as a director at Inlet Technologies, a company that creates video compression hardware and software. At first I thought Inlet hired me because I knew something about compression, but I quickly learned that everyone there had me beat, so I think they just wanted me because I think like a customer and it was easier to have me in the office than to kidnap somebody. They are a scary-smart collection of people, and I feel honored that I get to work alongside them.

But they aren't the first talented folks I've gotten to work with. Much of the video I use as examples in this book comes from the archives of Magnet Media, my previous employer and the home of Zoom In Online (*www. zoom-in.com*). Zoom In Online offers exclusive access to the latest in creative culture, entertainment, and technology through regularly published podcasts, Internet video, and blogs. All the programming on Zoom In Online features industry insiders who publish timely movie and album reviews, event coverage, and exclusive interviews with industry insiders and original programs from the world of entertainment. The site offers free RSS subscriptions to keep viewers up-to-date in various areas of the entertainment world: film/video, music/audio, Web/interactive, and photography design. There's also a special members-only section, ZIO Pro, dedicated to creative professionals that delivers current trends, best practices, job listings, professional development courses, and an award-winning library of video-based training on how to use the latest technology for better creative results.

In addition to the people profiled in the book, a variety of other real-world compressionists I know deserve heartfelt thanks. Jem Scholfield of Buttons Production loves to mull over new announcements and prognosticate their meaning with me (and he's not afraid to split a bucket of mussels and a few pints of beer). David Randolph (now of Revision 3) has answered a variety of Avid- and SAN-related questions for me over the years, and both Alex Moseman and Dylan Lorenz have provided a wealth of workflow ideas over the past few years. Bruce Bowman, Bob Donlon, and Kristen Jiles from Adobe Systems all still take my calls, as dumb as the questions occasionally are, as do Brian Hoffman, Dennis Backus, Glenn Bulycz, Fritz Ogden, Thuy-an Julien, Patty Montesion, and Anne Renehan from Apple, Inc.

I also sorely need to thank the nice folks at Peachpit Press who have patiently waited for me to complete this book. I met Mary Sweeney and Hannah Latham while working on another project, and they were nice enough to introduce me to Karyn Johnson, who helped make this book a reality. Special bonus thanks goes to Stephen Nathans-Kelly for holding my hand during this process and making me sound like I know what I'm talking about. Brian Hoffman of Apple, Inc. served as my technical editor and helped make sure I wasn't lying anywhere. Thanks also to Jan Ozer of Doceo Publishing for his contributions in Chapter 6.

And, of course, none of this would have been possible at all without the love and support of my wife, Lisa Weisman, who is not only excited and proud of me for writing this book also sick to death of me explaining "codecs," and whatever else it is I do, and is glad I found another audience to pour this all out on. She also wishes I'd write a book on (or at least explain) why TiVo insists on taping *The Simpsons* and cooking shows we never watch yet can't remember to tape *Best Week Ever* and *The L Word* consistently. Sorry, darling, some things are just going to have to remain a mystery…

CHAPTER ONE

Understanding Video and Audio

Video compression is one of the linchpins of the production world. It is the quiet savior (and killer) of projects every day and is a process that, if done correctly, goes unnoticed. When was the last time you watched a TV show and marveled at how great the compression was? Bad compression, by contrast, is unmistakable and can render almost any video unwatchable.

The primary function of video compression is fairly straightforward: to conform the video to the desired delivery method, whether TV, DVD, the Internet, your iPod, or your cell phone. The difficulty is trying to work within the technical specifications required and the limitations of the delivery medium to provide an audiovisual experience that's satisfying to the end user. If you're delivering your content over the Internet, for example, you need to consider file-size issues. You might have the greatest film of all time, but if it's so big nobody can actually download it, then who exactly will be watching this masterpiece? Likewise, if your content will be broadcast on TV, you need to guarantee all the fields and frames of your edited, compressed program are still intact after the lengthy creation process.

But now I'm just getting ahead of myself. You see, there are some fundamentals at play within any discussion of video that are important to be aware of before delving into the intricacies of video compression. If you have worked with video for a long time, these are all familiar concepts. In fact, you most likely don't even think of them consciously in your everyday work. If you are new to video, getting a foundation in the basics of video will make solving your next compression problem considerably easier.

Thank You, Philo T. Farnsworth

The first demonstration of the technology that gave rise to modern TV and video occurred on September 27, 1927, in San Francisco through the efforts of Philo T. Farnsworth, who had dreamed up the idea as a 14-year-old boy in Rigby, Idaho.

There were, of course, many other individuals and corporations involved in creating and refining Farnsworth's electronic TV, but the essential idea of video came from this one somewhat-forgotten young inventor. Farnsworth's ideas still are at the core of video technology today, despite the radical evolutionary leaps the technology has taken in the past 80-plus years.

Philo Facts

- The first image transmitted was a dollar sign.
- The transmission was comprised of 60 horizontal lines.
- Farnsworth developed the dissector tube—the basis of all tube-based TVs.
- He won an early patent for his image dissection tube; he lost later patent battles to RCA.
- He invented more than 165 different devices, including equipment for converting an optical image into an electrical signal, an amplifier, a cathode ray, vacuum tubes, electrical scanners, electron multipliers, and photoelectric materials.

ELEMENTS OF VIDEO

Unlike film, which is a projected image, *video* is an electronic signal. Though the term *video* originally was used to describe any signal broadcast (or *televised*) to a TV set, it has been more broadly redefined over time to encompass any images displayed electronically (such as those on video billboards, cell phones, ATMs, and so on).

Video has become a pervasive part of our lives, particularly since computers (and their video displays) came along. We use video daily for our interactions, for our entertainment, for our communication, and for tasks as simple as taking money out of the bank. The technology has shifted so much that we now regularly see video on the nightly news that was shot by citizens on their cell phones. As our uses of video have evolved, the technology that supports it has changed as well.

Frames and Fields

When a group of sequential images is displayed in rapid succession, an amazing phenomenon occurs. Instead of perceiving each individual picture, humans see smoothly moving animation. This phenomenon is known as *persistence of vision*, and it is the basis for how film and video work. The number of pictures shown per second is called the *frame rate* (seconds is the most common measurement of the frame rate, but not the only one). It can take as few as about 8 frames per second (fps) for the viewer to perceive smooth motion; however, the viewer will also detect a distinct flicker or jerkiness. To avoid that flicker between frames, you generally need a frame rate greater than 16 frames per second (though this is a subjective opinion, and many believe you need 24–30 fps or more in order to completely remove the flicker). The faster the motion you are attempting to re-create, the more frames you need to keep that motion smooth. Modern film has a frame rate of 24 fps, and TV has a frame rate of approximately 30 fps (29.97 fps) in the United States, Japan, and other countries that use the National Television Standards Committee (NTSC) standard. Phase-Alternating Line (PAL) and Sequentiel Couleur Avec Memoire (SECAM) are the other standards, and they use approximately 25 fps.

A frame can be presented to a viewer in two ways: *progressive* or *interlaced scanning*. You are probably more aware of this than ever before as we move toward high-definition TV (HDTV). If you have ever seen an HDTV's specs referred to as 1080i or 720p, the *i* and *p* stand for interlaced and progressive, respectively. (The 1080 and 720 represent horizontal lines of resolution; more on that later.)

Interlaced scanning was developed in the early 1930s as a way of improving the image quality on cathode-ray tube (CRT) monitors (basically every TV you owned until plasma and LCD TVs emerged). Inside the tube, an electron beam scans across the inside of the screen, which contains a light-emitting phosphor coating. These phosphors had a very short persistence, meaning the amount of time they could sustain their illumination was short (today's computer CRT monitors tend to have a longer persistence). In the time it took the electron beam to scan to the bottom of the screen, the phosphors at the top were already going dark. To solve this problem, the early TV engineers designed an interlaced system for scanning the electron beam. With an interlaced system, the beam scans only the odd-numbered lines the first time and then returns to the top and scans the even-numbered lines.

These two alternating sets of lines (as shown in **Figure 1.1**) are known as the *upper* (or odd) and *lower* (or even) fields in the TV signal. So, a TV that displays 30 fps is actually displaying 60 fps—two interlaced images per frame.

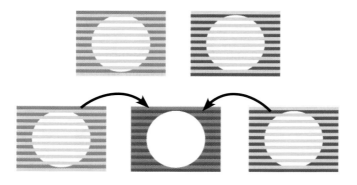

Figure 1.1 With interlaced video, the system scans the odd-numbered lines and then the even-numbered lines, combining fields to produce a complete frame. It takes both fields of the interlaced image to make a whole picture.

Benefits of Interlacing

NOTE It may seem strange to refer to your TV signal in terms of bandwidth, but that is exactly what it is. In terms of broadcast television, bandwidth is measured in hertz, while bandwidth for Web video is measured in bits.

All video systems have trade-offs, such as quality for file size or bits appropriated to video for those available for audio. One of the most important factors to consider is bandwidth, measured in megahertz for analog video or in bit rate for digital video (DV). The greater the bandwidth, the more expensive and complex the infrastructure needs to be, everything from the camera you capture on to the monitors the video is displayed on after transmitting the signal. Interlaced video reduces the signal bandwidth by a factor of 2 for a given line count and refresh rate.

A higher bandwidth can provide an interlaced video signal with twice the display refresh rate for a given line count (versus progressive scan video), which reduces flicker on CRT monitors. This higher rate improves the portrayal of motion because the position of the object in motion is rendered and updated on the display more often.

Problems Caused by Interlacing

There are, of course, disadvantages to working with interlaced images. Interlaced video is designed to be captured, transmitted, stored, and displayed in the same interlaced format. Because each interlaced video "frame" is composed of two fields that are captured at different moments in time, interlaced video frames will exhibit motion artifacts when both fields are combined and displayed at the same moment.

On the whole, the interlaced format is gradually being replaced by *progressive* video (where each captured image is rendered as a complete frame, rather than two fields). Even camcorders built to acquire only interlaced images are increasingly being equipped with faux-progressive modes that create composite frames at half the original refresh rate in-camera. All modern computers use progressive scan for video output, and the newer video displays, such as liquid crystal display (LCD) and plasma, are designed as progressive scan monitors, illuminating every horizontal line of video with each frame. If these progressive scan monitors display interlaced video, the resulting display can suffer from reduced horizontal resolution or motion artifacts, as shown on the left in **Figure 1.2**. These artifacts may also be visible when interlaced video is displayed at a slower speed than it was captured, such as when video is shown in slow motion.

Because modern computer video displays are progressive scan systems, interlaced video will have visible artifacts when it is displayed on computer monitors. Because most video editing is now done on computers, this disparity between computer video display systems and TV signal formats means that the video content being edited cannot be viewed properly unless separate video display hardware, such as a standard NTSC monitor, is utilized. Fortunately, most professional editing software and systems support previewing on external monitors for exactly this purpose.

Figure 1.2 Interlaced image (two fields) on the left; the same exported frame after deinterlacing on the right.

To minimize the artifacts caused by interlaced video display on a progressive scan monitor, most video-editing solutions feature deinterlacing filters. *Deinterlacing* is the process of converting those interlaced fields into a non-interlaced form sequence of frames, as shown on the right in Figure 1.2. This process is not perfect, and it generally results in a lower resolution, particularly in areas with objects in motion. The process typically requires the use of *temporal interpolation*, which is a fancy term for guessing where motion will occur and then applying blending and motion correction to smooth out the action taking place in the image. Deinterlacing systems are integrated into progressive scan TV displays in order to provide the best possible picture quality for interlaced video signals.

Interlacing also introduces a potential problem called *interline twitter* (also referred to as *moiring*). This aliasing effect shows up only under certain circumstances, when the image contains vertical detail that approaches the horizontal resolution of the video format. For instance, a person on TV wearing a shirt with fine dark-and-light stripes may appear on a video monitor as if the stripes on the shirt are "twittering." TV professionals are trained not to wear patterned clothing to avoid this problem. High-end video cameras can now also apply filters to the vertical resolution of the signal in order to prevent possible problems with moiring.

Finally, all video delivered over the Internet, either via streaming or via progressive download (more on these delivery methods in Chapter 2), is compressed and served in progressive format. Although opinions vary about whether it's necessary to shoot in progressive format or simply deinterlace your interlaced video during the editing process to produce effective Web video, the video must be in progressive format before it's delivered via the Web, as well as on mobile devices.

Progressive Scan Video

In progressive scan video, the entire video frame is captured in one go, rather than in two interlaced fields. Progressive scanning has many advantages over interlacing, in that it avoids "line twitter" and other complications. However, to deliver the same smoothness of motion, you need twice as much bandwidth to broadcast a progressive signal (although when played back, the progressive image would also be a slightly higher resolution than the interlaced one). **Figure 1.3** shows the difference between interlaced and progressive frames.

Figure 1.3 Note how much smoother the motion is in the progressive image (on the top) than in the interlaced image (bottom).

As the ball moves across the screen in Figure 1.3, the interlaced image (bottom) has to display fields that are slightly out of sync (because the ball is moving constantly). This can lead to slight distortions or other poor image qualities. The progressive image (top), by contrast, shows a complete frame each time, so the image quality will be improved and the motion smoother, though you are using more bandwidth in order to transmit the image.

Progressive video has superseded interlaced in much of the video world for a number of reasons. For one, most modern TV technologies are inherently progressive. As many manufacturers stop making traditional CRT-based monitors, newer display technologies such as digital light projection (DLP), plasma, and LCD are taking over.

Transmission technologies are also changing. When all TV was broadcast via analog signals, interlaced video provided an efficient lower-bandwidth way to deliver quality images and smooth motion. But now, as digital broadcasting and digital delivery (over Internet, satellite, cable, or via optical disc) take over, progressive video is more efficient. Plus, since consumer TVs are following the trend of progressive scanning started by computer monitors and higher-end wall displays, a workflow that maintains that standard makes the most sense.

Resolutions

The quality of the images you see in film and video is not based just on the number of frames you see per second or on the way those frames are composed (full progressive frames or interlaced fields). The amount of information in each frame, or *image resolution*, is also a factor. In **Figure 1.4**, you can see that image resolution varies greatly for different screen types. Standard-definition TVs are represented by the pink area (720 by 480), while modern high-definition TV falls into one of the two larger areas, either 1080p (1920 by 1080) or 720p (1280 by 720).

Figure 1.4 Here are some of the more common video image resolutions used, across TVs, DVDs, computers, the Internet, and handheld devices. The first number (across the top) denotes the width of the image as measured in pixels. The second number (on the right) is the height of the image, also in pixels.

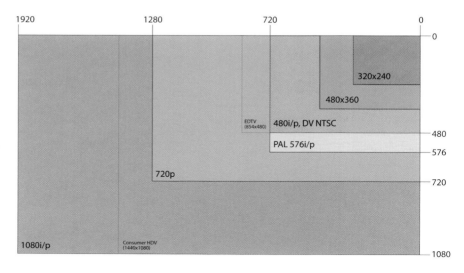

NOTE Why are there two different aspect ratios for SD? This has to do with the pixel aspect ratio, which you'll learn about in Chapter 2 (see "Square and Nonsquare Pixels").

The resolution of analog video is represented by the number of scan lines per image, which is actually the number of lines the electron beam draws across the screen or vertical resolution.

The resolution for digital images, on computer displays and digital TV sets, for example, is represented by a fixed number of individual picture elements (pixels) on the screen and is often expressed as a dimension: the number of horizontal pixels by the number of vertical pixels. For example, 640 by 480 and 720 by 486 are full-frame SD resolutions, and 1920 by 1080 is a full-frame HD resolution.

Vertical-Line Resolution for NTSC and PAL

The NTSC format is based on 525 vertical lines of resolution, displayed as two interlaced fields. However, some of these lines are used for synchronization and blanking, so only 486 lines are actually visible in the *active* picture area. (All video—not just NTSC—consists of more information than the visible content of the frame. Before and after the image are lines and pixels containing synchronization information or a time delay. This surrounding margin is known as a *blanking interval*.)

The PAL format is based on 625 vertical lines of resolution, displayed as two interlaced fields. As with NTSC, some of these lines are used for synchronization and blanking, so only 576 lines are actually visible in the active picture area.

Standard Resolutions in NTSC Broadcast TV

- **480p**: 480 lines of vertical resolution, scanned progressively
- **720p**: 720 lines of vertical resolution, scanned progressively
- **1080i**: 1080 lines of vertical resolution, interlaced

Aspect Ratio

The width-to-height ratio of an image is called its *aspect ratio*. Keeping video in the correct aspect ratio is one of the more important parts of video compression. As we scale the video to different sizes to accommodate different screens and resolutions, it is easy to lose the relationship between the original height and width of the image. When this happens, the distorted image can become distracting, even impossible to watch.

The 35mm still photography film frames on which motion picture film was originally based have a 4:3 (width:height) ratio, which is often expressed as a 1.33:1 or 1.33 aspect ratio (multiplying the height by 1.33 yields the width).

From the beginnings of the motion picture industry until the early 1950s, the 4:3 aspect ratio was used almost exclusively to make movies and to determine the shape of theater screens. When TV was developed, existing camera lenses all used the 4:3 format, so the same aspect ratio was chosen as the standard for the new broadcast medium. Today, we commonly refer to the 4:3 format as *full-screen* TV.

In the 1950s, the motion picture industry began to grow concerned over the impact of TV on their audience numbers. In response, the movie studios introduced a variety of enhancements to provide a bigger, better, and more exciting experience than viewers could have in their own living rooms. The most visible of these was a wider image. Studios produced wide-screen films in a number of "scope" formats, such as Cinemascope (the original), Warnerscope, Technicscope, and Panascope.

One major problem with these wide-screen formats is they don't translate well to TV. When wide-screen films are shown on standard TVs, the sides of the image are typically cut off to accommodate the 4:3 ratio of

TV, as shown on the left in **Figure 1.5**. This process is known as *pan and scan* because the focus of the image is moved around based on the action onscreen. To solve this, studios often use *letterboxing*—black bars positioned above and below the wide-screen image—to present the entire image as originally intended, as shown on the right in Figure 1.5.

Figure 1.5 Here's a wide-screen image cropped to 4:3 on the left, with the entire frame restored in letterbox on the right.

Why 16:9?

Dr. Kerns Powers of the David Sanroff Research Center in Princeton, New Jersey, a leading research lab on the advancement of TV, studied all the major aspect ratios in popular use and mapped them together. He then discovered something interesting. If he took a rectangle of a certain proportion and scaled it two different ways, he could encompass both the width and the height of all the other aspect ratios. That magic rectangle had the proportions of 16 units wide by 9 units high, or 16:9 (**Figure 1.6**). Because of this discovery, 16:9 was adopted as the new aspect ratio standard for HDTV, and most HDTV-capable TV sets have been designed with 16:9 screens.

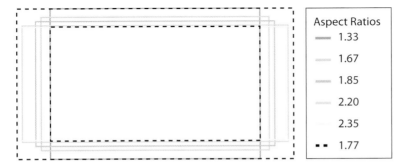

Aspect Ratios
━━ 1.33
── 1.67
▬▬ 1.85
── 2.20
2.35
▪▪ 1.77

Figure 1.6 Kern's approach to solving the aspect ratio problem was to take all the popular aspect resolutions of the day and lay them over each other. Upon doing so, he discovered all could be encompassed within a 16:9 rectangle.

The adoption of HDTV is driving us to migrate from 4:3 TVs to a newer wide-screen TV format. The aspect ratio of wide-screen TV is 16:9 (1.78), which is well suited for the most-popular film aspect ratio of 1.85. **Table 1.1** shows the range of current and emerging video formats, as well as their aspect ratios, resolutions, frame rates, and bit rates (where applicable).

Table 1.1 Modern Video Formats and Aspect Ratios

Format	Aspect Ratio	Horizontal Resolution (Pixels/Line)	Vertical Resolution (Scan Lines)	Frame Rate	Bit Rate (Megabits/ Second)
NTSC (United States, Canada, Japan, Korea, Mexico)	4:3	330	525 (480 visible)	30i	N/A
PAL (Australia, China, most of Europe, South America)	4:3	330	625 (576 visible)	25i	N/A
SECAM (France, Middle East, much of Africa)	4:3	330	625 (576 visible)	25i	N/A
				24p	18 Mbps
HDTV	16:9	1920	1080	30p	18 Mbps
				30i	18 Mbps
				24p	8 Mbps
HDTV	16:9	1280	720	30p	10 Mbps
				60p	18 Mbps
				24p	3 Mbps
SDTV	16:9	720	483	30p/30i	4 Mbps/4 Mbps
				60p	8 Mbps
				24p	3 Mbps
SDTV	4:3	720	486	30p/30i	4 Mbps/4 Mbps
				60p	7 Mbps
				24p	3 Mbps
SDTV	4:3	640	480	30p/30i	3 Mbps/3 Mbps
				60p	7 Mbps

Much of the production and postproduction equipment we use today attempts to acquire and output video to these standards. New media video options, such as cell phones and Web sites, have very different format needs and do not have as uniformed, standardized specifications.

Analog vs. Digital

As noted earlier in this chapter, a video signal is either analog or digital. An analog signal (**Figure 1.7**) is a continuously varying voltage that appears as a waveform when plotted over time. Individual lines of the video are stored with timing information to allow the receiver (your TV) to reassemble the information correctly.

Figure 1.7 Here's a rough comparison of analog (top) and digital (bottom) signals.

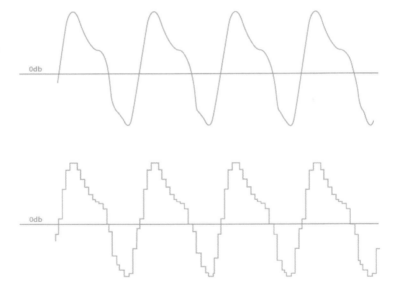

A digital signal, on the other hand, is a numerical representation of an analog signal. This means a digital signal is really a stream of *bits* (data stored as a long list of binary numbers). Each number in the list is a snapshot (called a *sample*) of the analog signal at any one point in time. The sample rate of a digital stream is the number of snapshots per second.

Digital has a number of advantages over analog. One of the most important is the quality you get when reproducing content—known as *fidelity*. An analog device, like a VCR, simply renders the variations in voltage as sound or pictures but has no way of distinguishing between the original signal and voltage that comes from electrical interference (such as a power line). Electrical interference or noise can come from an external source, from the tape, or from components in a recorder or the TV itself. When you duplicate a tape, the noise recorded on the original tape is added to the new tape. If you were to then duplicate the new tape, noise from the two previous tapes would be added to the third tape, and so on; each copy made adds to the loss in fidelity—known as *generation loss*—from the original.

With digital, the signal recorded on a tape consists of nothing more than a string of 1s and 0s that a digital player converts to numbers and then to sounds or pictures. Because a digital player reads only 1s and 0s, it can more easily discriminate between the original signal and noise. So, you can transmit and duplicate a digital signal as often as you want with no (or very little) loss in fidelity.

How Compression Works

At its most basic level, video compression works by analyzing the content of every frame and figuring out how to re-create it using less information (the technological equivalent of paraphrasing). This feat is accomplished by *codecs*—shorthand for *co*mpression/*dec*ompression algorithm—which address the problem in various ways. Let's say you have an entire black frame of DV-quality video (say, before your content has started); all the codec has to remember is the phrase "every pixel in this frame is the same shade of black." That's a lot less data than writing "0, 0, 0" 345,600 times (that's 720 by 480 for those of you following along).

But most video isn't just one solid color, is it? So, a codec has to look at where the values begin to differ within the frame—borders between light and dark shades, for instance—and describe those values more efficiently. It does this by dividing the scene into groups of pixels, called *macroblocks*, and representing them with numbers that can re-create the patterns within them (this is the foundation of Discrete *Cosine* Transform codecs, such as DV and MPEG, which are covered in more detail in "Lossless and Lossy Compression," later in this chapter). **Figure 1.8** shows an example of a macroblock grid.

Figure 1.8 Macroblocks represent the ability of codecs to break the image into a grid or into groups of pixels that are located near each other in order to process them more efficiently. Certain codecs have the ability to divide macroblocks into smaller groups called *partitions*.

So, now the codec has broken down the image into groups of blocks, from frame to frame (remember, this is all happening over time). With information about preceding frames registered in these blocks, the codec needs to record only the *differences* within those blocks, rather than the entire frame, to construct the complete frame. This works extremely efficiently in video with little or no motion—such as in an interview scene or in static titles.

Despite the complexity of this process, it's an established approach and works very well. But it doesn't give a good enough compression ratio to reduce high-definition video to manageable file sizes. This is where time travel comes in handy. You've just learned that video compression works by looking for easily describable features within a video frame. Very little information may need to be carried forward from frame to frame in order to render the entire image. However, in video with lots of motion, such as footage shot with handheld cameras or clips showing explosions, more pixels change from frame to frame (as shown in **Figure 1.9**), so more data must be passed along as well.

Figure 1.9 The sequence on top, with lots of motion and little redundancy, is more challenging to compress than the sequence on the bottom, which changes relatively little from frame to frame.

In the top set of frames, the football player is moving across the screen, and the camera is tracking his movements. This means virtually every pixel is changing from frame to frame as the sequence progresses, making it difficult to make a high-quality compression of it without using a lot of data. The bottom sequence, on the other hand, would compress more efficiently. The camera is locked down, and very little in the frame is changing except the motion path of the biker as he jumps the ramp.

That's how compression works in the most general terms, but there is of course a great deal more specific terminology used to describe how and what is occurring in the compression process. It's important to understand some of these terms described in the next sections, and how they may affect your production, the actual compression and delivery, or the archival process you might use with your video content. You don't necessarily need to be able to recite verse on the topic, but you should be able to identify the words when they come up. The more compression you do, the more they will come up in the context of your work, and being able to use them correctly can only help you.

Lossless and Lossy Compression

All the codecs I'm talking about in this book (as well as all the ones I don't talk about) are either lossless or lossy. Just like they sound, *lossless* video codecs are ones that, when decompressed, are a bit-for-bit perfect match with the original. Although lossless compression of video is possible, it is rarely used. This is because any lossless compression system will sometimes result in a file (or portions thereof) that is as large as or has the same data rate as the uncompressed original. As a result, all hardware used in a lossless system would have to be able to run fast enough to handle uncompressed video, which eliminates all the benefits of compressing the video in the first place. For example, digital videotape can't vary its data rate easily, so dealing with short bursts of maximum-data-rate video would be more complicated than something that was fixed at the maximum rate all the time.

With *lossy* compression, on the other hand, compressing data and then decompressing the data you retrieve postcompression may well be different from the original, but it is close enough to be useful in some way. Lossy compression is the most common method used to compress video, especially in preparing for final delivery such as on DVD, the Web, or mobile devices.

What Should You Remember About Lossy and Lossless?

Just keep in mind as you are working on your video projects that video can be stored as both lossless and lossy. Lossless may or may not come into play during your actual production. If it does, you will need some fairly powerful (and expensive) equipment to store enough of it and play it back fast enough. Even if you are using lossy compression in your production, it is still probably a higher quality (and higher data rate) than the finished product is going to be. Something that is being delivered as a finished project is probably a lossy format. Remember that this doesn't mean the quality is lower, just that the data making up the image isn't as large.

Spatial (DCT) and Wavelet Compression

NOTE DCT-based codecs are discussed further in Chapter 3.

Now that I've established the lossless/lossy distinction, I'll move on to explaining two other types of codecs, spatial and wavelet-based codecs. Spatial compression is the basis for what I described earlier as a general description of how video compression works—the frame-by-frame removal of redundant material over time. Discrete Cosine Transform (DCT) is a form of spatial compression that is always lossy.

Wavelet-based video compression is a more modern form of compression that's well suited for images and video, but which is less commonly used. Wavelet compression can be either a perfect, lossless data compression or a lossy compression, unlike DCT compression. Wavelet-based codecs are fewer and further between than their DCT-based counterparts; the files created with them are often much larger, and they typically take more processor power to play back. Thus, they're less suitable for common video applications and platforms. One example of a wavelet video codec is JPEG 2000, considered an excellent intermediate (or *mezzanine*) format.

What makes JPEG 2000 better than DCT-based codecs? Three things:

- **Superior compression performance:** At high bit rates, where artifacts become nearly imperceptible, JPEG 2000 has little fidelity over other codecs; however, at lower bit rates, JPEG 2000 has a much greater advantage.

- **Lossless and lossy compression:** Unlike DCT-based codecs, wavelet codecs can be both lossless and lossy, allowing for a broader range of options when working with video.

- **Side channel spatial information:** Wavelet codecs fully support transparency and alpha channels.

We'll look at more examples of wavelet-based codecs in Chapter 3.

What Should You Remember About Spatial and Wavelet Compression?

Spatial compression, specifically DCT compression, is much more common than wavelet compression, though wavelet will continue to increase in popularity. For the most part, you won't need to concern yourself with keeping track of whether you are using one or the other in your workflow. However, since spatial is much more pervasive now, you want to make sure you are delivering content to others in such a codec.

Quantization

The use of both DCT- and wavelet-based video compression involves quantization. *Quantization* is the process of approximating a continuous range of values by a relatively small set of discrete symbols or integer values; in other words, it's a way of mathematically finding an efficient way to describe all the pixels in an image.

Quantization plays a major part in lossy data compression and can be viewed as the fundamental element that distinguishes lossy data compression from lossless data compression.

What Should You Remember About Quantization?

Quantization is used as a measurement of quality when speaking about video. The lower the number, the better the quality of that image.

Interframe and Intraframe Compression

Earlier in this chapter, I described compression as being dependent on the ability to keep track of how the pixels evolve frame by frame over time. Interframe and intraframe are ways of describing how that compression relates the various frames of the video to one another.

With *interframe*, the most common method compares each frame in the video with the previous one. Since interframe compression copies data from one frame to another, if the original frame is simply cut or lost (either through editing or dropped during broadcast), the following frames cannot be reconstructed properly. Only video ready to distribute (and no longer edited or otherwise cut) should be compressed in an interframe format.

Some video formats such as DV, however, compress each frame independently using *intraframe* compression. Editing intraframe-compressed video is similar to editing uncompressed video, in that to process the video, the editing system doesn't need to look at any other frames to decode the information necessary to construct the frame at hand.

Another difference between intraframe and interframe compression is that with intraframe systems, each frame uses a similar amount of data. In most interframe systems, however, certain frames (called *I-frames*) don't copy data from other frames and so require much more data to create than other nearby frames. See Chapter 2 for more information on the types of frames that exist, including I-frames.

It is now possible for nonlinear editors such as Apple Final Cut Pro and Adobe Premiere Pro to identify problems caused when I-frames are edited out while other frames need them. This has allowed newer formats such as high-definition video (HDV), which uses a version of the MPEG-2 format, to be used for editing without requiring conversion to all I-frame intermediate codecs. However, this process demands a lot more computing power than editing intraframe-compressed video with the same picture quality because the processor is constantly looking to other frames to find the information needed to re-create the frame the user wants to edit.

What Should I Remember About Interframe and Intraframe?

Interframe compression works well for video that will simply be played back by the viewer but can cause problems if the video sequence needs to be edited. Video that is still in production and therefore may need to be edited or otherwise cut should be compressed in an intraframe method (such as MPEG-2 or DV).

AUDIO COMPRESSION

With all this talk of video compression, it's easy to forget that video has audio with it almost all the time. In fact, many filmmakers will tell you that audio is more important than the visuals in the film-watching experience. Certainly it's no less important, though the process for capturing and compressing it is less complex, only because there is less data present to work with.

The term *compression* has several meanings in audio, so it's good to be aware of that, especially when speaking with an audio professional. There is lossy data compression (just like I've been discussing for video), level compression, and limiting. I will touch on compression and limiting a bit in Chapter 4 as part of the preprocessing techniques for audio.

As with video compression, both lossy and lossless compression algorithms are used in audio compression, lossy being the most common for everyday use (such as with MP3). In both lossy and lossless compression, information redundancy is reduced, using methods such as coding, pattern recognition, and linear prediction to reduce the amount of information used to describe the data.

The compression of audio can quickly go too far, however, and the results are quite noticeable, especially in music, which has a more dynamic sound than spoken words. Music is similar to high-motion video; with more action in the content, the compressors have to keep track of more information continuously. In a monologue, by contrast, where much less is happening, less data is needed to capture what is happening. When very dynamic audio is restricted to too few bits to re-create it, the results sound distorted—either tinny or degraded by pre-echo or an absence of bass.

As mentioned earlier, good audio compression is just as important as video compression, and with the rise in popularity of podcasting, many people have come to pay attention to it much more than they have in the past. The key to good audio, perhaps even more than video, is to acquire good source material.

Evaluating Video for Compression

You've spent the better part of this chapter looking at the theoretical side of video and video compression. With that out of the way, in this section you'll put theory into practice and evaluate the video you are working with to determine, at a high level, how well it will compress. Then, throughout the book, you'll learn the steps you will need to take to compress it.

This is going to sound ridiculous, but you really need to sit down and watch anything you are planning to compress. I have neglected to do this at times—I get so busy with my work that if I'm handed a tape to encode or shown a clip in Final Cut Pro waiting to be exported, I instantly dive into the settings and all the "mathy" bits of encoding without ever looking to see just what the video is.

Simple issues of video quality that you can judge only with your own eye, as well as with practical knowledge of the source material, are as important as how well you know and use the technology in many cases. Before you get into the nitty-gritty of your technology-specific compression choices, knowing what you are encoding, how you want it to look, and what you want to do with it after it's encoded will help you target the settings and filters you apply in order to get the highest-quality video possible at the best file size. Generally speaking, there are three primary questions I ask myself and others when I am compressing a video. If I can answer these questions, I can provide a better file.

How Was the Video Shot?

Decisions about how to compress something go back as far as how the video was originally acquired. Factors that will affect how it gets compressed can be broken down into two main categories: equipment and production. Equipment issues include the types and quality of the cameras used to capture the video—the more professional-grade the equipment was, typically the better the source footage you are compressing.

Equipment-Related Issues to Keep in Mind

Was the video shot with a professional video camera or a consumer-level one?

What format was it captured in?

Was the audio mixed or wild?

Was there professional lighting, or was ambient used?

Production-Related Issues to Keep in Mind

Is the video image static or in motion?

Was it shot interlaced or progressive?

Is the camera movement smooth or jerky?

Is the video high- or low-contrast?

Are there lots of wide shots, or is it mostly close-up shots?

How Was It Edited?

After the video is in the can, how was it handled in postproduction? Editing styles vary greatly, depending on the content, the desired finished product, and the actual editor. Certain types of editing lend themselves more naturally to a type of video that will more easily compress than others. Being able to identify the differences between these allows you, the compression-ist, to devote the necessary time to the right files (or even ask for different edits, if this is possible).

Postproduction-Related Issues to Keep in Mind

Does the video have long or short edits?

Are there cuts or transitions (such as cross-fading dissolves)?

Are there a lot of graphics? If so, are they static or in motion?

Are there a lot of transparencies or layer images?

Has the video intentionally been degraded (or color-treated) as a technique (which is common in music videos and aggravating as all get out when you don't know this)?

Who Is the Intended Audience?

So, your video is shot, edited, and all ready to go. Now there's one last issue to consider—how and where are people watching this video? There is a lot of video consumed on TV still, sure, but if you are compressing your video, you're doing so in order to distribute it in some other way (or, more than likely, multiple other ways).

Distribution-Related Issues to Keep in Mind

How are viewers watching this—on a computer, a TV, a kiosk, or a mobile device?

Will it be an individual or group-viewing experience?

Will it be easy or hard to hear (in other words, is it a quiet or noisy environment)?

How big is the screen, and how far away are the viewers expected to be?

Which is more important: quality or speed of delivery?

CONCLUSION

Generally speaking, compressionists cannot be absolutists. There's no single right answer (or associated plan of action) to any of the questions just asked. Instead, compression is about weighing the information and balancing the video quality requirements against the realities of the preferred delivery method.

By remaining conscious of production and video elements and—more important—how they are likely to affect the outcome of your video compression, you will improve your chances of successful compression. You'll be aware of pitfalls in advance and find yourself better prepared to diagnose what the results may be like after encoding.

Asking these questions before you make and implement your compression choices should help maintain a high-quality video when the final compression is delivered.

That said, there is so much more to video compression than just how video works. The next step is to understand how the language of compression is likely to affect the video you encode and how you encode it.

CHAPTER TWO

The Language of Compression

All disciplines have their own specialized terminology and references for explaining various components and practices, and compression is certainly no different. It has its own specific language—and like most languages, it shares elements in common with other neighboring tongues, especially the video and IT network worlds.

But in some cases, the same terms have different meanings in the world of compression. Talk to a broadcaster or cable operator about video-on-demand, and he'll immediately assume you are referring to the video content made available on demand through cable channels. Talk to a streaming services or content provider about the same terminology, and she will assume you mean any video content available at any time to view via the Internet. The compressionist needs to know both definitions and be conscious of the context others refer to when they use these terms.

On the other hand, some words and concepts are very specific to compression, and these are the ones that typically cause communication problems between compressionists and others. Perhaps the most confusing terms concern the differences between video players on computers (and embedded devices), video and audio codecs, and video and audio formats. The words that describe these very different parts of compression are similar enough to puzzle anyone working in the field and confuse the living daylights out of a client who just needs work done and has no inclination or need to learn the compressionist's lexicon.

So in this chapter, I will clarify what exactly these three major concepts—players, codecs, and formats—mean, and then I will discuss some specific facets of compression that any compressionist should be prepared to discuss as part of the encoding process.

PLAYERS

Used generically, the term *players* refers specifically to the software applications on computers that make it possible to play back video and audio from a compressed format. In essence, video players are the TV within the computer that plays our videos. There are many out there; some come free from software and hardware companies, others are sold commercially, and some are open source products supported by a community of developers and enthusiasts. At minimum, a player is the application that you launch to play back files that are either available locally or remotely via the Internet. Sometimes these players will have compression capabilities of their own, making it possible to transcode a piece of video in addition to playing it back. And there's a term I should define right off the bat: *transcoding* is the common name for taking an existing video or audio file and recompressing it into a different format for delivery and playback in a different environment.

As mentioned, several players are available; there isn't one universal video player that will seamlessly play back all video and audio formats (though some try very hard to do just that). As a compressionist, you want to be familiar with all these players and have them available to test and play back content you are creating to make sure it will work for your clients (and their end users) upon delivery.

If you are widely distributing your content (and if you aren't, why are you reading this book?), then you should also be checking this content in these players on multiple types of computers. Don't test just on your Mac if all your viewers are likely to be playing it back on a PC; you have to mimic the end-viewer experience as closely as possible in order to assure a quality viewing experience.

There are four well-known Web-related players these days—QuickTime Player, Windows Media Player, Adobe Flash Player, and RealPlayer—each with their own characteristics and each popular with their own market segments and specific types of applications. But don't assume you can pigeonhole your end viewers with one player or another; if you are compressing video for anything other than DVD, it is almost certain that you need to support most or all of these formats in your work.

QuickTime Player

QuickTime Player is part of QuickTime, a multimedia framework developed by Apple to handle various formats of text, animation, still images, and interactivity. It is available for Classic Mac OS (OS 9), Mac OS X, and Microsoft Windows operating systems (Windows 98 SE and newer).

QuickTime and QuickTime Player are distributed free of charge and QuickTime Player will play back any audio or video that QuickTime can natively decode. This covers a large collection of codecs (see "Codecs" later in this chapter for specific examples), though only a handful of them are considered modern ones—the rest of the codecs are there as part of the legacy of video that QuickTime Player supports.

QuickTime Player (**Figure 2.1**) is most closely associated with the file type .mov, but it can play back a variety of other formats as well.

Figure 2.1 The basic QuickTime Player window.

Functionality: QuickTime Player vs. iTunes

QuickTime Player is a stand-alone desktop application and a plug-in. This means content can be played in a self-contained QuickTime Player or embedded in a Web page. QuickTime Player is not, however, a media library, allowing users to organize their content in addition to playing it back. That is the job of Apple's free application, iTunes, which is built on the QuickTime framework. iTunes allows users to import, play back, and manage their audio and video content (**Figure 2.2**). Additionally, iTunes allows users to synchronize the content with external devices such as the iPod or iPhone (for portable playback) or AppleTV (to view on their TV).

Figure 2.2 The iTunes interface.

QuickTime Pro

QuickTime is free to use. Apple made it hard to understand this by making the free player continually launch a window prompting users to upgrade for $29.99 to the QuickTime Pro version, which makes many more features available to the end user. This window prompt has always really annoyed end users because they thought they were using a piece of crippled software. Let me say it again for those in the cheap seats: If you are not in the business of making content or preparing content for delivery, you can use the free version of QuickTime until the end of creation, and you'll be just fine.

However, if you *are* in the business of creating or preparing content (and compressionists are in that category), then QuickTime is a key part of your toolkit, and you'll most likely need the Pro version to get your work done (**Figure 2.3**). QuickTime Pro keys are specific to the major version of QuickTime for which they are purchased. If you bought a Pro license for QuickTime 6, when QuickTime 7 came out, you would have to buy a new version. Since the version numbers for QuickTime roll over only every few years, this is still not an unreasonable price for all the functionality you get (though, again, this has really angered some users). Using the Pro key does not require downloading anything new; it just unlocks functionality of the player you already have.

Figure 2.3 QuickTime Pro extends the basic playback functionality of the player to allow exporting and basic video editing.

Features enabled by the Pro license include the following:

- Editing clips through the Cut, Copy, and Paste functions; merging separate audio and video tracks; and freely placing the video tracks on a virtual canvas with the options of cropping and rotation

- Saving and exporting (encoding) to any of the codecs supported by QuickTime

- Exporting video and audio to other wrappers and formats also supported by QuickTime (such as MPEG-4, 3GPP, AIFF, WAV, image sequences, and so on)

- Exporting to other normally unsupported formats through QuickTime component plug-ins (specifically, Adobe Flash and Windows Media Video)

- Exporting video to a video-capable iPod, AppleTV, and the iPhone (QuickTime Pro 7 only)

- Saving existing QuickTime movies (.mov) from the Web directly to a hard drive

QuickTime Components

The very flexible framework that QuickTime provides makes it easy to extend the playback and export features of the QuickTime Player by using component plug-ins. These plug-ins are small pieces of software developed by third-party companies that extend the functionality of the player. For example, Flip4Mac, a division of Telestream, makes available a component that allows QuickTime to play back most Windows Media Video (WMV and ASF) files on the Mac (**Figure 2.4**). Since Microsoft chose to discontinue the development of its own Mac-based player in 2003, this was a very valuable plug-in for any Mac user wanting to play back such content. Microsoft has even officially sanctioned the plug-in, making it available on its Web site for download at *www.microsoft.com/windows/windowsmedia/player/ wmcomponents.mspx*.

Figure 2.4 QuickTime components such as Flip4Mac add functionality beyond QuickTime Player.

Another good example is the open source project known as Perian (*http:// perian.org/*). Perian extends the QuickTime Player by making it possible to play back the following formats:

* AVI, FLV, and MKV

* MS-MPEG-4 DivX, 3ivX, H.264, FLV1, FSV1, VP6, H263I, VP3, HuffYUV, FFVHuff, MPEG-1 and MPEG-2 video, Fraps, Windows Media Audio 1 and 2, Flash ADPCM, Xiph Vorbis (in Matroska), and MPEG Layer II audio

* AVI support for AAC, AC3 Audio, H.264, MPEG-4, and VBR MP3

* Subtitle support for SSA and SRT files

More information on other component plug-ins is available at *www.apple.com/quicktime/resources/components.html*.

Windows Media Player

Windows Media Player (WMP) is the digital media player and media library application developed by Microsoft that is used for playing audio and video and viewing images on personal computers running the Microsoft Windows operating system, as well as on Pocket PC and Windows Mobile–based devices. Versions of WMP were also released for Mac OS and Mac OS X but have been discontinued. In addition to being a media player, WMP includes the ability to rip music from and copy music to CDs, build audio CDs on recordable discs, and synchronize content with an MP3 player (such as Microsoft's own player, the Zune) or other mobile devices. It also enables users to purchase or rent music from a number of online music stores. WMP replaced an earlier piece of software simply known as Media Player and is differentiated by additional features beyond simple video or audio playback (**Figure 2.5**).

Figure 2.5 Windows Media Player 11 sports a sleek black interface.

The default file formats are Windows Media Video (WMV), Windows Media Audio (WMA), and Advanced Systems Format (ASF). WMP also supports its own XML-based playlist format called Windows Playlist (WPL). Just like QuickTime and iTunes, WMP goes hand in hand with a playback/media library application called Zune, which is a modified version of Windows Media Player, but it adds support for Advanced Audio Coding (AAC) audio, MPEG-4, and H.264 video formats.

Unlike QuickTime, WMP is also able to utilize a digital rights management (DRM) service in the form of Windows Media DRM, allowing content creators to provide protection of their media if they choose.

Silverlight

Figure 2.6 Microsoft hopes that its Silverlight will compete head to head with Flash in the world of interactive video for the Web and computer.

At the National Association of Broadcasters conference (NAB) in 2007, Microsoft announced it would be relaunching its WPF format (Windows Presentation) as Silverlight—an Adobe Flash competitor that allows users to create interactive graphical environments that incorporate video. The Silverlight plug-in (**Figure 2.6**) will also play back WMV videos in addition to the WMP player. Of particular interest is that Silverlight is a cross-platform solution, meaning that for the first time in many years, Mac users now have the capability of playing back WMV video in an application created and supported by Microsoft. Silverlight launched as a public beta in September 2007 and became available in early 2008 as an official release. Several companies, including the Major League Baseball Association, have partnered with Microsoft to offer their content in a Silverlight-powered interface. For more details, visit *http://silverlight.net*.

Adobe Flash Player

Figure 2.7 Adobe Flash Player 9 continues to mature as an interactive product that enables both graphic and video interactivity. In late 2007, Adobe added support for H.264 to the player with its "RockStar" Flash 9.2 beta release.

Adobe Flash Player is a multimedia and application player developed and distributed by Adobe Systems. Flash has been around for 11 years and was initially not a video player but rather a plug-in that allowed Web developers and designers to create a more graphical experience. Flash 7 added the ability to play back video via the Sorenson Spark codec, but this was seen as a fairly low-resolution video experience. Flash 8 introduced support for the On2 VP6 codec, and the quality was greatly improved, though VP6 was still seen as inferior to codecs such as VC-1 and H.264. Adobe adopted On2's codec as its default for the player.

Adobe announced in August 2007 that Flash Player 9 (**Figure 2.7**) would begin offering support to H.264 MPEG-4 video as well and made a beta available. This would greatly improve quality even further, and it has been speculated that this was done to make Flash competitive with Microsoft's newly announced Silverlight and the VC-1 video format. An official release that supports H.264 was released in December of 2007 to the general public.

Flash Video content is most commonly embedded within SWF files for playback via the Internet. Notable users of the Flash Video format include YouTube, Google Video, Reuters.com, Yahoo! Video, and MySpace. The BBC has recently begun using Flash-based media on its news portal.

Adobe Media Player

In 2007, Adobe announced the creation of a stand-alone player known as Adobe Media Player (AMP). AMP (originally codenamed Philo) is a desktop media player that offers users the ability to manage and interact with their media content and allows content publishers to define branding and advertising in and around their content. AMP, shown in **Figure 2.8**, is one of the first applications launched by Adobe based on Adobe AIR, a cross-operating system runtime for applications to deploy on the desktop. Adobe Media Player is currently available as a public beta at *labs.adobe.com* and is expected to launch in early 2008.

Figure 2.8 Adobe Media Player. Similar to iTunes and Windows Media Player, Adobe Media Player allows viewers to stream, download, manage, and play rich media content. Users can queue up and download favorite content for Internet TV shows and video podcasts, and they can manage their personal video library.

Here are some of Adobe Media Player's most significant features:

- **FLV on the desktop:** Stream, download, manage, and play rich media content in the FLV format

- **Library:** Gather and manage collections of Flash videos

- **Tags and ratings:** Add keywords and ratings to Flash videos

- **Smart playlists:** Filter the Library and Favorites based on tags and ratings

- **Catalog:** Find and automatically download Internet TV shows and video podcasts

Adobe Media Player is also designed for media content publishers to distribute, track, and monetize their media contents:

- **Branding:** Deliver backgrounds and badges that are displayed dynamically around the distributed contents

- **Advertising:** Deliver banners, in-rolls, and bugs that are displayed dynamically in and around the distributed contents

- **Usage statistics:** Anonymously track and asynchronously report content usage

- **Content protection:** Ensure that advertisements cannot be replaced or removed and that content cannot be reused or remixed

- **Media RSS:** Increase viewership by delivering new content on an automatic and periodic basis via RSS technology

RealPlayer

RealPlayer, briefly known also as RealOne Player, is a cross-platform media player by RealNetworks that plays a number of multimedia formats, including MP3, MPEG-4, QuickTime, Windows Media, and multiple versions of the proprietary RealAudio and RealVideo formats.

The first version of RealPlayer was introduced in April 1995 as RealAudio Player, one of the first media players designed to stream content over the Internet. Version 6 of RealPlayer changed the naming scheme when it came out and was known as RealPlayer G2. Version 9 did the same and changed the naming scheme to RealOne Player. Free basic versions have been provided (users however were required to provide a legitimate e-mail address to install and authorize the free player). Paid versions, known as the RealPlayer Plus, were also available and offered advanced features, though they were not compression tools like QuickTime Pro.

The current version for Windows is RealPlayer 10.5. Slightly different versions are available for Mac OS X (**Figure 2.9**), Linux, Unix, Palm OS, Windows Mobile, and Symbian OS. The program is powered by an underlying open source media engine called Helix. In June 2007, RealNetworks announced that a new version of RealPlayer would be released. The first beta of version 11 contains a new user interface and some new functions such as Flash Video support, DVD burning, and video recording. A controversial feature that allows users to download video embedded on Web pages has met with much criticism, raising concerns about making it easier for users to steal content.

Figure 2.9 The standard RealPlayer on OS X.

Where Does RealNetworks Really Fit?

I am sort of being polite by including RealPlayer in the top tier of players, in all honesty. RealNetworks helped put video on the Internet and was an inventive and creative platform for developers and content creators to provide a unique experience through the Internet. Unfortunately, the others caught up with them, and RealNetworks stopped being regarded as an innovator several years ago. In addition, RealNetworks has caught a lot of flack in the past few years for the pop advertising and "sneaky" callbacks its software made reporting system information. RealNetworks made a big splash in 2007 by launching its first new player in some time, but it sort of feels like too little too late to gain back the traction it once had. Regardless of where the company is, we owe much of the functionality we see in QuickTime, Windows Media Player, and Flash Player to RealNetworks and its pioneering work.

Other Video Players

QuickTime Player, Windows Media Player, Flash Player, and RealPlayer may be the big four, but they certainly aren't the only games in town. As video playback on computers has gained popularity, several open source projects have crept up that support a wider range of formats or purport to have better features than the basic players from the big four.

MPlayer

MPlayer is a free and open source media player distributed under the GNU General Public License. The program is available for all major operating systems, including Linux and other Unix-like systems, Microsoft Windows, and Mac OS X. MPlayer is best known for supporting a wide variety of media formats. It is a very useful tool to the compression world because it has the ability to play back many files that aren't necessarily supported by the main players.

A helper application called MEncoder can take an input stream or file and transcode it into several different output formats. Though not typically used for or known as a transcoding tool, this feature is particularly useful if the content that needs to be transcoded cannot be recognized by any other player as a valid format.

MPlayer (**Figure 2.10**) was developed as a command-line application and has different optional GUIs for each of its supported operating systems. Commonly used GUIs are gmplayer (the default GUI for GNU/Linux and other Unix-like systems, and Microsoft Windows), MPlayer OS X (for Mac

Figure 2.10 Unlike players such as Windows Media Player and QuickTime, MPlayer has an information and controls window that opens separately from the video screen.

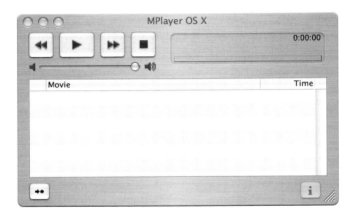

OS X), MPUI (for Windows), and WinMPLauncher (also for Windows). A nice feature of the MPlayer is its ability to play several movies queued in the control window, one after another.

VLC

VLC (**Figure 2.11**) is a free software media player from the VideoLAN project. It is a highly portable multimedia player, encoder, and streamer supporting many audio and video codecs and file formats as well as DVDs, VCDs, and various streaming protocols. Like MPlayer, it has versions for Microsoft Windows, Mac OS X, BeOS, BSD, Windows CE, Linux, and Solaris.

Figure 2.11 The VLC player controls.

VLC uses a large number of free decoding and encoding libraries. Many of its codecs are provided by the libavcodec codec library from the FFmpeg project, but it uses mainly its own muxer and demuxers. Version 0.8.6, released in December 2006, added support for WMV 9 and enhanced support for H.264.

One of the most popular features of VLC is its ability to play damaged or unfinished video content. This made it extremely popular with users in the BitTorrent community, but VLC is also popular with compressionists because it makes it possible to partially recover corrupted video files that may otherwise be lost.

VLC supports all codecs and all file formats supported by FFmpeg (MPlayer also uses FFmpeg). FFmpeg is a collection of software libraries that can record, convert, and stream digital audio and video in numerous formats. The name of the project comes from the MPEG video standards group, together with "FF" for "fast-forward," and was started by Fabrice Bellard (under the pseudonym Gerard Lantau).

NOTE In video processing, software that produces a transport stream or container is commonly called a multiplexor, or muxer. A demuxer extracts or otherwise makes available for separate processing the components of a transport stream or container.

WRAPPERS

If players are the TV set we are viewing the content on, then wrappers are similar to the cable or TV antenna bringing the content to us. A *wrapper* (also known as a *container* or *format*) is a computer file format that can contain various types of data, compressed by means of standardized audio/video codecs. The container file is used to identify and interleave the different data types and make them accessible to the player. Simpler container formats can contain different types of video or audio codecs, while more advanced container formats can support multiple audio and video streams, subtitles, chapter information, and metadata (tags), along with the synchronization information needed to play back the various streams together.

Some wrappers/containers are exclusive to audio:

- **WAV:** widely used on the Windows platform

- **AIFF:** widely used on the Mac OS platform

- **MP3 (MPEG-1 Layer 3):** considered one of the linchpins for the rise of digital music

- **M4A and AAC:** audio formats that improve audio quality over MP3 and take advantage of the MPEG-4 audio standards

Other, more flexible containers can hold many types of audio and video, as well as other media. Some of the more common containers include:

- **IFF:** the first platform-independent container format.

- **AVI:** the standard Microsoft Windows container.

- **ASF:** the standard container for Microsoft WMA and WMV.

- **WMV:** a compressed video file format for several proprietary codecs developed by Microsoft. The original codec, also known as WMV, was originally designed for Internet streaming applications as a competitor to RealVideo. The other codecs, such as WMV Screen and WMV Image, cater to specialized content. Through standardization from the Society of Motion Picture and Television Engineers (SMPTE), WMV has gained adoption for physical delivery formats such as Blu-ray Disc.

- **FLV:** the format specific to Flash Video. Uses either the Sorenson Spark codec or the On2 VP6 codec.

- **MOV:** the standard QuickTime video container from Apple.

- **MPEG-2 transport stream (TS) (aka MPEG-TS):** the standard container for digital broadcasting; typically contains multiple video and audio streams, an electronic program guide, and program stream (PS).

- **MP4:** the standard audio and video container for the MPEG-4 multimedia portfolio.

- **Ogg:** the standard audio container for Xiph.org codecs; can also contain video (as in Ogg Theora).

- **OGM ("Ogg Media"):** the standard video container for Xiph.org codecs.

- **RM/RMA/RMV:** the standard container for RealVideo and RealAudio.

- **Matroska/MKV:** which is not standard for any codec or system, but instead is an open standard and open source container format.

- **3GP:** used by many mobile phones.

- **DV:** the acquisition and editing format used on DV tapes, such as MiniDV, DVCAM, and SD DVCpro.

CODECS

Ah, here we are, the core component of the compression world—the codec. *Codec* is an acronym that stands for *co*mpressor/*dec*ompressor or *co*der/*dec*oder, depending on whom you ask. Though codecs also exist in hardware, when you hear codecs referred to, people are typically speaking about the software codecs that actually make it possible to translate stored video and audio from their digital form into moving images and audio. Codecs are often associated with the quality of the video, but this is not always strictly correct. True, different codecs are optimized for different levels of quality, but poorly compressed content that isn't taking advantage of what the codec may offer often gives particular codecs a bad rap that isn't necessarily deserved. Knowing when and when not to use different codecs is important throughout the postproduction, compression, and final delivery of your content.

Descriptions of the Commonly Used Codecs

A variety of codecs can be implemented with relative ease on PCs and in consumer electronics equipment. It is therefore possible for multiple codecs to be available in the same product, avoiding the need to choose a single dominant codec for compatibility reasons. In the end, it seems unlikely that one codec will ever supplant all others.

Current Popular Codecs

The following sections cover some widely used video codecs, starting with the ones that are currently most popular, followed by a chronological-order list of the ones specified in international standards.

- **MPEG-4 part 10/H.264/AVC:** MPEG-4 part 10 is a standard technically aligned with the ITU-T's H.264 and often also referred to as AVC. This new standard is the current state of the art of ITU-T and MPEG standardized compression technology, and it is rapidly gaining adoption into a wide variety of applications. It uses different profiles and levels to identify different configurations and uses. It contains a number of significant advances in compression capability, and it has recently been adopted into a number of company products, including the Xbox 360, PlayStation Portable, iPod, the Nero Digital product suite, and Mac OS X 10.4, as well as high-definition Blu-ray Disc.

  Though it has impressive quality at bit rates lower than older codecs like MPEG-2, it is very processor-intensive to edit, encode, and play back, and older computers or low-powered portable devices may have difficulty playing it back or may drain their batteries faster than normal when using it.

- **VP6:** This is a proprietary video codec developed by On2 Technologies and used in Adobe Flash Player 8 and newer.

- **VC-1:** This is an SMPTE standardized video compression standard (SMPTE 421M) based on Microsoft's WMV 9 video codec. It is also one of the three mandatory video codecs in Blu-ray high-definition optical disc standards (MPEG-2 and H.264 are the others). It is commonly found on the Web, in portable devices, and on computers that support the WMV format. Like MPEG-4 part 10, VC-1 uses the concept of profiles to differentiate different uses and data settings it will support though its configurations are more straightforward than MPEG-4 part 10/AVC/H.264.

- **MPEG-2 part 2:** Used on DVD, on SVCD, and in most digital video broadcasting and cable distribution systems, MPEG-2's sweet spot in the market is the quality of video it provides for standard-definition video. When used on a standard DVD, it offers good picture quality and supports wide-screen. In terms of technical design, the most significant enhancement in MPEG-2 over its predecessor, MPEG-1 (see the next section), was the addition of support for interlaced video. MPEG-2 is now considered an aged codec, but it has tremendous market acceptance and a very large installed base, and even the relatively new high-definition video acquisition format, HDV, is based on MPEG-2. Its use will decline as a delivery format as more efficient codecs such as AVC and VC-1 are adopted for HD video.

The Rest of the Pack

Plenty of other codecs are available. Some are older versions of the popular standards; others are geared toward specific uses so may not be as well known. Although you may not use or need many of these in your work, it's good to know the names and backgrounds of what's available. Many codecs have such similar names that it's easy to get them confused.

- **H.261:** Used primarily in older videoconferencing and video telephony products, H.261, developed by the ITU-T, was the first practical digital video compression standard. Essentially all subsequent standard video codec designs are based on it. It included such well-established concepts as YCbCr color representation, the 4:2:0 sampling format, 8-bit sample precision, 16 by 16 macroblocks, block-wise motion compensation, 8 by 8 block-wise discrete cosine transformation, zigzag coefficient scanning, scalar quantization, run+value symbol mapping, and variable-length coding. H.261 supported only progressive scan video.

- **MPEG-1 part 2:** This is used for video CDs (VCD) and also sometimes for online video. The quality is roughly comparable to that of VHS. If the source video quality is good and the bit rate is high enough, VCD can look better than VHS, but VCD requires high bit rates for this. MPEG-1 offers high compatibility, in that almost any computer can play back MPEG-1 files, and many DVD players also support the VCD format. However, it is an antiquated format that has been surpassed in terms of quality and file size by many others. MPEG-1 supports only progressive scan video.

- **DV:** The DV codec, in terms of file-based content (as opposed to tape), has two main versions: DV-NTSC, the 720 by 480-pixel default DV codec comes installed with QuickTime for use in accordance with the North American broadcast standard and 720 by 576 DV-PAL is also available for European playback standards.

- **Avid DV (the other version of DV):** This is considered one of the best (if not the best) DV codecs available. Previous versions were tied to an Avid dongle, but the company has decided to cut the codec free, making it available to anyone wanting to install and use it.

- **Cineform:** This is a high-quality production codec that works on both Mac and PCs and can scale from standard-definition to 4k film resolution. Cineform is a wavelet codec (not a DCT codec) that's often used as a digital intermediary codec for editing video captured in formats like HDV that, because of the way they're compressed, are difficult to edit on many systems.

- **H.263:** Used primarily for videoconferencing, video telephony, and Internet video, H.263 represented a significant step forward in standardized compression capability for progressive scan video. Especially at low bit rates, it can provide a substantial improvement in the bit rate needed to reach a given level of fidelity.

- **MPEG-4 part 2:** An MPEG standard that can be used for Internet, broadcast, and on-storage media, MPEG-4 part 2 offers improved quality relative to MPEG-2 and the first version of H.263. Its major technical features beyond prior codec standards consisted of object-oriented coding features and a variety of other such features not necessarily intended for the improvement of ordinary video-coding compression capability. It also included some enhancements of compression capability, both by embracing capabilities developed in H.263 and by adding new ones such as quarter pixel motion compensation. Like MPEG-2, it supports both progressive scan and interlaced video.

- **DivX, Xvid, FFmpeg MPEG-4, and 3ivx:** These are different implementations of MPEG-4 part 2.

- **Sorenson 3:** This is a codec that was popularly used by Apple Quick-Time prior to the launch of H.264. Many of the QuickTime movie trailers found on the Web use this codec.

- **Sorenson Spark:** This is a codec that was licensed to Macromedia for use in its Flash Player 6. This is in the same family as H.263.

- **Theora:** Developed by the Xiph.org Foundation as part of its Ogg project, based upon On2 Technologies' VP3 codec, and christened by On2 as the successor in VP3's lineage, Theora was designed to compete with MPEG-4 video and similar lower-bit rate video compression schemes.

- **RealVideo:** Developed by RealNetworks, this was a popular codec in the late 1990s and early 2000s but is now fading in importance as newer codecs have evolved and because of a lack of recent updates to its quality and performance.

- **Cinepak:** A very early codec used by Apple's QuickTime, Cinepak was very popular with interactive CD-ROM authors in the mid 1990s.

- **x264:** A GPL-licensed implementation of H.264 encoding standard, x264 is only an encoder.

- **Huffyuv:** Huffyuv (or HuffYUV) is a very fast, lossless Win32 video codec written by Ben Rudiak-Gould and published under the terms of the GPL as free software, meant to replace uncompressed YCbCr as a video capture format. A more up-to-date version of Huffyuv is also available called Lagarith.

- **SheerVideo:** A family of fast, lossless QuickTime and AVI codecs developed by BitJazz, SheerVideo is a production-based codec that is popular because of its support of Y'CbCr 4:4:4 and 4:2:2 formats, for both 10-bit and 8-bit channels, and for both progressive and interlaced data. It is also available for both Mac and PC, making it ideal for cross-platform production environments.

A Time and a Place for Everything

Each of the previous codecs has its advantages and disadvantages. Comparisons are frequently made between which are the "best" (best being a sliding scale depending on who published the findings). Generally speaking, the trade-off between image fidelity, file size, processor usages, and popularity can be used to draw comparisons between various codecs. What do I mean by that?

- **Image quality:** Obviously, preserving image quality is of paramount concern when compressing video.

- **File size:** Quality has to be balanced by how large the file actually is.

- **Processor usage:** As the video is playing back, it is being decoded from its binary form to be displayed. Each codec requires different amounts of processor support to perform this. It can't be so intensive that it's impossible for the device or computer to actually keep up with the decoding process, so this should be considered as well.

- **Popularity:** The most popular codecs are the ones that have the widest-reaching audience, though they are not always the best-looking or the ones capable of delivering the best quality in the smallest files. A video format or codec that requires additional steps to install a custom player may not get the viewers that a lower-quality but widely supported player may get.

So with these criteria in mind, you can begin organizing codecs into a few categories that make it easy to decide when—or even more importantly, when not—to use a certain codec. The following are the essential categories for video codecs.

Delivery Codecs

Delivery codecs should be used to distribute video and audio content to an audience. These codecs provide the tightest balance between small file sizes and image quality. They are widely adopted and supported codecs that will reach the widest audience possible.

Codecs I would categorize as good delivery choices include the following:

- **VP6:** Although not the best video quality compared to some of the other options cited here, Flash VP6 has a huge market penetration and makes it easy to share the same content across both Mac and PC computers.

- **H.264:** Though it can be a resource hog, you can't argue with the quality you get for the file size (many say you get two times the quality of MPEG-2 for the same file size). This codec can easily be served in several different file formats, depending on how and where you'll be using it.

- **WMV 9 (aka VC-1):** VC-1 is a very flexible codec that allows users to scale from mobile all the way to high-definition video. It is decidedly friendlier and easier to view on the PC than the Mac; however, with the advent of Silverlight, it will become more standardized and accessible to Mac users.

Authoring Codecs

The main purpose of authoring codecs is to preserve image quality (usually) regardless of file size. Authoring codecs are used as intermediary steps during the production process and are not suitable for delivery because of their often-immense files sizes or lack of wide public support as playback formats. You would use an authoring codec if you wanted to export video to be used in another program but you didn't want to introduce any compression artifacts. The various DV codecs are considered authoring codecs, though they are considered a fairly low common denominator.

Codecs I would categorize as authoring include DV (in both AVI and MOV wrappers), DVCPro 25/50 (a much higher-quality version of the consumer-friendly MiniDV), Huffyuv, Animation, Blackmagic 10-bit and 8-bit, Avid Meridien Compressed, AJA uncompressed (for working with video captured on an AJA Kona card), and Cineform for higher-resolution video like HD.

> **NOTE** Remember how I said compression was about tradeoffs? Well, DV is not the highest quality, but it is so ubiquitous and easy to work with on modern editing systems that it can get the job done easily for you if you can live with a slight knock on the image quality.

Legacy Codecs

Once great but now past their prime, these legacy codecs were once widely used and are still widely available but have been surpassed in almost every other area by other codecs. Though they will continue to see support so older content can be played back, newer codecs should replace them in your standard workflow in order to take advantage of all they offer.

Generally speaking, anything not listed in the previous sections is considered a legacy codec as far as I am concerned, but I'm going to call out a few in the hopes that I may add a nail to their respective coffins:

- **MPEG-2:** We have newer codecs that do much better at the image-to-file-size ratio, so let's put our dear friend MPEG-2 to rest, shall we? This can't happen overnight, given the huge infrastructure built around it and deep roots in the broadcast industry, but it's time to begin adopting newer, more forward thinking formats for your productions. Let

VC-1 and H.264 duke it out to see who unseats this broadcast codec powerhouse.

- **MPEG-1:** If MPEG-2 is old, this is ancient by technology standards. Surprisingly, it still creeps up as a request for those working with older workflows, particularly if they need playback on a wide range of computers. However, it could easily be replaced by Flash Video and retain the same user base.

- **Sorenson Pro 3:** This was the best-looking QuickTime codec for a long time, but H.264 has officially unseated it. The only time you should be using this is if you are supporting QuickTime 6 or earlier (H.264 works only in QuickTime 7 and newer). If you need to support QuickTime 6 only, then switch to MPEG-4 part 2 instead.

- **Cinepak:** A precursor to Sorenson Pro 3, this should also no longer be considered a viable delivery codec.

- **Windows Media 7 and 8, Microsoft MPEG-4 version 3:** All of these have been far surpassed by WMV 9/VC-1.

- **Sorenson Spark:** This original Flash video codec was replaced by VP6. It still sees a large audience base in user-generated content sites because it is much faster to transcode content to it. However, the quality is not up to snuff in my opinion, and either VP6 or H.264 should be considered for Flash Video these days.

It's a Multiformat, Multicodec World We're Living In

In the recent past, technologists argued over which video player, format, or codec would win out over another. The fact is it's a multiplayer, multiformat, multicodec world now. We don't need just one option; we need different options and scenarios for all the very different ways we want to use and consume audio and video.

What works when we are watching a movie on our TV with surround sound isn't the same as when we are watching a movie on our portable player. And neither of those scenarios may work for the video used in the billboards surrounding Times Square.

We are collectively getting smarter about how video works now that it is not just something that plays back on our TVs, and we will continue to get smarter about how it works. So, take a deep breath and hang in there.

Why Is This So Confusing?

Players, wrappers, and codecs often are the components of video compression most difficult to understand. This is for a number of reasons. For one thing, you can see that several of them share identical or similar names, making it hard for someone not deeply rooted in the video compression realm to differentiate between the terms. It is also hard for those who just want to watch a video clip on their computer to grasp (or even care about) the relationship between the three terms, and frankly, I don't think they have to understand it. If we as compressionists and content creators/distributors are doing our jobs, the content should just work (like turning on a TV). It shouldn't be hard to make it work. This is something Apple has really succeeded at, making audio and video work across a mixture of TV, computer, and mobile devices without the end user really needing to fully understand how it happened.

Generally speaking, it is useful to remember that players are a long-term prospect—they are something that will be around for a long time (as evidenced by the longevity of such players as QuickTime Player). They will rise and fall in popularity depending on the quality and types of video they may offer. Formats can also have a long shelf life, if they were developed with an eye to the future. Formats that limit the codecs and data they support other than audio and video (metadata) have fallen out of popularity as other more flexible formats have gained popularity. Codecs are perhaps the most expendable part of the equation. Codecs will continually be updated and created to take advantage of the newest, fastest computers and higher-resolution video monitors we are all using.

COMPRESSION PARAMETERS

Now that I've touched on all the formats, wrappers, and codecs you are going to come into contact with, let's drill into compression parameters. This is a term that is commonly used to describe the settings available with a codec. Many are global, meaning they are identical or at least similar from codec to codec. Some, however, are quite specific to an individual codec family. It's important to understand all the basic settings, because these are directly going to affect the quality of the finished video you are creating.

It's also a good idea to familiarize yourself with the advanced settings possible within the codecs you work with most often. This will allow you to get in there and optimize the finished product (and potentially make you stand out from some of your colleagues or competitors).

Much of what I refer to in the following sections is most applicable to Internet or mobile content delivery; however, it still applies to things like standard definition DVD or Blu-ray content. The only differences for those platforms are that the hardware needs such a specific group of settings that there isn't a whole lot of room for optimizing the settings. It just comes down to what the best hardware or software encoder is for the job at that point.

Data Rates

Data rates are the amount of bits you are allowing the software to use to describe each frame of the video. If you use more bits, your detail and picture quality go up, but so does your file size. If you use fewer bits, the size goes down, but the image detail may suffer as well. Certain codecs are better at providing a better-quality image with less data than others.

TIP In the world of acronyms, a little b means bits, and a big B means bytes. Don't get them confused; there are 8 bits in a byte, so if you get it wrong, you are off by eight times!

Data rates are typically represented in bits (whereas storage on a hard drive is typically represented in bytes). The two abbreviations you will see most often in reference to this are kilobits per second (Kbps) and megabits per second (Mbps).

VBR and CBR

Variable bit rate (VBR) encoding varies the amount of output bits per time segment, using an average target bit rate as a goal but apportioning different amounts of bits to different portions of an encoded video. VBR allows a higher bit rate (and therefore more storage space) to be allocated to the more complex segments of media files, while less space is allocated to less complex segments. The average of these rates is calculated to produce an average bit rate for the file that will represent its overall audio and video quality.

Constant bit rate (CBR), on the other hand, means that bits used per segment are constant, regardless of the complexity of the audio or image. Why would you use one versus the other? VBR is useful for Web-based content that is downloaded, not streamed in real time because the ratio of image quality to file size is very high—you are being as efficient as possible with the bits being used (the most bang for your bits, as it were).

So if that's true, why would you ever use CBR? If a player expects the same amount of data constantly, it is easier for the player to maintain smooth, continuous playback of the video. Older devices with lower processing power than modern, top-of-the-line DVD players and computers, as well as portable devices that have to balance processing power against power consumption, are ideal candidates for CBR video because the processor won't get any "surprises" along the way.

TIP Need a small-sized video with a decent picture quality? Try a VBR file with a low minimum data rate and a high peak. This will keep the average fairly low while allowing the codec to decide when it needs to spend more bits to get the image right.

Frame Rates

Most digital video is shot at 60 interlaced fields per second, or less commonly at 30 progressive frames. This means the screen refreshes 30 times per second, as described in Chapter 1. If the video you're compressing is sourced from film, it may come in at 24 progressive frames per second. Some popular prosumer digital video cameras also shoot in 24 fps or faux-progressive modes. Some video producers believe that 24 fps video looks more like film than interlaced 60-field video, which makes sense since it's shot at the same frame rate. On the other hand, high-motion video shot at 24 fps can look choppy to some eyes.

Much of the video that's compressed and delivered on the Web is delivered at lower frame rates. If you're content to deliver your video at a lower frame rate of, say, 15 fps—which admittedly works better for lower-motion than higher-motion clips—this will actually give you more bits to allot to each frame, since you're delivering half the frames per second.

One aspect of all video that's delivered on the Web is that it must be progressive, noninterlaced video. Web delivery simply doesn't accommodate the split frames (aka fields) of interlaced video—your viewers will see artifacts everywhere.

Frame Types

When encoding video, there are a few different types of frames that will appear within the content—intra (I) frames (also called *key frames*), predicted (P) frames, and bipredictive or bidirectional (B) frames. I-frames are frames that do not refer to other frames before or after them in the video. They contain all the information needed to display them. P-frames, however, use previous I-frames as reference points to complete them (in other words, they describe the changes made in an image since the last I-frame). Because they are describing changes only since the last I-frame, P-frames take fewer bits to create. B-frames are predictive frames that use the last two I-frames to predict motion paths that may occur. These take even less data to create than P-frames.

All My Frames

Intra frames (aka slices, I-frames, or key frames) have the following characteristics:

- Are pictures coded without reference to any pictures except themselves.
- May be generated by an encoder to create a random access point (to allow a decoder to start decoding properly from scratch at that picture location).
- May also be generated when differentiating image details prohibit the generation of effective P- or B-frames.
- Typically require more bits to encode than other picture types.
- Often, I-pictures (I-frames) are used for random access and are used as references for the decoding of other pictures. Intra-refresh periods of a half second are common on such applications as digital TV broadcast and DVD storage. Longer refresh periods may be used in some environments. For example, in videoconferencing systems it is common to send I-pictures very infrequently.

Predicted pictures (aka slices or P-frames) have the following characteristics:

- Require the prior decoding of some other picture(s) in order to be decoded.
- May contain both image data and motion vector displacements and combinations of the two.
- Can reference previous pictures in decoding order.
- In older standard designs (such as MPEG-2), use only one previously decoded picture as a reference during decoding and require that picture to also precede the P-picture in display order.
- In H.264, can use multiple previously decoded pictures as references during decoding and can have any arbitrary display-order relationship relative to the picture(s) used for their prediction.
- Typically require fewer bits for encoding than I-pictures do.

Bipredictive pictures (aka slices, bidirectional, or B-frames) have the following characteristics:

- Require the prior decoding of some other picture(s) in order to be decoded.

(continued on next page)

All My Frames *(continued)*

- May contain both image data and motion vector displacements and combinations of the two.

- Include some prediction modes that form a prediction of a motion region (for example, a macroblock or a smaller area) by averaging the predictions obtained using two different previously decoded reference regions.

- In older standard designs (such as MPEG-2), B-pictures are never used as references for the prediction of other pictures. As a result, a lower-quality encoding (resulting in the use of fewer bits than would otherwise be the case) can be used for such B-pictures because the loss of detail will not harm the prediction quality for subsequent pictures.

- In H.264, may or may not be used as references for the decoding of other pictures (at the discretion of the encoder).

- In older standard designs (such as MPEG-2), use exactly two previously decoded pictures as references during decoding, and require one of those pictures to precede the B-picture in display order and the other one to follow it.

- In H.264, can use one, two, or more than two previously decoded pictures as references during decoding, and can have any arbitrary display-order relationship relative to the picture(s) used for its prediction.

- Typically require fewer bits for encoding than either I- or P-pictures do.

Aspect Ratios

As discussed in Chapter 1, a number of aspect resolutions are available; however, 4:3 and 16:9 are the two primary ones used. As part of the compression process, you want to be conscious of preserving the intended aspect ratio as you scale the video resolution; nothing can be as distracting as trying to watch video that has a distorted image.

But there is also one other issue to keep an eye out for: letterboxed video. Letterboxed video is 16:9 content that has black bars above and below the image to conform it to 4:3 standards. Letterboxing became popular in the 1970s to help preserve the full image of a feature film being played back on a broadcast TV. When a letterboxed video comes through your compression workflow, the goal should not be to preserve the 4:3 aspect ratio of the original video;

rather, you should try to correct it to the intended aspect ratio of the wide-screen content. Pillar bars are another form of letterboxing, which became popular with the arrival of wide-screen TVs (**Figure 2.12**). Most compression applications have a built-in cropping tool that allows you to remove the black bars from the original image as well as alter the intended aspect ratio to the new dimensions needed to keep the video image from distorting.

Figure 2.12 Vertical black bars appear on either side of the image to maintain the 4:3 aspect ratio content on wide-screen TVs.

You Can't Win Them All, But You Should Try

Removing black bars is the right choice when compressing video for delivery to the Web and mobile devices; the bars do nothing to improve the image quality except increase the size of the file. However, sometimes you just have to bite the bullet and keep them in place. Some content publishers may have a mix of 4:3 and 16:9 videos that get published to their sites but have only one standard player they get embedded in (this is most true if they use some sort of content management system that treats all the video content the same). In this instance, you may need to keep the letterbox black bars in place in order to keep the content identical in ratios. It's not going to make the individual video clips look better, but it is going to guarantee that the end user experiences them all the same, which is also important. When possible, however, urge your customers (or company) to make allowances in their formatting and design for both aspect ratios so that we can all eventually get rid of irrelevant black bars in our encoded video.

Square and Nonsquare Pixels

Pixels in the computer world are square. A 100-pixel vertical line is the same length as a 100-pixel horizontal line on a graphics monitor (a 1:1 ratio).

Pixels in the broadcast video world (also known as Rec. 601 and formerly CCIR 601) are not square. A 100-pixel vertical line may be longer or shorter than a 100-pixel horizontal line on a video monitor, depending on the video standard (an 8:9 ratio). As you convert video meant for one delivery format to another, you may need to convert the pixel aspect ratio as part of the process. Many compression programs will already correct for this automatically; however, some may expose an option that allows the users to either select it manually or override the default options available.

Resolution

Refer to Chapter 1 for more background on screen resolutions. In terms of compression parameters, you need to be aware of the type of playback device you are targeting with your video and balance that against the bit rate used to compress the file.

Generally speaking, the larger the screen resolution, the more data will be required to re-create it (remember, the bigger the canvas, the more paint needed).

Modern computer displays are much higher resolution than the ones we were using even just a few years ago. As monitor resolutions increase, the resolutions we use for video on the Web need to be reevaluated as well. For example, in 2001, 800 by 600 was still the predominant screen resolution for most consumers, so a video that was 320 by 240 looked pretty good embedded in a Web page. However, most screens have moved to 1024 by 768 or higher as the default display, leaving that same video looking much smaller and having less of an impact to the viewing.

Resolutions such as 400 by 300 and 480 by 360 have become popular for Web-based video playback for standard resolution video. For high-quality video, meant for playback on both computers and TVs, 1280 by 720 and 960 by 540 have become popular resolutions.

Online Delivery: Streaming vs. Download

This parameter is applicable only to content you are planning to share on a network (either the Internet or a local closed network of some type). Video and audio content can be delivered in two ways on the Internet: as a streaming file or as a progressive download file.

Internet Basics

Web site addresses usually begin with *http://* (for Hypertext Transfer Protocol) or *https://* (for secured pages). The server computer is running Web server software such as Microsoft Internet Information Services (IIS) or Apache. A Web browser such as Firefox, Internet Explorer, or Safari is used to access Web sites hosted on the server. The same technology is often used to host computer files including executable programs, Adobe Acrobat (PDF), and Microsoft Word files.

The same technology used to share Web pages can be used for distributing media. The content can be embedded in a Web page or can play directly through one of the players described earlier, directly from the Web server. This process is called *progressive download* and doesn't require a special server, other than the standard Web server.

With progressive download, the client handles the buffering and playing during the download process. If the playback rate exceeds the download rate, playback is delayed until more data is downloaded. Files that are downloaded over the Web are, generally speaking, able to be viewed only after the entire file is downloaded. Some forms of progressive download video allow the user to start watching before the entire video has downloaded.

Streaming media works differently. In this scenario, the server, like the standard Web server, is connected to a high-speed Internet connection. However, in this case, the computer is running streaming media server software such as Windows Media Services (Microsoft) or the Flash Media Server (Flash Video).

Streaming addresses appear like this:

mms://x.x.x.x/streaming_media_file_directory/media_file_name.wmv

or

rtsp://x.x.x.x/directory/filename.flv

A streaming server works with the client to send audio and video over the Internet or an intranet and play it almost immediately. Streaming servers allow real-time "broadcasting" of live events and the ability to control the playback of on-demand content. Playback begins as soon as sufficient data has been transmitted. The viewer can skip to a point partway through a clip without needing to download the beginning. If the data cannot be transferred fast enough, a streamed Webcast sacrifices quality in order for the viewing to remain with the original timing of the content.

You Should Use Streaming If You're...

- delivering long files—for example, video clips more than 10 to 15 minutes long
- delivering video to many viewers—for example, 100 or more simultaneous viewers
- providing advanced features such as bandwidth detection or quality-of-service monitoring for delivering the best possible experience
- serving live video, such as a Webcast

You Should Use Progressive Download If You're...

- using a small Web site with low traffic requirements
- delivering only short videos (less than 10 minutes)
- using higher-quality video than a streaming connection to your end users would allow

Internet Video Myth: Online Video = Streaming

People constantly get this wrong: If it's on the Web, it must be streaming. Well, now you know it's not, and the only way to dispel this widespread misconception is to pay it forward. The next time you hear people referring to YouTube as streaming video, tell them it's actually just progressive download video.

Most content you see on the Internet is actually progressive download video. As you can see in **Figure 2.13** from Frost and Sullivan's 2006 report on the content delivery, three quarters of all content consumed on the Web is progressive download.

Figure 2.13 Frost and Sullivan have identified that most of Web video consumption is progressive download versus streaming.

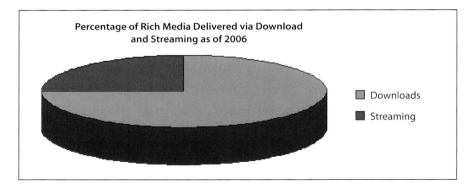

Percentage of Rich Media Delivered via Download and Streaming as of 2006

☐ Downloads
■ Streaming

CONCLUSION

These are the basic tenets of the compression part of video compression. To use them effectively, you need to consider how they apply to your daily workflow. Now that you are better informed about the fundamentals of video compression, in Chapter 3 I'll identify what type of equipment and process you need in place to use that knowledge.

CHAPTER THREE

Best Practices

The Boy Scouts have it right: Always be prepared. Most first-time compressionists assume that preparing to compress video means choosing your equipment and firing it up or shooting and editing the video you intend to compress.

But the most important step you need to take before you start compressing video is to identify what type of compressionist you are. Secure in the knowledge of who you are and what kind of compression you need to do, you can come up with a few scenarios for how best to get your compression work done. Even though all compressionists ultimately use similar setups, different jobs have different needs, so in this chapter I'll identify those needs. With these preliminaries out of the way, you can then turn a critical eye on your equipment and make some decisions about what gear you'll need to compress your video effectively.

Once you do all that, you'll be well prepared for video compression. In this chapter I'll also offer some suggestions for optimizing both your equipment and your workflow.

WHAT ARE YOUR COMPRESSION NEEDS?

Different types of deliverable content have different needs in terms of how you handle them and what type of equipment you use. So, let's figure out just exactly what type of compressionist you are and what kind of compression you'll be doing by answering some questions.

Long-Form or Short-Form Content?

Determining the length and type of content will help you make some basic decisions, especially once you also know the target delivery medium. Different lengths of video lend themselves better to different delivery platforms. Generally speaking, video meant for the Web is shorter than video meant to be viewed on a TV, though this is not a hard-and-fast rule by any means. If you are planning on delivering long-form content that is meant for playback on the Web, you will have to encode the video at a much lower data rate than short-form content in order to keep the file size down to a manageable download. This refers to progressive download clips, such as those posted on YouTube and popular social networking sites.

What Is Your Final Delivery Target?

Knowing your target delivery medium will help you determine the video quality limitations of the final product. It might be broadcast, Web, mobile, or DVD. Some combinations—such as sending full-frame, high-bit-rate video to mobile or dial-up end users—just aren't practical. Most likely, you are not just compressing your video for one particular targeted delivery. Identify all the places to which you'll ultimately deliver your content, and then determine what specific needs each has to make sure you are correctly compressing the video.

How Is Your Content Delivered to You?

There are a lot of ways to deliver content to a compressionist. Some of the most common are tapes (MiniDV, Beta, Digibeta, and so on), hard disk, flash media, DVD, and FTP. The medium used to deliver content to you matters for several reasons.

First, you have to be prepared to accept the delivery format your clients or colleagues commonly use, and then you also have to know the practical limitations of it.

Do you have the right equipment to accept your content source's format of choice? Your client might like using Digibeta, but do you have access to a Digibeta deck that can capture the video? If not, you need to ask for something else or plan on spending the time to locate a vendor who can convert it to a source format you're equipped to accept.

Is the delivery format too low quality to make it possible for you to deliver the finished content in the desired format? That this problem still arises surprises even me—a client will try to deliver their clips already encoded for Web playback and ask you to prepare them for DVD or HD. I don't care what kind of golden touch you have—the results in this scenario will always stink. Make sure the client is delivering a file or tape format that is high enough quality that you can encode a decent finished deliverable from it.

Are the files too big to deliver practically via FTP? If the client wants you to download 10 GB of files from their Web server, it just isn't going to work. Realistically, it will take you longer to download those files than it would take someone to copy it to a hard drive or DVD and send it to you via FedEx. The Web sometimes makes us think all things digital are better, but the reality is that sometimes overnight delivery still makes for a better source file than an FTP download.

How Much Content Are You Compressing?

How many minutes or hours of content are you working with actively in a given week? What about at one time? Do you even have enough equipment to do the workload?

Why ask these questions? Well, overcommitting your time and your equipment will lead only to delayed or disappointing results. Determine how much work you have to accomplish, and then make sure you have the appropriate amount of hardware and software available to accomplish it. Some video clips take longer to compress than others, so budget your time based on the length of video, ingest format, export format, and complexity of compression in order to decide whether you can keep up with your workload. Unfortunately, there isn't a fast or easy way to determine this—you have to learn the capabilities of your setup over time.

Is Compression All You're Doing?

Where does compression fit into your job description? Is it your only responsibility in the project at hand? Are you also playing some other role? If you are going to be doing things other than encoding video, where does video compression rank in your job priorities?

Quality or Timeliness?

Which is more important to you, or to the client for whom you're compressing video: quality or on-time delivery?

There's much more to video compression than subtracting or reassigning bits, and often, the better the compression, the longer it will take. When it comes to crunch time (and almost every project you do will find you working hard against a deadline), does your client (or you, if you're the content owner or project initiator) simply need all the work done in the agreed time frame, or is it better to take an extra few hours or days to get the right results?

Are You a Content Owner or a Cog?

Are you independent or in a department? Are you solo or part of a bigger group? How many clients do you have? How are you tracking jobs and work? Are you confident you understand all the requirements if the content is coming from a client?

If you're working as an independent contractor for an outside client and you aren't 100 percent sure that both of you know exactly what the expected results and delivery requirements are, send some tests before committing a lot of time and resources to completing a job that you might otherwise do unsatisfactorily.

How Knowledgeable Is Your Client?

If your answer to the owner/cog question is that you work for yourself, and if you, as compressionist and de facto client, aren't knowledgeable about video and what's involved in encoding and delivering it, you're in trouble.

A little knowledge is super dangerous in any field, and compression is no exception. Some clients know a little of what they want, or they understand an older set of standards, but this kind of knowledge does more damage than good. A good example of this is a client insisting you post MPEG-1 files because those are the only files that will play back correctly on his laptop. Help educate your clients on best practices so they can be good clients who work with you to get what they need, instead of making arbitrary demands based on poor or outdated information. This, of course, means *you* need to be up to date and knowledgeable, too—which is as good a reason as any for you to be reading this book and asking these questions well before your actual compression work begins.

It has been my experience that most people are looking for a compressionist to drive the car. By that I mean they may have an idea of the results they ultimately want, but they don't know the specifics they need to get there. You as the compressionist—and, consequently, the person most knowledgeable about the compression process—should be in a position to make suggestions to the client or colleague who needs a particular end result. So even if you aren't the project champion, offer your opinion on the deliverable if appropriate—you may be surprised to discover you have information the others in the chain don't have that will make the process easier or the results better.

> **NOTE** To stay up to date, be sure to visit this book's companion Web site at *www.peachpit.com/ rwvideocompression*.

EQUIPMENT AND WORKFLOWS FOR DIFFERENT SCENARIOS

Though the equipment may not vary that much from one compressionist to another, it's good to identify the type of setup that will best suit your work needs. The following sections highlight some real-world scenarios to illustrate how to match encoding equipment to the demands of the job at hand.

Encoding as an Editor

Let's say you're an editor and you need to encode video. Maybe you're sharing rough cuts with a client, maybe you're delivering dozens of finalized short clips meant for the Web, or maybe you're a blogger packaging your own content for delivering. Regardless of the reason, you're working with video in a nonlinear editing (NLE) system, and your ultimate goal is to not go back to tape but to go "somewhere" else, be it DVD, Web, mobile, or e-mail. If this is the case, then video compression is almost always a second- or third-tier priority in your workflow. Not to diminish its role, but if you're busy trying to get the message laid out in a carefully edited video, get all the titles finished and in place, and make sure the audio levels are good. By the time you're ready to encode, you will probably have run out of steam. The compressing part is an afterthought—something you do while you get up and stretch after a long editing session.

You probably aren't encoding a whole heck of a lot of content at once. Most likely you will edit a sequence together, encode it, send it off to the next postproduction stage (whether that's the graphic artist, the colorist, the sound editor, or your client for review), and then carry on editing. Or you might edit together a variety of clips all pertaining to similar jobs, queue them up for encoding either overnight or during a break, and then carry on with work. The point is, the encoding is something that's not primary here—when the time comes for encoding the video, the work you specialize in is done. The good news is that if you are using an NLE, you don't really need much more specialized equipment to also be a good encoder; your NLE will feature encoding presets for all kinds of contingencies (**Figure 3.1**) and usually will have the ability to tweak them to your specifications, if your attention to encoding extends that far. The one thing I'll caution you on is storage. Editors use up a lot of storage for their edits typically, but this is very transient—once the job is done, you can back up the primary editing drive to offline storage media, or you can delete the project and its source files altogether.

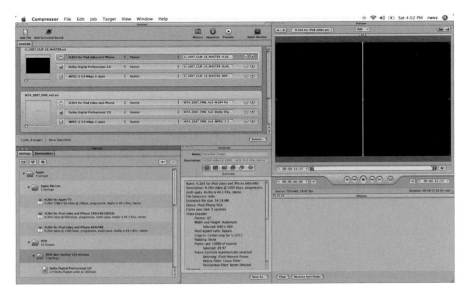

Figure 3.1 Here's where you choose encoding options in Apple Compressor, the compression tool that ships with Apple Final Cut Studio and Final Cut Server.

If you are a hobbyist just editing together your own movies, you may not want to invest in an overly expensive setup. In fact, you may not have to invest any money at all. Many consumer DV cameras come with free editing software, such as Ulead VideoStudio or CyberLink PowerDirector, and most Windows PCs ship with Microsoft MovieMaker. And if you are on a Mac, all new Macs ship with a version of iLife that includes editing software (iMovie). You can buy iLife separately for $79, but if you have bought a Mac in the past few years, double-check your Applications folder. You may not have the most recent version, but you no doubt have some version of it. All these tools come with some video compression capability—usually the ability to encode video for DVD and VideoCD authoring, plus WindowsMedia or QuickTime. Your encoding options might be limited to good/better/best or similar categories, but this is enough to get you started compressing video that's reasonably suited to your output choices.

Maybe you are getting paid occasionally for your editing skills. Or perhaps you're just the type of avid hobbyist who wants the best equipment possible for your productions. Then you're categorized somewhere between the amateur and pro—you're the prosumer. Don't be shocked, saddened, or upset in any way by this moniker. Equipment manufacturers and software creators love the prosumer because they tend to spend more on equipment than the average hobbyist-type consumer. All you ask for in return is a better set of features, but not as many features as, say, a full-time professional might need. You are probably spending somewhere between $1,000 and $3,000 for your editing equipment and might even use compression tools that match (**Figure 3.2**).

Figure 3.2 Transcode settings in Adobe Media Encoder, the encoding tool found in Adobe Production Premium.

Or maybe you're a professional editor and your equipment reflects it. You might have somewhere between $25,000 and $200,000 parked in a climate-controlled suite somewhere (or you just rent other people's gear). You might even have multiple systems in your studio—the high-end Avid setup for the full-on, high-paying clients and then a smaller Final Cut Pro setup, maybe on a laptop that you use to bang out the in-between jobs (**Figure 3.3**).

Figure 3.3 The professional editor may simply choose to use the default export settings within their NLE of choice in order to expedite the compression process.

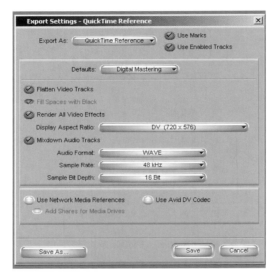

In all these cases, you're an editor first and a compressionist second (or third or fourth). But you'll need to output video in a compressed format at some point, and the higher up the editing food chain you are, the more encoding options you'll have, and most likely, the more you'll need to know about compression so you can choose wisely among the choices you have and get the type of high-acuity results your projects and clients demand.

Encoding as a Compressionist

Maybe you don't bother with editing and content creation. Maybe you just take the stuff already made and transmogrify it into something else. Well, you, my friend, are a compressionist—*mazel tov*. You probably don't need quite the same equipment your friend the editor needs, but the setups will still look shockingly similar (although you will have a wider variety of tools on hand). Because the editor is typically her own encoding customer, she just needs to accept content from one primary source—her NLE. You, however, do not have this good fortune. You need to be equipped to decipher nearly any type of video content from any source, whether tape-based, disc-based, or file-based (**Figure 3.4**).

What are the basics you need to consider? These are the fundamental requirements:

- You need to be able to successfully open and play back any content thrown your way.

- You need to get that content into a format from which it's easy to encode.

- You need to encode it (duh).

- You need to organize and archive it.

- You need to deliver it.

In short, if you're encoding as a compressionist, you'll need to know more about encoding than your editor counterparts and be prepared for more scenarios.

As we shift to IP video as a major delivery option for traditional broadcast, we will see the demand for professional compressionists increase.

Figure 3.4 The compressionist will have many types of settings that are based both on workflow and on file type, similar to the templates installed by default in Telestream's Episode Pro.

Automating the Encoding Process

Many modern encoding applications have automation tools built into them that are meant to further speed up the encoding workflow by removing the human element from the process when possible. In actuality, you're not so much removing yourself from the process as allowing the computer to handle the simpler mundane tasks and jobs, which leaves you free to focus on the more difficult segments or to manage a larger volume of work.

The most common automation feature is the Watch folder. This is where, through the application, the compressionist designates a folder on the computer as an incoming compression source and assigns a template or groups of templates to the folder. With the Watch folder activated, the encoding application monitors the folder looking for new files. When files are copied to this folder, the application automatically begins encoding the content based on the templates that were assigned.

Some systems further support automation by allowing finished files to be copied across the local network or remotely to FTP servers for delivery. Such automation is particularly useful with time-sensitive content (such as dailies in the postproduction world).

Since the content is always the same, the system can be relied on to deliver consistent results. If, as part of your regular encoding, you receive a variety of types of content, this automation may not be useful, because the results cannot be relied on to be consistent.

Enterprise Systems: The Big Leagues

Although automation on a single encoding system may help you speed up a production environment, it may not be enough. Some broadcast facilities and other outfits dedicated to the business of encoding have to deal with 200 or more hours of content a week. When you hit that scale of work, it's time to invest in an enterprise encoding solution that enlists multiple computers in the encoding process. Anystream's Agility and Telestream's FlipFactory are two popular enterprise solutions, but many others have emerged recently. Being an enterprise solution means more than just being able to split compression jobs over several computers (known as *grid encoding*). It also means giving the compressionists running this system some tools for managing the whole process from end to end. Such tools aren't cheap—expect to spend at least $40,000 to $60,000 just to get started, but then if you are encoding that much content at a time, you probably need to spend the money.

> ## Encoding on the Road
>
> Thanks to the increased storage and processor speeds of modern high-end laptops, compressing video is not something confined to large desktop computers any longer. A fairly new laptop with a good amount of random access memory (RAM) will serve as a fast encoding tool on the go for compressionists who need to balance portability with power.

ESSENTIAL ENCODING EQUIPMENT

Unless you're working in a studio that specializes in high-end DVD or Blu-ray Disc authoring, you're probably not working with a hardware encoder. More likely, you're doing your encoding within your NLE, with a supporting application that shipped with your NLE (such as Apple Compressor or Adobe Media Encoder) or with a stand-alone encoding application such as Telestream's Episode Pro, Sorenson Squeeze, Inlet's Fathom series, or Apple QuickTime Pro. But that doesn't mean you aren't using hardware to support your encoding work or that your hardware setup isn't critical to the process. And make no mistake, video encoding is nothing if not a processor-intensive application, so making sure you have enough power in your system to support the process is a key step in your preplanning efforts.

Hardware

If you're about to build (or buy) your encoding system, it's a good time to be doing so. Most computers on the market today ship with two or more processors; these dual-core, quad-core, and eight-core systems deliver a noticeable improvement over older single-core and even hyperthreaded systems, which do a decent job of acting like multiprocessor systems but aren't the real deal. Video encoding demands lots of encoding horsepower and, more to the point, needs the full attention of your processor, or as close to it as possible. Whenever possible, your encoding system—even a multiprocessor one—should be a dedicated one, since asking your computer to perform other tasks while encoding just slows down the process. Multicore systems are great for focusing the full resources of one or more encoders on the encoding tasks at hand while relegating routine operations to other system resources that don't interfere. Keep in mind that not all encoding software is optimized for quad-core and eight-core systems, but we can expect to see that change as new iterations of the tools emerge.

Another advantage of multicore systems is that the processors themselves don't need to be as honkin' fast; in other words, clock speed is less important than the number of processors you have. If you have multiple older, single-processor systems you want to use for encoding applications, you can network them for grid or distributed encoding, but keep in mind that this process—which actually breaks up an encoding job into multiple segments, sends the pieces to the other systems on the network for encoding, and then retrieves the encoding segments and pieces them back together—might not increase your efficiency as much as you'd imagine. For one thing, the longer the clip to be encoded, the more the time spent shipping it back and forth across the network will cut into your encoding time savings; in addition, breaking up the clip will reduce your encoder's ability to identify redundancies in the data that make efficient compression possible.

The Ideal Setup

The ideal CPU setup for video encoding is one honkin' horsepower machine and a few lower-powered grinders. Then there's one 20-inch or wide-screen monitor that powers all the machines via a KVM (keyboard-video-mouse) switch. If you are capturing high-resolution files, your ideal setup also has a dedicated, multiterabyte Redundant Array of Independent Devices (RAID) and some active encoding storage (either internal or high-speed external) of 1 TB per CPU.

If you feel like setting up and tending it, go with a storage area network (SAN)—that way the encoders all share the same workspace. All of this should have a backup storage in place: either big FireWire drives you manually back up to or a network-attached storage solution with backup management software.

Monitors aren't as important as processor power, though a nice-size LCD is handy. Use a KVM (keyboard-video-mouse) switch, and let multiple machines use one screen keyboard if you can.

Storage

Figure 3.5 Storage may be the most important feature to the compressionist. All the encoding horsepower in the world doesn't mean a thing if you do not have enough space to properly store the source material as well as all the files you plan to create in the encoding process.

As for storage, there's no way around it: you need a lot (**Figure 3.5**). Fortunately, hard drives have gotten much cheaper in the past few years. You can purchase external FireWire hard drives for about $200 per half terabyte (500 MB). In addition to capacity, you must consider the type of connection to the drive, because you will be moving around very large files. **Table 3.1** shows the different transfer speeds for various common hard drive interfaces in addition to both 100-bit and gigabit Ethernet connections. FireWire and USB 2.0 provide relatively good transfer speed; however, if you can afford to, invest in eSATA or FireWire 800 drives in order to get the most bang for your buck.

Table 3.1 Transferring 4.4 GB from Drive to Drive

Transfer Speeds for Common Hard Drive Interfaces

Interface	Speed	Time (hours:min:sec)
eSATA	3000 Mbps	0:30
FireWire 800	800 Mbps	1:47
FireWire 400	400 Mbps	2:39
USB 2	480 Mbps	5:21
USB 1	12 Mbps	1:58:53
100 Base Ethernet	100 Mbps	14:16
Gigabit Ethernet	1000 Mbps	1:25

Higher-Capacity Storage

Depending on how high quality the source is, you may need a RAID if your work requires playing back the video in real time. At the very least, you'll want a network-attached storage (NAS) solution for offloading work. A storage-area network (SAN) can be annoying (well-specialized knowledge is needed to set up and manage one) but handy. All these systems share the same basic concept: using multiple hard drives combined to act as one large storage device (**Figure 3.6**).

Figure 3.6 If compression is your main job, consider investing in a high-capacity storage system such as a SAN.

The higher the volume of work you are performing at any given time, the larger capacity storage your encoding system needs to be, and potentially the more encoding stations you need. The number of jobs and length of content will dictate how much active space you need, but 1 terabyte (TB) per CPU is a good start.

Note how I said *active* storage space. Once you have encoded video for a while, you'll discover that doing so means creating a lot of files. It is quite easy to run out of space, lose files, or generally become confused about where everything is. As part of staying organized with your files, you should also create and follow a storage policy. A storage policy is a guideline for how files get treated as part of your workflow. Depending on how long your project cycles are, try storing files based on what is active and keeping those files close at hand. Then, in descending order, create a storage hierarchy for files older than 30, 90, and 120 days. Active files are regularly needed for work and are on the main system, as are files that are less than 30 days old. You can back up older files to external hard drives such as a NAS solution once you no longer need to access them regularly. Every six months or so, it is worth reviewing this *cold storage* to decide whether the files still need to be retained on a drive or can be burned to DVD (even colder storage).

In addition to backing up the video and audio files you are working with, don't forget to back up your settings and applications as well. If you can afford to do so, keep an external hard drive available as part of your backup system that is an exact copy or clone of your entire encoding system, and plan on recloning it once every 30 or 60 days. This way, if anything happens, you have a perfect image of your entire system that can be used to quickly get you back online. Apple's Leopard (OS X 10.5) comes with a built-in backup system known as Time Machine, but many other backup systems are available for both the Macintosh and the PC.

Input/Output

Although you may not specifically have to purchase this separately, be very conscious of your system's hardware I/O ports, because each protocol typically has different supported read/write speeds, which will greatly affect your performance for copying files back and forth and compressing files on external drives. FireWire is a great ubiquitous connection these days (and external FireWire drives are quite cheap now), but it has been surpassed by newer protocols such as FireWire 800 and eSATA.

Software

Hardware, of course, is only one piece of the compressionist's toolkit. You're also going to need a variety of software to help you get the job done.

Operating System Agnosticism

Although choosing an operating system is a religious issue for many people in this industry, no operating system is inherently superior for video encoding. The most important thing is to choose the one that best matches your existing workflow. There are more transcoding options on the Mac side, and the software is typically a little cheaper; however, the hardware will cost more. Like many things, it's a trade-off.

Players

The first part of being able to encode video is being able to play it back. With the range of file formats and codecs in use (see Chapter 2 for more details), you may often find yourself presented with a file that doesn't conform to your production standards. Keeping a variety of video players handy (not just the usual suspects) is a useful way to verify that the video file you need to encode works and is in a format that will work in your particular workflow.

Rippers

The term *rippers* sounds like the evil tools of pirates and misguided college kids, but the fact of the matter is they are a perfectly legal and necessary tool that should be part of any compressionist's toolkit. A ripper is a specialized encoder that allows you to convert DVDs into a format readily understood and usable by your encoding workflow. Though not the best source material for encoding video, DVDs have become a popular way of moving files around because they are small and lightweight (easy to ship) and nearly universally playable. The problem with using DVDs as source material for reediting and reencoding is not playability but access. Although a DVD can act as just another data storage medium, just like hard drives or flash media, DVDs written in the DVD-Video format recognized by hardware and software DVD players store MPEG-2 files in video objects (VOBs), which include metadata that makes the discs readable in consumer players. These VOBs need to be disassembled—a process often described as *unpacking* or *ripping*—to extract MPEG-2 video files that can be edited and reencoded on your computer.

A popular (and useful) DVD ripper on the Macintosh is DVDxDV (*www. dvdxdv.com*), which allows you to extract whole sections or just small clips by marking in and out points from a video DVD. You can export the files as a number of high-resolution file types, making it easy to then transcode them to whatever formats are needed. Several PC ripping tools are also available; however, many automatically transcode the video to another editing or delivery format on the fly, which means they're optimized for speed rather than quality. Although this seems appealing and can save time, I haven't been impressed with the results of such direct-from-DVD encoding and, as such, prefer to keep the extraction from DVD to high-quality format and do my transcoding later.

Compression Tools

Chapter 5 discusses compression applications in specific detail, but I'll lay the groundwork for that chapter now by discussing the categories of compression tools in use today. Some applications—usually the cheaper and free tools—are meant to encode only one video clip at a time. Some applications meant for other purposes, such as editing, creating graphics, or authoring DVDs, can also encode video clips. These single-encode tools are useful for one-off projects and jobs that have simple settings but are typically used as part of some other workflow, not just video compression.

If you are reading this book, you probably have more than just one clip at a time that you need to deal with, so you'll likely need a batch encoding tool to get your compression jobs done. Using a batch encoder will allow you to create settings as a template that is stored separately from the videos, then apply them to a lot of files at the same time, and finally send them off to encode. The application encodes the video one format at a time but will keep the rest queued and begin encoding them one after the other until all files have been completed. Batch encoding is incredibly handy because hours of content can be queued at night or on dedicated machines while you do more important things. Some batch encoders, such as Inlet Technologies' Fathom, also have what is called *concurrent-mode encoding*. Certain codecs do not support encoding across multiple processors on the same machine, so in effect you may not be getting the most use out of your system. Concurrent mode recognizes this and allows the computers to begin working on multiple video encodes simultaneously until the processors are maxed out.

Although you will most likely pick one compression tool as your primary workhorse, it's a very good idea to have a few of these tools installed so that you can switch between them as needed. Certain applications perform better than others for certain types of files and certain types of video. For example,

I used to receive uncompressed video files from record labels in New York regularly for encoding to various sizes meant for Web delivery. One band regularly sent over videos that were shot and edited in such a way that the standard deinterlacing options available in my normal compression application did not do a very good job of combining the fields into a progressive image. I knew that when that band's content came in, I'd want to use some other application that had a wider range of deinterlacing options available.

Another reason to be familiar with a couple of the major compression tools is that over time, support and features may change enough to merit switching from one to another for your day-to-day work. The flexibility to switch between different applications to get the best performance and results will help set you apart as a top-notch compressionist.

Analysis/Quality Control

It's not enough just to encode the video—you need to make sure it actually works. This is the fundamental premise of quality control (QC). QC isn't just about making sure the video file opens and plays back either. True QC means replicating the environment in which the video will be consumed and testing its performance there. As a compressionist, this means having access to a variety of DVD players, computers, and mobile devices—or whatever gives you the broadest representation of your target platform(s)—to assure that the content you are creating will play back on them. The files have to be tested in their entirety; it's very tempting to test just the first few seconds of any clip, but until you've reviewed the entire video to verify full playback without losing audio/video sync, dropping frames, and so on, your compressed video has not passed QC. After all, nothing can be more embarrassing than delivering files that do not work.

As you can imagine, this process can be quite time-consuming. It may be impossible to check every single frame of every video you encode, so you have to decide what level of spot-checking you are comfortable with in order to catch any serious problems. Several companies have also developed software and hardware designed to perform the same QC in a matter of seconds that would take a human being all day to do; however, some of these products can be expensive, so again it's a matter of how important QC is to your work when deciding how much time and money you invest in performing it.

Video meant for playback on the Internet should also be checked to see whether the file sizes you have encoded the video to will allow the user to watch the video comfortably as it downloads (if that is the intended goal). Regardless of how great the video looks, if the file is too big to download and watch simultaneously, then the video ultimately fails to deliver the desired experience. It's better, instead, to reduce the quality slightly in order to get the file down to a manageable size and thus make the viewing experience more enjoyable.

Some encoding tools, such as Rhozet Carbon Coder and Inlet Fathom, have some analysis tools built into them, allowing the QC process to be done as part of the encoding process. Stand-alone products such as Inlet's Semaphore analyze video after the encode process to verify specific settings.

Aspect Ratio Calculator

In the course of scaling and cropping all that video, you end up doing a lot of math to determine the new dimensions. In the past few years, several handy tools have cropped up to make this easier on those of us trying to crunch the numbers quickly. Although it might not be the kind of tool you use daily in your workflow, this type of product can come in handy from time to time. Several aspect ratio calculation tools can be used online, and others are available as small downloadable applets. Some of the better ones I've tried include the following:

- The Aspect Ratio Calculator (cross-platform), *www.wideopendoors.net/design/aspect_ratio_calculator.html*

- The Screen Aspect Ratio & Dimension Calculator (online tool), *www.silisoftware.com/tools/screen.php*

- Bitrate and Aspect Ratio Converter (Windows-only), *www.afreecodec.com/win/428/bitrate-amp-aspect-ratio-calculator*

Video Storage Calculator

VideoSpace is a free widget for Mac OS X that calculates the disk space required for a given duration, codec, frame rate, and audio setting. It works in both directions, so you can calculate time to space or space to time as indicated by the direction of the arrow between the two input areas.

You can find the video storage calculator widget here:

www.digital-heaven.co.uk/videospace

You can find other storage calculators as online tools as well, though I'm particularly fond of the easy-to-use nature of the Digital Heaven widget.

Pick Your Poison

Now that you are fully armed with information about the tools of the trade, it's time for you to build out or at least enhance your encoding workflow. What is important to note here is that every encoding solution can be as specific as you need it to be. There is no need to pick a specific platform or operating system that *you have* to support to make your encoding solution work. If you are more comfortable on PCs, stay on PCs. If you're a Mac fan boy, then geek out and let your Mac flag fly.

Supporting the compression of lots of video on a regular basis is hard enough, so there is no need to make the process harder on yourself by adding some specific solution that is marketed as *the* encoding solution. No single encoding solution is superior to all others in every situation. The solution that's right for you is the one you develop to answer the needs you have. So, get out there and check out all the options available, and start testing them until you find the one that works for you.

PRODUCTIVITY TIPS

Now that you have your compression setup and workflow in place, let's review some good ideas to follow while encoding.

Minimizing Quality Loss Without Overdoing It

Typically, though not always, the goal of video compression is to get the best possible quality out of the smallest amount of data (the most bang for your bits, as it were). So what exactly does that mean in terms of encoding?

To begin with, you want the best ingest-quality source you can get your hands on. I oftentimes like to use a painting metaphor to describe the bits that make up a video clip. The more paint (or bits) making up the source, the better the end result will be, regardless of the file sizes involved.

Until the moment you are creating your delivery format (the clip the end user will actually view), you want to stay in what is referred to as *production* or *authoring* formats and codecs that will retain as much data as possible. They typically take a fairly powerful machine to open and play back, but that's OK—you aren't sharing this version outside your postproduction workflow, so leave it big and buy another hard drive if you need it. You want all the data possible available right up until the moment you create the final version. At that point, you are going to subject this super-high-quality, super-high-data-rate file to all the magic, trickery, and science you can in order to maintain superior video and audio quality while removing as much of the data (bits, paint, whatever) from the process as possible.

That said, don't be silly and take low-resolution source files and convert them to some high-quality format in the hopes that you will get a superior end result. You can't invent bits that weren't there to begin with. You will waste your time and end up with large, just-as-ugly video as the end result. The quality of the source you get, whether it is uncompressed, DV, or something else, is the highest quality you should concern yourself with for the duration of that job.

Stay Organized

As I mentioned earlier in the "Storage" section of this chapter, if you are doing any kind of serious encoding, regardless of the volume of work, you are going to make a whole heck of a lot of new files. It becomes very easy, very quickly to lose files, or worse, erase something you didn't mean to erase. How do you need to stay organized when it comes to encoding?

- **Don't work on your desktop.** It is very tempting to keep all the files you are working with on your desktop. Do not do this! The desktop is a temporary space that can get cluttered very quickly. Instead, set up a work folder in your user account.

- **Use source and export folders.** Within your work folder, set up both an incoming work area and an outgoing work area (just like the little baskets people used to have on their desk). This way all your source material has an assigned spot to live in for the time you need it, which can be regularly erased to make more space. Your newly created files have a special location to go until you have time to back them up, upload them, or do whatever needs to happen after encoding. This is

an area that will also be regularly deleted to make room, but since you
know all the files that live here were newly created, make sure they have
been archived somehow before deleting.

- **Create client or project folders.** If you have a lot of different unre-
lated projects, maybe across multiple clients, it's also a very good idea to
give each its own unique folder within the incoming and outgoing sections. Nothing is more embarrassing than delivering the wrong content
to the wrong person.

- **Develop a storage policy.** As described in the "Storage" section, make
keeping your storage organized part of your daily or weekly schedule.
Regularly remove files you no longer need on your active system to
some sort of backup, and then review the backup from time to time to
make sure it is also organized.

File-Naming Conventions

Choose a method for naming your files, and stick to it as best you can. It's
very easy to get lazy about naming files and give them generic names like
Finished Movie.mov, but will you remember what that was in a month
when you need to use the file again? Probably not—especially if you've
used similar names for other video files. Even just a few years ago, we were
limited to only a few characters for filenames. Both OS X and Windows
XP made it possible to have much longer filenames, but often only the first
dozen characters or so will be visible in the operating system, making it
hard to differentiate between similarly named files.

Filenames should be long enough to help you describe what the file is without opening it but short enough to work in the computer environment. File
spaces were also once a taboo of computers but have become acceptable to
use on local machines. However, files on remote servers such as a Web or
FTP server typically cannot read across a space in a filename, so substituting
an underscore is a good policy.

Also, remember that at minimum when encoding, you are going to have
two very similar files: the source and the export. And these days you typically have more than just one export; you may have half a dozen exports
from one source clip, accounting for a variety of data rates, formats, and
resolutions. File extensions will help you easily differentiate most of the different formats, but all the movies exported for the Web will be in the same

format but at different data rates meant to target different qualities of the same source. In this scenario, it's common to denote the different qualities with a numeric value of the target data rate. So if you have three encodes of the same movie—one meant for dial-up connections, one for middle-of-the-road DSL/cable, and one super-high-quality movie meant for high-bandwidth DSL/cable modem—you can easily differentiate between them by adding their target data rate to the filename—which, in this example, would mean adding something like _56, _200, and _800 to the end of the filenames to denote the data rate differences between versions. It's also a good idea to keep the numeric value in the same base, so convert the earlier data rates in megabit per second to their equivalents in kilobits per second (for example, 1.5Mbps would become 1500Kbps for naming purposes).

Experimenting Can Be a Good Thing

Even the most proficient compressionist has to do some trial-and-error encoding from time to time to optimize the settings for a specific video. The newer you are to encoding, the more trial-and-error work you may need to perform in order to get the exact results you want from a clip. Save yourself a lot of time and effort by performing these dry runs on short clips rather than on your entire video. Many encoding tools allow you to mark in and out points around a specific part of a video, but if yours doesn't, find a way (through either an editing tool or QuickTime Pro) to create a short, self-contained clip you can use to tweak and perfect your settings.

If the image of your video content changes dramatically from beginning to end (for example, cutting between fast-moving outdoor scenery and indoor headshot interviews), then you may want to perform experiments on one or two sections of the video to make sure you are optimizing it for one specific type of scene at the detriment of the others. Using these short clips allows you to quickly adjust and reencode your content several times very quickly until you get the results you want. Then set the entire video (or multiple videos) to encode to the final setting.

Keep a few clips around as test encodes for new applications as they come out (or even upgrades of the same application). These clips should run the gamut of the same types of video you are likely to receive for encoding (for some, this may mean from super-high-quality, gorgeous HD content all the way down to video shot on a cell phone). I find it useful when new products or upgrades come out to run this baseline test video through once at some fairly standardized settings so I can see what type of results I may expect from the application during my regular work. This basic diagnostic experiment can quickly help identify pitfalls in your workflow before they cost you time and money in the middle of a big project.

Make Your Own Recipe Book

I thought at some point I was being clever by referring to compression settings as *recipes*, but then I discovered that several of my friends who also had encoding jobs referred to them as recipes. If you are going to have recipes for video compression, you might as well organize them into a cookbook. You may not have to refer to it every time you work with content, but it's comforting to know that you have a reference somewhere when you need it.

My own cookbook is a handwritten book full of the settings that I have found to work specifically for certain clients over the years. I've also included specs sent to me by clients as the deliverable they wanted (though often these get tweaked slightly over time). Mine is a handwritten list because I have found I retain things that I have to write out longhand better, but I have met others who just keep a running text file or Word document that has all their favorite usual settings. Check out Chapters 6 through 9 for some starter recipes for your cookbook.

Mezzanine, or In-Between, Files

It isn't practical for most people to try to keep uncompressed versions of every video they create; it is possible to "lightly" compress the same video to some format in between the finished deliverable and the source. These files are known as *mezzanine* versions. Mezzanine is an architectural term for an intermediate floor found between two main floors of a building. In the encoding world, it describes a file that is high enough quality to act as an archive and encoding master but sufficiently smaller than the original source to be stored and handled practically.

Some people refer to this as an *intermediate* format, but this can get confusing because the term digital intermediate (DI) is used in the postproduction world to describe the high-resolution digital version of a film that can be manipulated digitally (e.g., *color grading*, the act of altering or conforming the colors of the image) but can still be printed to film with no visual loss.

More recently DI has also referred to codecs such as Cineform that make acquisition formats like HDV easier to process and edit. To avoid confusion, compressionists have adopted the term *mezzanine*, and though it hasn't been accepted as a standard, it's widely enough used that others should generally know what you're talking about if you use it.

I-frame-only MPEG-2 video is a popular mezzanine format for many encoding facilities because it is still edit-friendly but relatively small in file size when compared to 10-bit uncompressed video. ProRes 422 and Cineform are also high-quality codecs that are popular both in postproduction and in compression as mezzanine formats.

Archiving and Transcoding

Video clips that get used as part of marketing such as movie trailers or commercials may be first released in one format or size, but over the life of the marketing initiative, may need to be sent out in as many as 20 or more different resolutions and formats. Rather than repeatedly digitizing the same source again and again, you can save a step by storing a mezzanine version of the content somewhere safe and then transcoding from it repeatedly whenever needed. This can potentially save a great deal of time as part of your workflow.

CONCLUSION

By now you should have some idea of what type of compressionist you are and the gear you need to get the job done. But there is still one area of knowledge the compressionist needs if he or she is to be considered a world-class professional. This one area is the difference between just being able to convert video simply and efficiently from one format to another and being able to take any video and draw out the best quality and the most detail from each frame when you compress or transcode it to a deliverable format. Skill in this area is invariably referred to as the "magic of video compression" because the results are sometimes nothing short of a miracle. But when we aren't calling this special knowledge a "dark art," we in video compression just call it *preprocessing*, and although it can be a little specialized (and sometimes a hit-or-miss process), it can be taught to mere mortals. How do you think I learned it?

CHAPTER FOUR

Preprocessing

You have your video shot, captured, and edited, and it's ready to compress, encode, and deliver. But one more step is left before encoding can begin. This step is called *preprocessing*, and it consists of a variety of optimizations you need to perform on the video and audio before you can hand them off to the encoder. These optimizations include deinterlacing, inverse telecining, cropping, scaling, aspect ratio adjustments, noise reduction, brightness and color corrections, and corrections to audio.

Preprocessing is almost always necessary to getting your video to look its best. The goal of preprocessing is to both clean up any noise in the video and optimize its basic elements for playback on the devices you are targeting (TVs, iPods, computers, and so on). Preprocessing is often referred to as the "magic" part of compression because it takes lots of practice to achieve the desired results. This is the most artistic, and frequently misused, part of the compression process, and it's easy to go overboard with the changes until you get a feel for how much you really need to do to your audio and video to optimize it for encoding.

Fortunately, preprocessing is a craft that can be learned, and practice will only make you better at it. Understanding why you preprocess video and audio and how the various types of optimization that occur at this stage affect your final product will help you make your preprocessing choices.

When and What to Preprocess

To some degree, every piece of video will need some preprocessing, but the amount is wholly dependent on both the source video and the format you are creating. There are basic things like scaling and changing the frame rate that will often be required, but color and luma changes should be used judiciously in order to avoid taking away from the intent of the content. Often, new compressionists will want to pull out all the bells and whistles when preprocessing and the results may be negligible at best. Add to that the fact that any additional processing you are asking the machine to do to the content will lengthen the overall encoding process.

Remember the goal of preprocessing is to improve the quality of the video and audio, but not to overpower it, so use a light hand most of the time.

DEINTERLACING VIDEO

As discussed in Chapter 1, most digital video is interlaced when it's created because it is assumed that at some point it is meant for playback on a standard TV. This will not always be the case, and the trend toward progressive (noninterlaced) video will continue; however, for now, most of the clips you compress will come to you as interlaced video. Because interlaced video is unacceptable for Web delivery, deinterlacing video for playback on the Web or other progressive displays is a fundamental and necessary step.

If the source video is left with interlacing lines intact, the output will appear as jagged lines. The lines do not make for a good viewing experience and are also difficult to encode for a couple of reasons. Because moving objects will keep merging and reassembling (the two fields moving out of step), motion estimation will become difficult, making the encode very inefficient. The interlaced image will also have more detail than is necessary to display the image, so additional bits are wasted when relaying this redundant detail.

You can perform a deinterlace in several ways. Each is designed to optimize different types of images and different types of motion within the video. All in all, there are approximately eight ways to perform a deinterlace, though those eight have several different names by which they are recognized, depending on who you are working with.

Blend

The first common deinterlace method is referred to as *blending*, also known as *averaging* and *combining* fields. This method involves both fields being overlaid. This method gives you good results when there's no movement, but it results in unnatural, low-quality movements. The advantage of this approach is that it's a fast way to deinterlace and is good for low-motion scenes, such as interviews, but you will get ghosting every time an image moves.

Weave

The next commonly used method is *weaving*, which shows both fields in each frame. This method basically doesn't do anything to the frame, leaving you with jagged edges but with the full resolution, which can be good.

Area-based

Next is *area-based* deinterlacing, which blends nothing but the jagged edges. You do this by comparing frames over time or by space/position. It gives you good results in quiet scenes with little movement, because in those circumstances there is nothing to blur.

Motion Blur

The *motion blur* method blurs the jagged edges where needed, instead of mixing (that is, blending) them with the other field. This way, you get a more film-like look. You may have to apply Motion Blur with a program such as Apple Final Cut Pro or Adobe After Effects before using a compression application.

Discard

With the *discarding* method, you discard every second line (leaving the movie at half the original height) and then resize the picture during playback. Because this is the same as skipping Field 2, Field 4, Field 6, and so on, you could also call this Even Fields Only or Odd Fields Only. Although you won't get artifacts from trying to blend or merge the images, you'll lose half the resolution, and motion will become jerky.

TIP It is rare for a compression application to offer all the deinterlacing options listed here and they may have their own naming scheme for them. Experiment with the options to find the ones that work for you.

Bob

The *bob* approach displays every field (so you don't lose any information) one after the other (that is, without interlacing) but with double the frames per second. Thus, each interlaced frame is split into two frames (that is, the two former fields) at half the height. Sometimes bobbing is also called progressive scanning. However, since the bob approach doesn't analyze areas or the differences between fields, the two approaches are not really the same (see the next section).

Progressive Scan

Progressive scanning analyzes the two fields and deinterlaces only the parts that need to be deinterlaced. The main difference between progressive scanning and area-based is that progressive scanning gives you a movie with twice the frames per second instead of the standard 25 fps or 30 fps movie, thus leaving you with perfect fluidity of motion. To say it more academically, it has high temporal and vertical resolution.

This method is also variously called motion-adaptive, bob and weave, and intelligent motion-adaptive.

Motion Compensation

NOTE If you control the video production process for your content and know you don't plan to distribute via a traditional broadcast, then try to keep your whole project in progressive mode to avoid issues with deinterlacing.

The *motion compensation* method analyzes the movement of objects in a scene, while the scene consists of a lot of frames. In other words, it involves tracking each object that moves around in the scene, thus effectively analyzing a group of consecutive frames instead of just single frames.

Although effective for horizontal motion, some software for this technique does not handle vertical motion at all and may fall back on selective blending or other techniques when it is unable to resolve the motion vectors.

TELECINE AND INVERSE TELECINE

Telecine is the process of transferring motion picture film into electronic form. The term is also used to describe the machine used in this process. Traditional motion picture film runs at exactly 24 fps progressive scan, which doesn't convert to the 59.94 fps of NTSC or the 50 fps of PAL.

Converting from film to PAL is easy. The video is sped up 4 percent to 25 fps and converted into progressive PAL.

The telecine process for NTSC is more complex: the film is first slowed down 0.1 percent to 23.976 fps and is then converted to 59.94 fps by using *3:2 pulldown* (**Figure 4.1**). In this process, the first frame of film becomes three fields of video, the next frame becomes two fields of video, the next becomes three fields, and so on, resulting in two out of five frames having fields that come from different source frames.

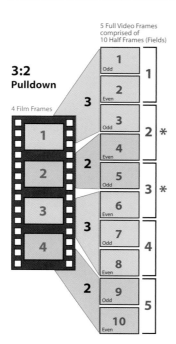

Figure 4.1 In the 3:2 pulldown process inherent to NTSC telecine, each 4 frames of film become 10 fields/5 frames of video by using a 3-then-2 field pattern to maintain the smooth motion of the film in the newly created video.

To correctly compress video that has been telecined, it is crucial to be able to identify these duplicate frames and then remove them. Inverse telecine basically reconstructs the four frames from every five to turn the source back into progressive video.

CROPPING

Cropping is a way of identifying a specific region of the video to use in the compression, excluding the other areas of the source frame. TVs do not display the entire image that is transmitted. Instead, they are *overscanned*, meaning slightly larger than the viewable area of a standard TV. This is done for several reasons, all of which culminate in needing to hide irregularities that exist in the edges of the video frames. Production people are aware of this and have created three regions of a video image that affect how they frame shots and incorporate graphic overlays: overscan, action safe, and title safe (**Figure 4.2**).

Figure 4.2 This type of image will be familiar to anyone who has looked through a video camera viewfinder. It depicts the action- and title-safe areas that a camera operator needs to be conscious of when framing a shot. Compressionists need to be aware of these regions as well and use them as a general guideline for cropping nonbroadcast content.

SAFE IMAGE
SAFE TITLE

Mary Jane Skalski
Producer, The Station Agent

Keep text within this boundary
Keep graphics within this boundary

The outermost region of the video is known as the *overscan* region. It will not appear on standard consumer TV screens, and it is often used to store information that isn't meant to be viewed by the general public, such as the edge of the set or cables and other equipment. Professional-grade monitors have a mode that allows the overscan to be viewed, known as *underscan* mode. These monitors may also include white lines like the viewfinder that show where the title-safe and action-safe areas are located.

The *action-safe* area is the larger rectangle within the image area. This area displays approximately 90 percent of the video image and is where camera operators will make sure to keep the primary action framed up in order to keep it viewable on TVs. As of 2007, most TV stations and networks will also place information within this area, such as news tickers, station IDs, and advertisements.

The smaller rectangle in the image is the *title-safe* area (comprising about 80 percent of the visible image). It is far enough in from the four edges of a standard CRT TV set that text or graphics should show neatly without any distortion caused by the curved glass at the edges of the screen. Modern TVs—CRTs included—display more than the title-safe area without any distortion, so though not specifically necessary, it is still applied as a good rule of thumb in many productions.

When compressing video not meant for rebroadcast or playback on a standard TV, it's necessary to crop the active picture area at minimum to the action-safe area. However, depending on the action in the frame, it may be possible to crop even more aggressively, thus focusing on the action better (and possibly improving the picture quality).

SCALING

Scaling is another key part of the preprocessing process, and it refers to resizing the cropped source rectangle to the proper output frame size—for example, going from a 720 by 480 (standard-definition) source frame to a 320 by 240 output frame for Web video (**Figure 4.3**).

Figure 4.3 These images demonstrate how a 720 by 480 source clip (left) can be scaled down to 320 by 240 (right) for Web delivery with no loss in quality.

Scaling up video to higher frame sizes (as shown in **Figure 4.4**) is not recommended, but in the case of user-generated content (such as that captured via mobile phone), it is sometimes necessary. Be prepared for poor results when you go the upscaling route.

Figure 4.4 Upscaling, unlike downscaling, is a bad idea—you can't add pixels that weren't in the image to begin with without compromising quality.

A key question when scaling video for Web playback is just how big should you resize to? There are all sorts of possibilities, but here are two general rules of thumb: the larger the frame size, the bigger the output file will need to be to maintain good quality, and the slower it will play on some machines. Of course, very small frame sizes will always be low quality, so you need to find a good balance that works for your projects. Here are some general guidelines, regardless of aspect ratio:

- **Widths of 640 pixels:** This is a great high-quality encode if you don't need to worry about file size or playback speed (some older computers will have difficulty playing back files this large without dropping frames).

- **Widths of 400 to 480 pixels:** Though smaller than SD, these frame sizes are still large enough for good viewing on modern computer displays. Widths of 400 to 480 will also fit in well with modern Web site designs.

- **Widths of 320 pixels:** Ironically, just seven years ago, 320x was considered "large" for video files for the Web, but no more. This makes a small but viewable video file.

- **Widths of 300 pixels and smaller:** On a computer screen, these will look more like moving postage stamps—not a rich video experience. These are more suited to mobile video, given the screen resolution and bandwidth.

For more details on general guidelines for frame sizes, see **Table 4.1**. These ratios assume correct pixel aspect ratio (PAR).

Table 4.1 Common Sub-SD Frame Sizes

Output	Full-Screen (4:3)	Wide-Screen (16:9)
Near-DVD quality	640x480	640x360
Large broadband	480x360	480x272
Medium broadband	400x300	400x224
Small broadband and large mobile	320x240	320x180
Web dial-up and medium mobile	240x180	240x134
Small mobile	160x120	160x90

Image Aspect Ratio Correction

It's not uncommon in modern postproduction to deliver letterboxed content (for example, a 16:9 image that has black bars above and below the image to fill a 4:3 screen). Some cameras actually shoot in letterbox, but more often the bars are added in postproduction to make an edit more cinematic (wide-screen being so heavily tied to film).

Some broadcast facilities will also ship finished content on tapes in *anamorphic* format—that is, wide-screen content that is horizontally squished to fit in 4:3. During playback, specialized hardware is used to restore the wide-screen aspect ratio. When working with content that is either letterboxed or anamorphic, it's important to correct the image appropriately. In the case of letterboxing, this probably means cropping out the black bars, and in the case of anamorphic, it means changing the aspect ratio from 4:3 to 16:9 to correct the image.

Pixel Aspect Ratio Correction

An important element of scaling is pixel aspect ratio correction. Generally speaking, production formats such as DV use nonsquare pixels. For example, you already know DV-NTSC is 720 by 480. Just by looking at the numbers, you would assume that the aspect ratio is 3:2. But that's not the case. DV-NTSC is either 4:3 or 16:9, depending on how it was produced. In 4:3 mode, the pixels are more narrow than square, and in 16:9 mode, they're more wide than square. Nonsquare pixels are also used for MPEG-2 for DVD and MPEG-1 for SVCD, with different shapes for MPEG-2 for SVCD.

Web video formats, however, use square pixels, which makes it easier to do the math. For example, 320 by 240 is 4:3 in square pixels.

Make sure you get the aspect ratio correction right when you convert to square-pixel sources from nonsquare-pixel sources by verifying that the output frame size matches the source aspect ratio. So if you use a 4:3 source, a 4:3 frame size such as 160 by 120, 320 by 240, 400 by 300, or 640 by 480 (all square pixel) are acceptable choices, even if the source frame size is 720 by 480, 720 by 486, 640 by 480, or 352 by 480 (all nonsquare pixel).

Creating Square-Pixel Footage for Nonsquare Output

Because most applications create still images that consist of square pixels, most of the animations and still images in a project have a square-pixel aspect ratio. Some applications, however, give an option for selecting between square and nonsquare pixel compositions. If you use square-pixel footage with a resolution of 720 by 480, your video will appear slightly larger than footage in a 720 by 480 DV-NTSC project because of the difference in pixel dimension.

When creating square-pixel still images to combine with DV-NTSC footage, use a frame size of 720 by 534 and disable Maintain Aspect Ratio for the images.

NOISE REDUCTION

Noisy video is a big headache for video compressionists. Random noise causes pixels to change rapidly and constantly, making it difficult for the codec to encode the clip correctly.

Noise reduction encompasses a variety of techniques to remove that noise from an image, making it easier to compress. Very simple noise reduction algorithms are just blurs that hide grain but make the image softer as well, such as when a median filter is applied (**Figure 4.5**). More advanced algorithms try to blur only the parts of the image that have grain and may take advantage of differences among frames.

Figure 4.5 Here are two versions of a DV-NTSC clip. On the right it has had a median filter applied. Note the increased softness in the image on the left but the smoother quality of the image also.

Noise Reduction Before Compression

If the damage from video noise is significant enough, such as dust or scratches in film, no amount of blurring will help remove them completely from the image during compression. In this case, you may want to use a stand-alone application, such as Adobe After Effects or Photoshop CS3, to digitally remove the scratches either manually (with a clone tool) or with an automatic scratch removal filter. Once you've treated the source footage to remove the damage, you can then compress the footage as you normally would.

Noise reduction is not always required. If you have a clean video source to work with, simply skip the noise reduction step when preprocessing your work. If you do have damaged footage, it may take several experiments to find the right balance of cleaning up the source without degrading the finished video image.

LUMA ADJUSTMENTS

Image adjustment is the process of using controls, similar to those in image-editing applications, to change aspects such as brightness and contrast. Digital video is described in either RGB or in Y'CbCr (aka YUV) color space. A *color space* (or *model*) is a way of describing and specifying a color. RGB and the Y'CbCr color space formulas contain three variables, also known as *components* or *channels*. RGB's variables are red, green, and blue, while Y'CbCr breaks down as follows: Y is luma (or black and white or lightness), and CbCr is chroma or color (Cb is blue minus luma, and Cr is red minus luma).

This representation addresses the human eye predisposition to green-light sensitivity, which is why most of the information about the proportion of green is in the luma (Y), and only the deviations for the red and blue portions need to be represented. The Y values have twice the resolution of the other two values, Cb and Cr, in most practical applications, such as on DVDs.

Because different color spaces are used by different codecs and video playback devices, image adjustment may be required as part of the preprocessing.

Luma Range Expansion

The RGB color space breaks the steps from black to white into 256 even steps (0 to 255, with 0 being black and 255 being white). Standard TV has only 220 steps from black to white, using black as 16 and white as 235 within the same scale (**Figure 4.6**). Generally, modern postproduction applications automatically keep black and white consistent. However, if blacks and whites appear either crushed (too black) or faded (too white), the luma range may need to be remapped.

Figure 4.6 Television and computer-based video use different luma ranges to depict the range between black and white. When not compensated for in preprocessing, this distortion of the luma range can leave video either washed out or too dark.

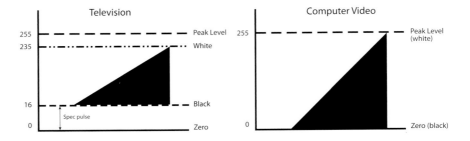

The Digital Color Meter

Apple users have some built-in help when figuring out luma and chroma values. In the Utilities folder (Application > Utilities) is the Digital Color Meter (**Figure 4.7**). This little application launches a small magnifier and a table that shows the specific RGB value of the samples part of the screen. This application is a handy way of checking values, rather than just trusting that your display is calibrated correctly.

Figure 4.7 Apple's Digital Color Meter makes it easy to check luma and chroma values.

TIP Using noise reduction in addition to adjusting the luma may make achieving proper levels easier.

GAMMA CORRECTION

Gamma is a measurement of how the luma range turns into brightness when it is displayed. Although black and white will look the same under different gamma values, the middle of the range will look different. Different computer platforms and TVs all have different default gammas (though Windows is very close to TV). Apple computers use a value of 1.8 by default, whereas Windows uses a range from 2.2 to 2.5 (TV is 2.2).

As a result, some video may appear to have brighter midtones on an Apple computer than on one running Windows. If you are encoding for a mixed environment or are unsure of what playback device the end user has, it's best to split the difference by targeting a value of 2.0.

Brightness and Contrast

Brightness filters adjust the overall intensity of each pixel in a frame by a fixed amount. *Contrast*, on the other hand, increases or decreases each pixel's value by an amount proportional to how far away from the middle value it is (the farther away, the bigger the change). These values are often used together, rather than separately, because just brightening an image without adjusting the contrast can leave the black levels too muddy gray, rather than the desired black.

Chroma Adjustment

Chroma adjustments affect the color of a video image, similar to the way luma affects the brightness. Changes to the color of the video aren't commonly required—in fact, some compression tools do not even include these filters.

Saturation

NOTE Digital video has a narrower saturation range than RGB, so slightly increasing the saturation will make video look more vibrant on computer screens.

Saturation controls the intensity of a color. Increasing saturation will have the effect of brightening a color artificially, while decreasing it (or desaturating) will remove the color, all without affecting the luminosity of the image.

Hue

Hue is the way of describing a color (for example, red or blue). The hue adjustment in compression tools shifts the color spectrum of the image. It is used to do simple color correction, most often when white levels or flesh tones do not appear correctly. This is a pretty coarse adjustment and should be used with care or not at all.

AUDIO PREPROCESSING

Audio is a huge part of any production and can make or break the viewing experience. There isn't typically a lot of preprocessing that needs to be done with well-produced audio, however. Raw captured audio may need some preprocessing (known as *sweetening*) to clean it up, but this is typically done during the edit process, rather than during preprocessing for compression.

Producing professional audio is its own specialized art, and those needing help with it should seek additional references. To learn how to get the most out of your audio production, try Peter Kirn's excellent book, *Real World Digital Audio*.

Adjusting Volume

Volume is one of the elements easily adjusted in preprocessing, and you can do so in a few different ways. The quickest way is to raise or lower the volume, either by a decibel (dB) or percentage amount. This is another fairly coarse adjustment, akin to turning up or down the volume on your radio. For those needing a little more finesse, there are other possibilities, such as normalization and compression.

Normalization

Normalization is the act of adjusting the audio levels in the content and then raising or lowering the volume of the entire clip so that the loudest sound matches the level you have specified. This is a global adjustment, affecting the volume of the entire track the same way, rather than affecting the relative levels.

Compression

This is a totally different type of compression than what we have discussed so far in this book; with regard to audio, *compression* refers to a specific type of audio filter known as a compressor. Loud noises in a digital audio track can cause distortion, and likewise, quiet sounds, such as whispering, can be lost. An audio compressor can smooth out these issues in an audio track by acting as a dynamic range. By pulling down large spikes and lifting those quiet parts up, compression will ensure that the average loudness is fairly constant.

Noise Reduction

Just as with video, there are also noise reduction filters for audio, although these are more often found in professional audio-editing tools, not in compression tools. Unwanted noise in audio tracks is just as bad for compression as noisy video—bits will be wasted, and the end result will be lower quality than desired. Some compression tools have simple hum-removal filters that will help clean up the audio during encoding, but truly bad audio may need to be preprocessed separately in a professional application such as Digidesign Pro Tools, Apple Soundtrack Pro, or Adobe Audition.

CONCLUSION

Being aware of these preprocessing techniques is great and will no doubt make you a better compressionist. However, the application you use determines how well you will succeed with your content almost as much as the skill set you're developing. Each application, through supporting multiple formats, typically has one or two specific workflows or techniques it does better than most, so knowing how to use several applications can be crucial to successful compression. In the next chapter, we'll dive into the various applications and then spend time focusing on some specific delivery platforms.

Interview with a Compressionist

Name: John Howell

Location: Jacksonville, FL

Title/role: Graphic Designer III (I know, it is incredibly descriptive)

Company: Information Display Systems

URL: *www.ids-sports.com*

How did you get involved in video compression?

I picked it up when I worked for Deepend in London. There was one other guy doing compression at the time, and the workload grew to be too big for just one person, so I picked up some of the work. My first solo job was the trailer for *Gladiator* for the distributor's UK Web site, and it had to be perfect. So, it was pretty intense on-the-job training.

What was your biggest project?

This year was my first year at IDS. My first job for the company was one of our biggest events of the year. We do the production for all the video walls at the Players, one of the bigger tournaments on the PGA Tour schedule. We introduced a new display technology that allowed us to basically play unlimited amounts of preproduced video content on our "Monsterboard" giant video boards along with the scorecards and statistics and leaderboards we usually show.

The content came from our client on a hard drive and was about 500 GB of uncompressed AVI video files. That was more than we had room on the drives of the computers that ran the video boards, and the uncompressed files wouldn't play back in real time anyway. I had a problem in that for some of the video I needed to preserve an alpha channel, but the majority of the video needed to just be compressed. After some experimentation with file formats (WMV, DiVX, QuickTime), I settled on using animation-compressed QuickTime files for the movies that needed the alpha channel, which cut the file size to a tenth of the original. For the straight-up compressed files, I chose H.264-compressed QuickTime files, which turned out absolutely beautifully.

Our client had some reservations about using compressed video, but when I broke out the Pepsi Challenge and showed them a side-by-side comparison of their original video to my H.264 video, they couldn't tell the two apart.

What was your favorite project?

I used to do a lot of music video compressions. Tapes would come in from a bunch of different record labels, and I would just digitize and compress all day. It was a very simple, straightforward workflow. I got to see a lot of videos I wouldn't have otherwise seen because MTV stopped showing music videos. So, it was kind of win-win for me.

What's your format of choice?

I would have to say QuickTime even though it isn't really a format and more a playback option. But I like that Apple (at least for now) will allow me to do pretty much whatever I want with my media. I can edit and transcode from one format to another to put content on my computer, television, or phone. Windows Media and Real Player don't let people do that. Wow, am I still beating that dead horse? Guess so.

What does your average workday look like?

Most of my time is spent designing and building shows for our golf events. I work very closely with a programmer, and that is pretty much what the two of us have done for the better part of a year. I recently started the process of training and overseeing a couple of other designers to do what I do, which should be nice to spread out the workload. I also spend a lot of time in meetings because I am one of the technical authorities in the company, and people generally run things by me and sometimes I have useful advice.

What does your encoding hardware look like?

At my current job, I don't actually have any encoding hardware. To do any compression I need, I have to use my personal hardware. I am currently using a dual 2 GHz Apple G5 for work I can take home or my 2 GHz MacBook laptop for things in the office or if work comes up when I am on the road.

What's your encoding software of choice?

I pretty much exclusively use Compressor. Occasionally I have to produce WMV files for people at work, and I run those out of After Effects on the PC they want me to use.

What role does compression play in your work?

It plays a pretty big role these days. The technology of the outdoor video displays we use has advanced to the point where we can pretty much show any video content on the boards and it will look great. So, it is important for us to be able to manage and play back the content we receive from our clients. Hard drive space is a concern, and quality has to be pretty close to broadcast. So not just compression but well-done compression is becoming something we cannot overlook.

What surprises you most about video compression today?

A lot of products in the field have gone to real-time compression. The computers and special video cards have advanced to amazing levels. Just pull a video off a tape, and you have files straightaway. When I started doing this, we would digitize our content during the day, tweak our settings, and then leave the files to compress overnight and hope the computers didn't crash. To some degree, that is still how I work because most of what I do is one-off, and we haven't invested in a real compression solution. Real-time stuff just blows my mind, though.

CHAPTER FIVE

Compression Tools

By now we've discussed pretty much every concept associated with video compression. We've also talked about the various hardware and software that supports it, but one key topic we have not addressed in depth is the compression tools. More video compression software applications are on the market now than ever before. Each has its pros and cons that make it ideal or less than ideal for different solutions. The tools available today run the gamut from free, easy-to-use, one-click tools (for people who want to convert small amounts of content quickly without knowing much about how the technology works) to enterprise-level applications (designed for business-class customers who have hundreds of hours of content daily or weekly to convert, manage, and maintain). Unfortunately, most users do not understand what differentiates the free applications from the expensive ones; therefore, it is important to explore all the tools available, look at all their capabilities, and understand what sets them apart from each other.

This chapter will identify the major compression tools you are likely to run into in your regular work. I'll point out their distinct characteristics as well as let you know where they are weak. We'll quickly set up a different type of compression job with each application, keeping in mind that the next four chapters will go into further detail on compressing video for delivery to specific platforms (such as the Web, TV, DVD, and mobile devices). I'll include a variety of recipes to help get you started with your compression, and while evaluating these tools, I won't focus on the quality of one over another (with a few exceptions that I'll mention specifically). Generally speaking, each of these products is fairly good at what it's designed to do, so we are instead focusing on the nature of how they operate and calling out formats and features they may have that make them better choices than their competitors in specific situations. In addition to analyzing the most commonly used tools, I will also briefly cover the cheap tools that have come out as well as the very expensive enterprise tools so that when you finish this chapter, you'll have a full understanding of the spectrum of compression options you have at your fingertips.

Remember that no one tool may be the answer to all your needs when it comes to video compression—in fact, it can be a detriment to how you operate over the long run if you use a single tool for all your compression tasks. If you become reliant on just one application, you then become reliant on its developers to ensure they stay up-to-date with modern codecs and features that allow you to do your job and improve the process over time. Spreading your knowledge and workflow out over a few applications breaks that reliance and allows you to use the most appropriate tool for each job. It's only natural that one application may dominate your workflow, serving the majority of your encoding needs, but it's valuable to be aware of competitive tools and how they operate.

Video compression software has matured and now supports a wide range of output formats, from Web and mobile standards such as MPEG-4, Windows Media, QuickTime, and Flash to VC-1 and H.264 for next-generation Blu-ray Disc.

Adobe Media Encoder

The Adobe Media Encoder (AME) (**Table 5.1**) isn't a stand-alone encoding tool, but it's important to discuss here because it is the primary export tool for Adobe's Premiere Pro and Encore. To learn how to encode Blu-ray video from Premiere for use with Encore, see Chapter 6. Those using Adobe's tools will want to make themselves familiar with how it works and when to use it. With the launch of Premiere Pro CS3, Adobe brought the editing application back to the Mac platform for the first time in five years.

Adobe has a very tight integration with its other video and audio applications, so AME is very useful for those also working in After Effects, Flash Professional, Encore, Audition, and Soundbooth. You can launch it directly from within Premiere Pro. A key feature AME supports is the ability to export to Flash with an alpha channel, which makes it easy to incorporate composited video into Flash projects from Premiere Pro or After Effects.

Table 5.1 Adobe Media Encoder Specs

Price	$799 (as part of Premiere Pro CS3)
Developer	Adobe Systems, Inc.
Current Version	N/A
OS	Mac OS X 10.4.1 or later/Windows XP or later
Formats	MPEG-1, MPEG-2 (for DVD, SVCD, and Blu-ray Disc), QuickTime, H.264 (for Web, mobile, and Blu-ray), Flash 8, Real Media, and Windows Media (Real Media and Windows Media are supported for export on Windows only)

What Does It Look Like?

AME was redesigned and given a great deal more features with the launch of Premiere Pro CS3. It is a self-contained, one-panel interface that includes several different tabs for the various settings you need to adjust as well as a preview monitor showing you what a frame of the exported video will look like. Anytime you adjust a setting, the preview monitor will update to show the change.

The following sections give a full breakdown of each tab in the Adobe Media Encoder (**Figure 5.1**).

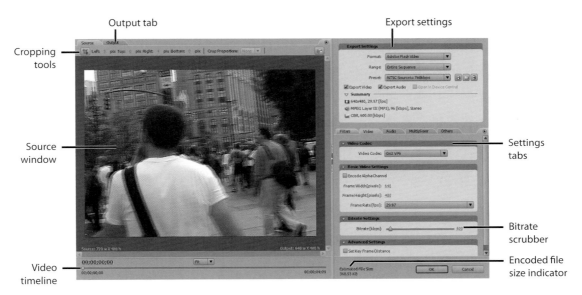

Figure 5.1 The Adobe Media Encoder interface

Source: The Source tab on the left side of the screen shows the incoming video that you are planning to encode. Below the video is a timeline and a marker that allows you to scrub through the video frame by frame to see different scenes of the video. Above the video is a cropping tool. When you click the Crop icon, a white frame appears on the video and denotes the area of the video that will be cropped out of the final encode.

Output: The Output tab shows an example of what the video will look like after it has been encoded to the selected specifications. Curiously, this is also where you can choose to deinterlace the video. If you are working with interlaced content and planning to show it on the Web, make sure the Deinterlace check box is selected. If you have also cropped the video image in the Source tab, you will want to most likely scale the video to fit the new resolution, unless you are purposely adding letterbox bars to the video to conform it to a different resolution.

Export settings: The Export Settings tab defines the format of your exported video and what basic preset you are using to export it. Finer details and changes can be made to the presets in the tabs below this section; however, this will be the first stop in exporting your clip. In the Format pop-up menu, you can select from the various formats AME supports. In Range, you choose whether to export the entire sequence or the workspace you're using. In Preset, you identify what type of specific deliverable you are making. You will notice that the presets also identify the source video as well.

Since different types of video need to be treated differently during compression, AME has templates for each type of source as well as multiple export options. Though the presets vary from format to format, generally you'll always see HDV, NTSC, and PAL source presets. Select the preset that best identifies your source and the type of deliverable you want to make. If you make changes to the preset, the name will automatically change to Custom to denote that it is no longer the saved template.

AME allows you to save your own custom templates by clicking the disk icon to the right of the Preset pop-up menu. Below Preset are radio buttons that allow you to select the tracks to be exported. Though you will typically be exporting both audio and video, sometimes you might want to have just one or the other. And finally, a Summary area shows the basic details of your encode profile.

Settings tabs: Below the Export Settings tab is a group of five tabs: Filters, Video, Audio, Multiplexer, and Others. Depending on the format you choose, the Multiplexer tab may disappear and be replaced with something else; when choosing QuickTime, for example, this tab becomes Alternatives, and when choosing Real Media or Windows Media, it becomes Audiences.

It is within these tabs that you would make specific changes to the presets that you chose on the Export Settings tab. Note that if you change settings, the Preset pop-up menu immediately changes to Custom. If you decide you want to keep the custom setting you have made, you will need to click the Save icon next to the Preset pop-up menu.

How Does It Work?

To better understand the AME workflow, let's use it to export a sequence for the Web. Let's assume we need to produce a Flash Video targeted toward broadband users and that we are starting with a DV-NTSC sequence.

To export a file for Web delivery, do the following:

1. Select the sequence in the Timeline panel or Program Monitor in Premiere Pro.

2. Specify a range of frames to export. (In a sequence, set the work area; or, in a clip, set an in point and an out point.)

3. Choose File > Export > Adobe Media Encoder (**Figure 5.2**).

Figure 5.2 AME is an export option in Premiere Pro 2. Select this option to export to files and formats such as Flash, Windows Media, and QuickTime.

4. In the Adobe Media Encoder Export Settings area, specify the following options:

- Set Format to Flash.

- Set Range to Entire Sequence.

- Set Preset to Select NTSC Source to 512kbps.

- Make sure both Export Video and Export Audio are selected (**Figure 5.3**).

Figure 5.3 AME's Export Settings tab

5. Crop the image by clicking the Crop icon in the preview window. Then either drag the crop border (the white marquee on top of the video image) or enter specific numbers (representing the number of pixels in from each side). To maintain the proper aspect ratio when cropping, also select a crop proportion ratio. Since our sample is standard DV, I have chosen to maintain a 4:3 aspect ratio when cropping (**Figure 5.4**).

Figure 5.4 The Source tab is for cropping and previewing the incoming video source.

6. To deinterlace the image, select the Output tab, and then select the Deinterlace check box. Since we also cropped the image slightly, select the Scale to Fit check box to ensure the image fits the new image size (**Figure 5.5**).

Figure 5.5 The Output tab allows you to deinterlace the source, scale the video to fit the new image resolution, and preview the applied settings.

7. Click OK.

8. Identify a location to save the file, and click Save.

9. While the video is rendering, a Rendering dialog indicates the progress (**Figure 5.6**). Clicking the small arrow in the dialog opens more details about your render, including when it was started and the time elapsed. This information may be particularly useful on long encodes.

Figure 5.6 The Rendering dialog displays the progress of your encode.

What Makes It Special?

For those working in After Effects and Premiere Pro CS3, the Adobe Media Encoder is an excellent choice for quickly rendering your current sequences and edits to a specific file format and setting. Artists using Flash CS3 Professional to include green-screened (or composited) video may also want to consider using AME to export Flash Video with an alpha channel. And finally, DVD authors working with Encore to create either standard-definition or Blu-ray Discs will want to take advantage of the presets defined in AME's interface that make it very easy to create author-ready material.

What Should You Watch Out For?

AME's biggest shortcoming is that it's not a batch encode tool. You can work on only one piece of content at a time rather than being able to queue up multiple videos to compress. This is very limiting, requiring a compressionist to be on hand to start up new jobs as each old job ends.

Additionally, although AME is encoding a video clip, no other work can be done in Premiere Pro, effectively locking up the machine for editing for the duration of the encode. One final downside is that jobs that are encoding cannot be paused, only canceled. This means that if you have to stop a job, you lose all the work that was done up to that point with no option of picking up and restarting where you left off.

What Should You Remember?

Because it can encode only one video at a time, AME is probably not going to be your primary encoding tool, because it won't handle the volume you need for most jobs. However, if you are using Premiere Pro CS3 or After Effects CS3 regularly and need to quickly export your work to a specific deliverable, then AME is the right tool.

QUICKTIME PRO

QuickTime is the audio and video playback application created by Apple, Inc., in the early 1990s. QuickTime Pro (**Table 5.2**) is essentially the same application, but it adds several incredibly important and useful pieces of functionality to the application, including simple editing and advanced exporting options. We covered the basics surrounding the QuickTime Player in Chapter 2. Now let's look at encoding options for QuickTime Pro more in depth.

Table 5.2 QuickTime Pro Specs

Price	$29.99
Developer	Apple, Inc.
Current Version	7.4
OS	Mac OS X 10.4.9 or later, Windows XP and Vista
Formats	MPEG-1, MPEG-2 for DVD (via a plug-in from Apple), QuickTime, MPEG-4, H.264, WMV9 (via third-party plug-in), and Flash 8 (via third-party plug-in)
Link	*www.apple.com/quicktime/pro/*

QuickTime has been the core of many video- and audio-related applications, including Final Cut Pro, iMovie, and iTunes. Though most consumers do not need QuickTime Pro to view their content, many professionals have relied on the easy-to-use tool for years as part of their production and compression work. QuickTime Pro is available for both Mac and PC users, though it admittedly performs better in its native Apple environment.

Though QuickTime Pro is primarily designed for encoding video in QuickTime-friendly formats such as MPEG-4 and the variety of codecs supported in MOV files, it does have the ability to encode video as other formats such as Flash Video and Windows Media Video through the QuickTime components. Apple developed the software as an open framework, allowing third parties to develop *components*, or plug-ins that extend the existing functionality of QuickTime—primarily in the types of video it decodes or encodes. Third parties have created a multitude of free and for-pay plug-ins, many of which are listed on Apple's site here: *www.apple.com/quicktime/resources/components.html*.

Unlike Adobe Media Encoder, QuickTime Pro is a stand-alone application, although it is also embedded in many other applications as an export option, just like AME. For example, in Final Cut Pro (FCP) users may choose to export a number of ways, but choosing the QuickTime Conversion option launches a window that presents the standard QuickTime Pro options that regular users of it will be familiar with (**Figure 5.7**).

Figure 5.7 QuickTime Pro can be used within other applications, such as Final Cut Pro.

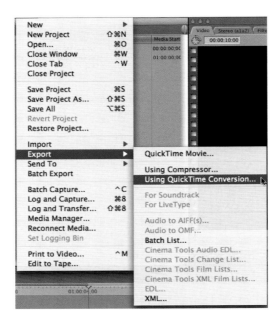

Though QuickTime Pro originally allowed you to export only one piece of video at a time, versions since 7.0 have allowed users to export multiple clips simultaneously. Though each source file would need to be opened separately and have settings applied, it is still useful to be able to continue to work with media when files are queued up and begin exporting.

What Does It Look Like?

Because QuickTime Pro is just an extended set of functionality, you may not immediately notice a difference between the free and Pro version when launching QuickTime. However, once you have registered QuickTime Pro, a number of additional menu options that were once grayed out will now be available, including Share, Export, and Export for Web (**Figure 5.8**).

Figure 5.8 Three options in QuickTime Pro allow you to encode video: Share, Export, and Export for Web.

Both Share and Export for Web are groups of simplified export profiles that make it easy to quickly export your video for e-mailing, embedding in a Web page, or using on an iPod or iPhone. Although you may be happy to use whatever basic settings Apple has provided, most of you will probably want or need access to more advanced features. For that reason, I will focus on the Export option in this section.

Selecting the Export option in the menu opens a dialog in which you get to choose the name of the file you are creating; it also contains a pop-up menu of all the export format options you have (**Figure 5.9**). This is similar to the presets in other applications because several of these options are the same formats but are optimized for different tasks (such as playback on iPhone or Apple TV). If you have installed QuickTime components, which extend your exporting options, those will also appear in this pop-up menu. For example, I have installed Flip4Mac's plug-in, so I have Movie to Windows Media listed as an option.

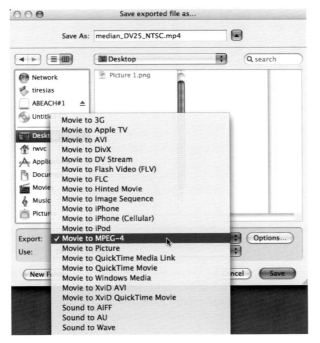

Figure 5.9 QuickTime Pro's Export pop-up menu gives you a choice of several formats and delivery options, including MPEG-4, iPhone, Apple TV, Windows Media, and WAV files. Options may vary depending on the QuickTime components you've installed.

In most cases, once you have selected a preset, you'll need to click the Options button to the right. This launches a new window and gives you access to advanced settings that you can change to the specific parameters needed for your content. It is worth noting that QuickTime Pro will save your most recent settings in memory, so if you need to export several clips with the same parameters, it is necessary only to open and click the Options button during the first file you export.

Figure 5.10 You can see the difference between the export options for an MPEG-4 movie (on the left) and a QuickTime movie (on the right).

Also note that not all the presets listed are movie options. Some of the preset options include still images, an image sequence, or audio-only options such as WAV files. All of these can be useful during the course of production to share certain parts of your work with others, but they do not often get utilized when finishing a piece of content for distribution to a larger audience.

Different profiles will also open different types of option windows. In particular, the Movie to MPEG-4 and Movie to QuickTime Movie options are very different, partially because there are more options available when exporting a MOV file versus an MP4 (**Figure 5.10**).

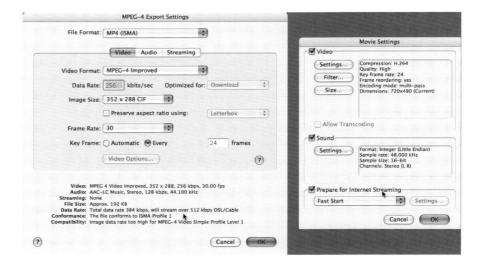

Below the Export pop-up is another pop-up menu called Use. This menu is typically empty. For a few export options, it will have specific templates for specific uses (which is where it gets its name). I have found these do not get updated very often, and because there is no way to save or update them yourself, I typically avoid using them and instead have used specific settings in the options menus.

How Does It Work?

To better understand the QuickTime Pro workflow, let's use it to export a movie. We'll start with a DV-NTSC clip that we want to export as a Quick-Time movie meant for playback on the Web. Let's assume the video will eventually be embedded in an HTML page and that we are targeting both dial-up and broadband users in the same clip. Since we are doing that, we'll have to be conscious of keeping the file size small enough for dial-up end users, while making the image large enough for broadband users to enjoy. Also, let's assume we do not have a QuickTime streaming server, so the file needs to be saved as a buffered download clip, not a streaming clip.

1. Starting with a movie open in QuickTime Player, choose File > Export.

2. Select a name and destination for the file you're creating.

3. If not already selected, choose Movie to QuickTime Movie from the Export pop-up menu, and then click the Options button (**Figure 5.11**). The Movie Settings window is now open and displays a summary of the settings already enabled (see the dialog on the right of Figure 5.10). Make sure both the Video and Sound check boxes are selected to ensure both your audio and video tracks are exported.

TIP Many people will name the file after applying all the various settings. I have found that it's easy to forget to do that later, so as a rule of thumb, I pick a name and location right from the get-go.

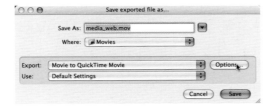

Figure 5.11 The Save exported file as dialog.

4. In the Video section, click the Settings button to open the Standard Video Compression Settings dialog (**Figure 5.12**). In the Motion

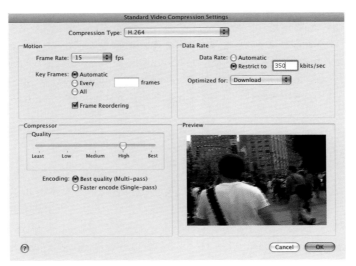

Figure 5.12 The Standard Video Compression Settings dialog gives you access to the basic compression for your video.

section, change the frame rate to 15 fps via the pop-up menu, and in the Key Frames option, select Automatic. With a frame rate of 15 fps, we will have a key frame every four seconds.

5. If it's not already active, select the Frame Reordering check box as well. In the Data Rate section, select Restrict To, and enter **350**. Note that all entries in this box are expressed in kilobits per second (Kbps).

6. Choose Optimized for Download from the pop-up menu.

7. In the Compressor section, select Best Quality (Multi-Pass) for Encoding. The Preview pane displays the first frame of the source video with which we are working. Note that the image is interlaced. We cannot change that here, but we should remember it so that we adjust that before completing our settings.

8. Quickly review all the changes you have made, and if satisfied, click OK to close this window and return to the Movie Settings dialog.

9. In the Movie Settings dialog, click the Filter button. A small window opens that allows you to apply various image filters such as brightness and contrast (**Figure 5.13**). You won't use this feature often, but briefly click through it to be familiar with the options. Note that as you make changes to various settings, the small preview on the lower left updates to reflect the new settings. Click Cancel to return to the Movie Settings dialog without applying any settings.

Figure 5.13 The rarely used Filters window. Use sparingly, but be aware of what's possible, just in case.

10. Click the Size button to open the Export Size Settings dialog (**Figure 5.14**), and using the pop-up menu, choose 320 x 240 as your dimensions. Then select the Deinterlace Source Video check box. There is no need to select the Preserve Aspect Ratio Using check box in this instance; however, you can use this when changing aspect ratios (such as from wide-screen to full-screen). Click OK to return to the Movie Settings dialog.

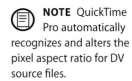 **NOTE** QuickTime Pro automatically recognizes and alters the pixel aspect ratio for DV source files.

Figure 5.14 The Export Size Settings dialog.

11. In the Sound section, click Settings to launch the Sound Settings dialog (**Figure 5.15**). Choose AAC from the Format pop-up menu. Next, choose Mono from the Channels pop-up menu. Since this is just people talking, I'm dropping it to Mono to save on file size, but if music or more dynamic audio were part of the video, I would leave it set to Stereo for richer sound.

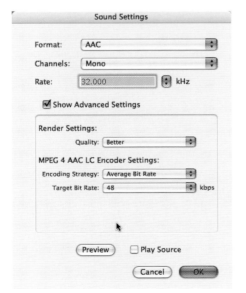

Figure 5.15 The Sound Settings window.

12. For the Rate option, type or choose 32 kHz. Select the Show Advanced Settings check box to expose more options for the audio compression.

13. Under Render Settings, choose Better from the Quality pop-up menu. Under MPEG AAC LC Encoder Settings, select Variable Bit Rate from the Encoding Strategy pop-up menu and recommended from the Target Bit Rate menu. QuickTime Pro will then select the most appropriate data rate, which in this instance is 48 Kbps.

Again, if this were more dynamic audio, I might want to increase both my kHz and my Kbps to something else; however, for audio consisting only of people talking and background noise, I'm willing to decrease the quality for file size.

14. Click OK to return to the Movie Settings dialog.

15. If it is not already active, select the Prepare for Internet Streaming check box, and then choose Fast Start – Compressed Header from the pop-up menu (**Figure 5.16**).

Figure 5.16 The Prepare for Internet Streaming section of the Movies Settings dialog.

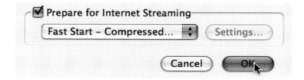

16. Click OK to save all your settings and return to the Save As dialog.

17. Click the Save button to begin the encode process. A progress window will open, displaying graphically the progress of your encode (**Figure 5.17**).

Figure 5.17 The export progress window.

18. When the encode completes, launch your encoded clip in QuickTime Player by double-clicking it or by choosing File > Open and navigating to the save location.

19. Play back the file to confirm that the quality and playback experience is as desired. If the file is lower quality than desired (remember, we were targeting *both* dial-up and broadband users in this exercise), you can experiment with increasing the data rate or key frames to improve the quality. However, keep in mind that the file size will also increase proportionally.

It may also be useful to open the Movie Inspector window (choose Window > Show Movie Inspector) to confirm that the basic settings you applied to the movie are correct (**Figure 5.18**).

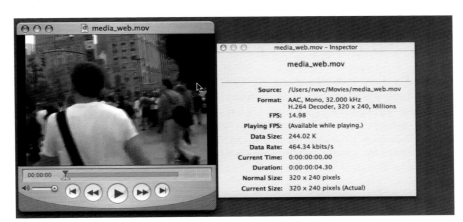

Figure 5.18 The completed movie and the Movie Inspector window (used to confirm the basic settings of the movie).

TIP To see more examples of saving Quick-Time and other formats for the Web, see Chapter 7.

What Makes It Special?

As I mentioned at the beginning of this section, QuickTime Pro is a very useful tool for those in video and audio production, not just compressionists. It is an easy way to quickly edit audio and video files—with simple stitching together of different clips and adding and removing different audio and video layers from files. To fully understand all that QuickTime Pro offers, check out *Apple Pro Training Series: QuickTime Pro Quick-Reference Guide* by Brian Gary, Steve Martin, and Jem Schofield.

What Should You Watch Out For?

QuickTime Pro is not going to be the fastest encoding option for you, and it won't offer you the deepest set of advanced options. The inability to save and store your own custom presets also keep it from being a more robust application. That said, Apple already has a batch application tool that does those tasks called Compressor, so I'm willing to cut QuickTime Pro a little slack here.

Though it does have fairly good format support, QuickTime Pro still doesn't handle them all—especially files associated with disc media (such as DVD MPEG-2s and H.264 files meant for Blu-ray Disc). These files often won't open, and cryptic error numbers (like -2048 or -2003) are your only explanation as to what has happened. You might be able to find some help on the Web that describes the problems, but there is usually not much advice to offer other than trying another application.

What Should You Remember?

QuickTime Pro will most likely never be your primary encoding tool, but it is nonetheless an essential application for anyone who works seriously in the audio and video world. And though many have balked at the price tag, at $30 it is also a bargain by all other standards. My advice is to skip lunch for a few days or one night out at the movies and buy this product!

For Better or Worse, QuickTime Has Come a Long Way

Those who have worked with QuickTime for more than 10 years have seen it change dramatically. It went from a simple playback device to the architecture for the MPEG-4 specification, an interactive platform, and the basis of video and audio in several applications. QuickTime, like many of Apple's products over the years, seems to have suffered from being ahead of its time.

The early part of this decade was really the heyday for QuickTime in many ways, with MPEG-4 first taking off and the interactive capabilities it offered. Many content creators, myself included, took advantage of these features to create unique QuickTime movies that combined video and audio along with Internet-enabled functionality to allow users to have an experience more akin to a DVD than just a linear movie playing (though even more interactive and often much more well-designed).

Unfortunately, as products like the iPod took off and increased the popularity of iTunes (which is actually quite reliant on QuickTime), combined with the rise in popularity of Flash-powered audio and video, interest in interactive QuickTime waned. As a result, support has progressively stalled. Interactive publishers reliant on QuickTime often fear new releases of QuickTime that may further break or drop support on which they had relied.

Man, I sound like a real Debbie Downer, don't I? The reality is that Apple has made a decision to change the focus of QuickTime from an interactive platform of its own to more of an interactive team player, working in compliance with Javascript, AJAX, and other Web development standards. This isn't a bad thing to do (in fact, it's a fairly smart move), as it will give those who want to integrate QT directly in a Web page a smoother workflow. Ultimately, I don't blame Apple for changing their innovation path, though I do wish Apple had openly discussed these changes so that developers and creators using QuickTime had a better understanding of all the possibilities (interactive or otherwise). A clearer roadmap would give those who wish to follow the path a chance to adjust their workflows accordingly.

COMPRESSOR

Compressor (**Table 5.3**) is the stand-alone encoding tool bundled in Final Cut Studio and Final Cut Server. It was initially developed primarily as a batch compression tool for creating DVD-ready MPEG-2 files, but it has expanded over the years to include file formats such as MPEG-4 to offer delivery to other platforms, such as iPods and the Web. Because Compressor is bundled with Final Cut Studio, it's tightly integrated with Final Cut Pro, making it easy to quickly export your Final Cut Pro projects and making it good for encoding.

Table 5.3 Compressor Specs

Price	$1,299 (as part of Final Cut Studio)
Developer	Apple, Inc.
Current Version	3.0.2 released November 2007
OS	Mac OS X 10.4.9 or later
Formats	MPEG-1, MPEG-2 for DVD, QuickTime, MPEG-4, H.264, WMV9 (via third-party plug-in), and Flash 8 (via third-party plug-in), ProRes 422, DVCPRO HD
Link	*www.apple.com/finalcutstudio/compressor*

Like many of the encoders covered in this chapter, Compressor relies on predefined templates as the compression instructions. It comes installed with hundreds of ready-to-use templates, as well as the ability to create new ones easily for custom parameters. There are a variety of advanced preprocessing controls as well as some special controls for passing through, editing, and creating chapter markers for DVDs and QuickTime movies (a popular feature with podcasters).

Another feature unique to Compressor among desktop encoding applications is the concept of grid encoding (submitting jobs to multiple CPUs from one interface). Normally, only enterprise solutions have this feature, but Qmaster, a protocol developed by Apple, allows for distributed processing of high-volume projects (such as video encoding and graphics compositing). Using Qmaster, an operator at one station can submit encoding jobs to any other Compressor/Qmaster-enabled system on the same network.

What Does It Look Like?

At first glance, Compressor's interface can be a little intimidating. With the release of Compressor 3 in 2007, Compressor got a pretty significant UI update. Though presented as a single full-screen interface, the sections are actually separate windows, allowing you to pick and choose what you keep open and visible. Its default layout is designed so users can both enter new jobs and monitor jobs already encoding (**Figure 5.19**).

Batch window   Preview window

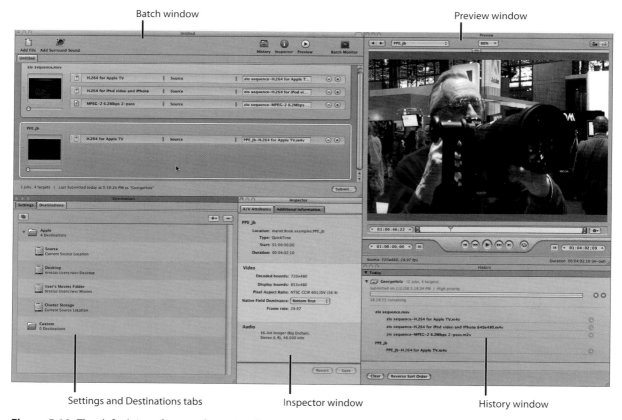

Settings and Destinations tabs   Inspector window   History window

Figure 5.19 The default interface configuration for Compressor.

Starting in the upper left, Compressor's interface consists of the following:

Batch window: The Batch window allows you to import source media files, add settings and destinations, and name the batch.

Settings and Destinations tabs: The Settings tab allows you to manage all your settings. By default, Compressor ships with templates geared toward specific device (like iPods) and format (like MPEG-2) settings. You can create new settings and keep them all organized within this space. The Destinations tab allows you to create, modify, or remove destination settings; set a default destination; and add file identifiers to your output media filename.

Inspector window: The Inspector is both a summary of your settings as well as the way to change advanced parameters such as preprocessing filters, image resolutions, and cropping. If you are changing settings for a template applied to a piece of video already, changes you make will automatically appear in the Preview window.

Preview window: True to its name, the Preview window allows you to play your source media file in its original format or preview your source media file with settings that have been assigned to it. A small tab at the top of the window allows you to view both source and preview results simultaneously by splitting the image between the two. You can see the effects of settings—such as filters and frame resizing—and make adjustments to these attributes while previewing the media file in real time. You can also use the Preview window to add and view various kinds of markers (particularly helpful to DVD and podcast creators).

History window: Slightly misnamed, the History window allows you to view a full log of all batches submitted from your computer, including progress bars of those still being transcoded. In this window, you can also monitor active encoding jobs, as well as pause and cancel them.

How Does It Work?

Let's walk through the basic Compressor workflow to understand it better. We will start, once again, with a DV-NTSC clip, and this time let's plan on making a video designed for playback on iPods and iPhones. Let's also make sure that when it is played back on either computers or TVs (through an Apple TV), it looks as good as possible, which means we'll need to target the maximum specifications these mobile devices can handle.

1. Start either by dragging your content into the Batch window or by clicking the Add File button in the toolbar and navigating to where the movie is stored on your hard drive.

2. Next, in the Settings window, locate the Apple Devices folder in the Apple settings. Notice that there are two iPod/iPhone settings—one for 320 by 240 video and one for 640 by 480. Click the H.264 for iPod

video and iPhone 640 by 480 setting, and drag it onto your source clip in the Batch window. Release the mouse button when a green plus icon appears, indicating that you will be applying that setting to your video (**Figure 5.20**).

Figure 5.20 Drag the setting onto your source movie in the Batch window.

3. By default, Compressor chose the source location as the destination. In an effort to stay more organized, let's change that to a new specific location. Right-click (or Control-click) your setting. Choose Destination > User's Movies Folder from the contextual menu (**Figure 5.21**).

Figure 5.21 Change the default location to a new location.

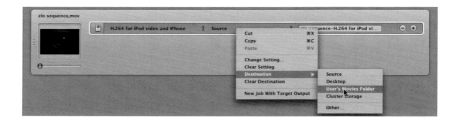

4. Use the Inspector window's Summary tab to verify that all the settings are what you need (**Figure 5.22**).

Figure 5.22 The Inspector window's Summary tab.

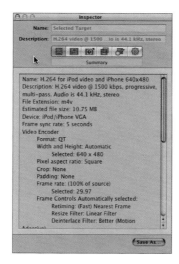

5. Scrub through the clip in the Preview window to confirm the quality of the settings applied (**Figure 5.23**). For this particular file, no custom settings are needed (to see customized settings in Compressor, check out Chapter 8, "Delivering Files for Mobile Devices").

Figure 5.23 The Preview window showing a split view of the video (before and after encoding).

6. Back in the Batch window, click the Submit button. A small dialog appears asking you to name the job as it is sent to be processed (**Figure 5.24**). If you had added multiple source files and settings to Batch window, all of them would be submitted into this one batch. Leave the "Include unmanaged services on other computers" check box deselected. Also, leave the Cluster menu set to This Computer and Priority set to High (see the "What Makes It Special?" section to learn more about encoding using a Qmaster cluster). Click Submit.

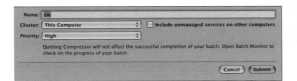

Figure 5.24 Naming and submitting a job to the queue.

7. The job will now appear in the History window. It appears as a collapsed name showing the batch name and the percentage of file(s) encoded. Click the down arrow next to the batch name to view a list of all the movies associated with that batch (**Figure 5.25**). If you had used multiple source movies, each would appear with its applied settings organized beneath its name.

Figure 5.25 The History window, showing the current batch encoding.

8. Once the batch job has finished encoding, click the magnifying glass next to the movie name, and a Mac OS X window for the destination folder opens. Double-click the video to launch it and confirm that it plays back as desired, or launch iTunes and drag the video into the Movies tab. Once located there, the file can be played back locally (**Figure 5.26**) or synced to an iPod or iPhone for mobile playback. Since we chose to make the file 640 by 480, playback on a TV would be almost the same as standard-definition video (similar to DVD or broadcast TV).

Figure 5.26 The finished encode playing back in iTunes.

What Makes It Special?

Because it is so tightly integrated with Final Cut Studio, Compressor is an obvious choice for Final Cut Pro editors needing to export video for DVD, MPEG-4, and other QuickTime-friendly codecs and formats. Because it is a separate application, it is technically possible to continue editing while encoding, though if you are attempting to export very high-quality content, you will notice slower performance than normal. The existing templates are an excellent jump-start for anyone needing to use them, and creating custom settings is just as easy.

There are also many production formats supported within the Compressor interface. For example, it is quite easy to convert 1080i HD clips to anamorphic SD formats and to convert HDV to DVCPRO. Previous versions of Compressor lacked inverse telecine capabilities, requiring the compressionist to use Cinema Tools. Fortunately, version 3.0 adds this feature. 3:2 pull down is located in the Frame Controls tab of the Inspector. Simply unlock the frame controls, then turn on Frame Controls and use the pull down under Deinterlace in order to perform an IVT.

NOTE Compressor 3.0 also ships with a new API that allows third party companies to create plug-ins that work with Compressor. Telestream was the first company to take advantage of this, by creating a plug-in that allows Compressor users to access their Episode templates. Additionally, Compressor now has command line control, allowing users to script encoding events and control the encode process without ever accessing the UI.

Compressor is also a fairly fast encoding tool when used on modern Intel Macs and even on the previous generations of G5 models. Compressor even runs fast on Macs with multiple G5 or Intel processors. If you are in a studio environment with multiple Final Cut Studio systems running, you can also enable encoding clusters through Qmaster. Basically, this allows a single user to take advantage of all the encoding resources on their network by submitting jobs to all the active encoding nodes. Qmaster takes a little setup and advanced knowledge, but it pays off greatly by speeding up your encoding workflow through distributed processing.

Compressor's ability to add chapter markers to video is also a unique and valuable feature. In the world of DVD authoring, chapter markers are used to determine points within the video to start playing based on user interaction. Likewise, chapter markers can be used in movies designed to be video or audio podcasts to create a series or shortcuts to quickly jump to specific parts of the timeline. Although you can also apply DVD chapter markers in DVD Studio Pro, podcasters don't have any other option for enhancing their content with chapter markers.

NOTE See Chapter 8 for a recipe on enhancing a video podcast with Compressor.

What Should You Watch Out For?

Though its image and preprocessing controls have been improved over past versions, Compressor still lags behind other stand-alone applications such as Episode Pro, making it less suited for specialized work where a great deal of noise filtering or other preprocessing is required. Also, several obvious audio-preprocessing capabilities are missing here, requiring users to switch to either Final Cut Pro or Soundtrack Pro to address these audio issues. If these features were integrated into Compressor, it would be much stronger, though, from Apple's point of view, less dependent on Final Cut Studio as a whole.

Compressor cannot make transport streams suitable for broadcast (CableLabs specifications or otherwise). Many in production agree that Apple's implementation of MPEG-4 and H.264 leaves much to be desired and they would prefer using another company's encoder, such as MainConcept or Nero. Compressor's biggest failing, perhaps, is the way Flash and Windows Media are handled via QuickTime export components such as Flip4Mac WMV Studio and On2 Flix Exporter. Though you can create custom settings for both, you must purchase the additional plug-ins, and then all interactions are controlled through one panel of the Inspector where you choose an encoder type and then use an Options button to open the same windows you would use in QuickTime Pro to enable QuickTime component encodes (**Figure 5.27**).

Figure 5.27 The QuickTime components interface in the Inspector. Although it leaves much to be desired, it does at least allow you to incorporate new formats into your existing Compressor workflow.

NOTE See Chapter 7 for instructions on setting up an encode using the QuickTime Export Components.

What Should You Remember?

If you're already using Final Cut Studio for other work, it would be silly not to use Compressor for much of the formats and encoding you are performing. However, standard formats such as Flash Video will require additional software to be supported, and certain specialized uses such as broadcast delivery may not be supported at all.

MICROSOFT EXPRESSION ENCODER

Microsoft Expression Encoder (**Table 5.4**) is a new encoding application from Microsoft. It was released in September 2007 as part of the Silverlight release. It is a batch application that is specifically designed to encode VC-1 video that is compatible with the Web, Silverlight, and Zune media players. It is part of the new Expression Studio, which is a complete design suite. Expression Studio is a mixture of design and programming tools that allow for the collaborative creation of interactive Web sites. It can be run both through the GUI and as a command-line service.

Table 5.4 Microsoft Expression Encoder Specs

Price	$299 (as part of Expressions Media)
Developer	Microsoft, Inc.
Current Version	1.02905.0
OS	Windows XP or later
Export Formats	VC-1 (WMV9)
Link	*www.microsoft.com/expression/products/overview.aspx?key=encoder*

Expression Encoder can import most video formats, including QuickTime movies, AVI files, MPEG-1, MPEG-2, and, of course, WMV files. Multiple files can be imported and have profiles (predefined templates). Custom templates can be made and saved as well. Nice-to-have features such as file stitching and graphic watermarking are available, and custom Silverlight player templates can be generated and saved with finished movies. It's not just a file-based transcoding tool; you can also create and encode a live multimedia session that you can stream to users from your workstation or from a Windows Media server.

Encoding in Expression Media Encoder consists first of assembling your videos into a job and then, if necessary, performing trimming and cropping edits, including adding markers, captions, overlays, and even script commands.

What Does It Look Like?

As I mentioned earlier, Expression Encoder can be run both via its interface and via the command line. The interface is a single pane with several tabs that display all the information needed to encode your video (**Figure 5.28**).

Figure 5.28 Microsoft's all-new Expression Encoder.

Starting at the upper left, the sections are as follows:

Timeline and Transport controls: Use this area to play/view your source and preview the results of your settings.

Media Content pane: The Media Content pane lists all the videos you have imported. This collective list is known as a *job*. You can save this list as an individual job file in XML format. Once you have applied all the settings necessary, you will also initiate the encoding process from this pane.

Settings tab: The Settings tab contains all the preset templates available to apply to your source video as well as the advanced settings needed to change these and make your own unique templates.

Metadata tab: The Metadata tab allows you to add key information such as the title, the copyright, and authoring information (virtually any piece of metadata you want to store can be saved). Additionally, you can manually add or import and manage markers and scripting commands to specific parts of the video.

Output tab: The Output tab allows you to export thumbnail JPEGs as part of your encoding process and generate Silverlight player templates. Automatic JPEG creation is useful for creating the thumbnails often needed for Web media. The Silverlight templates immediately allow content creators to integrate their content into Expression Studio Web sites.

How Does It Work?

To better understand the Expression Encoder workflow, let's encode some video and create a Silverlight template to house it. We will target broadband video users and will be starting with DV-NTSC source footage. Starting in the Expression interface, let's do the following:

1. Click the Import button to load a clip in the Media Content pane. A dialog appears. Navigate to the location where your media is saved on your hard drive, and select it. Click OK, and the file will appear in Expression Encoder (**Figure 5.29**).

Figure 5.30 Select the appropriate settings template in the Settings tab.

Figure 5.29 Media loaded into Expression Encoder.

2. In the Settings tab, choose the Web Server Broadband (MP) option under Video peak bit (**Figure 5.30**).

3. Review the settings that have been applied to assure they meet your needs. If necessary, adjust the data rate, video size, or other parameters necessary to match your deliverable needs (**Figure 5.31** on the next page).

Figure 5.31 Expression's Settings tab for video and audio.

4. Click the arrow next to Video Profile to activate that section of the Settings tab. Select Stretch from the pop-up menu to have the image fill the new video frame.

5. Next, click the Crop button. This will activate a red line on the Preview window (**Figure 5.32**). Drag the crop markers into the desired area to crop the edges of the video.

Figure 5.32 The Video Profile settings and the video preview with a crop marker. After activating the crop, a red box appears on the preview monitor. You can make changes by dragging the red box to the desired crop or by keying specific numbers in the Crop settings area.

6. Select the Output tab. In the Job Output section, choose Glassy from the Template pop-up menu (**Figure 5.33**).

Figure 5.33 Select Glassy Template in the Job Output section of the Output tab.

7. After selecting the template, you will see a small preview of it in the same window. Make sure that Preview in Browser, Save Job File, and Sub-folder by Job ID are all selected (**Figure 5.34**).

Figure 5.34 Preview the Silverlight template.

8. Click the Encode button in the Media Content panel. The job will begin encoding. A progress bar in the job will indicate the status (**Figure 5.35**). Once the job completes, it will automatically launch a preview in your default Web browser.

Figure 5.35 Watch the status in the Media Content panel.

9. View the results of the completed encode in your default Web browser to ensure the playback is as desired (**Figure 5.36**).

Figure 5.36 The completed video will automatically preview in your default Web browser.

10. All the finished files (video content and the Silverlight template) are located in a new folder at your designated save location (by default, the source video's location). Open the folder to see the files associated with the movie and its new Silverlight player (**Figure 5.37**).

Figure 5.37 Viewing the movie and template files created during the encode process.

What Makes It Special?

Expression Encoder is one of the only application that allows you to generate a Silverlight template with your encoded video (the Flip4Mac plug-in also creates templates for Mac users). Because it has been developed by Microsoft (creators of the VC-1 format), it is also one of the most robust VC-1 encoding applications available, particularly for this price.

What Should You Watch Out For?

Remember that this is specifically a single-format encoder, specializing in VC-1. You will most likely need to have other applications to handle the other formats you will invariably encounter in your production workflow.

What Should You Remember?

If you are trying to experiment with Silverlight or if Windows Media is an important format in your deliverables, it is worth investing in Microsoft's Expression Encoder.

SQUEEZE COMPRESSION SUITE

Squeeze (**Table 5.5**) is a batch compressing application from Sorenson Media. It has been around since late 2001. Squeeze is one of the only cross-platform compression tools available besides QuickTime Pro, and it has by far the most easy-to-use and attractive interface of any product on the market today.

Table 5.5 Squeeze Compression Suite Specs

Price	$749.99 as tested (prices vary)
Developer	Sorenson Media
Current Version	4.5.7
OS	Mac OS X 10.4.9 or later
Formats	FLV, MOV, MP4, SWF, RM (PC and non-Intel Macs only), MPEG-1, MPEG-2, WAV, MP3 (features vary from product to product)
Link	*www.sorensonmedia.com*

Flash (both the older Spark Pro codec and the newer On2 VP6 codecs) and QuickTime (specifically with Sorenson's Pro Video 3 codec) were the first formats Squeeze supported; however, new formats have steadily flowed into the product line over time, making it a fairly robust tool set. Squeeze has an additional nice little option for Flash creators: it can generate a SWF template for the video you are encoding, choosing from 21 included templates (as well as instructions to create your own if desired). Windows Media is supported as well (through Flip4Mac's plug-in on the Macintosh), and MPEG-4 output includes presets for QuickTime and H.264 for iPod, 3GPP phones, and Sony's PlayStation Portable (PSP). MPEG formats are a fairly new feature in the product line, and support is less complete.

Dolby Digital (AC3 audio) and multichannel audio are not yet supported, and although there are templates included for Blu-ray presets, they are reliant on high-bit-rate MPEG-2, not the more preferred VC-1 or H.264 codecs needed for better efficiency. Squeeze also supports Real Media, though only for PC and PowerPC users (non-Intel Mac hardware).

Squeeze suffers from a slightly confusing product matrix. Though the overarching name has always been Squeeze, different descriptors over the years have described versions that were specific to one format or the other (such as Sorenson Squeeze for Flash). Generally speaking, now there are three lines: one limited to Flash (Squeeze for Flash), one slightly limited in formats but lacking several add-on features (Squeeze Suite), and one complete package (Squeeze PowerPack). See **Table 5.6** for a complete breakdown of the formats and features of each configuration available.

Even the PowerPack has one additional upgrade required by large-volume users. By default, the entire Squeeze family is limited to 1,500 transcoding jobs per month via automated Watch folders (all products have unlimited transcodes through the GUI, however). If users want to encode more than 1,500 files per month via watch folder, they are required to purchase a yearly subscription to Squeeze Unlimited.

Table 5.6 Squeeze Configurations

	Squeeze Suite	Squeeze PowerPack	Squeeze for Flash
Standard List Price	$499	$599 Windows $749 Mac	$199
Format Support			
Windows Media output	Yes	Yes	No
Flash output (Spark)	Yes	Yes	Yes
Flash output (VP6)	No	Yes	$100 upgrade
QuickTime output	Yes	Yes	No
Real output*	Yes	Yes	No
MPEG-1 output	Yes	Yes	No
MPEG-2 output	Yes	Yes	No
MPEG-4/H.264 output	Yes	Yes	Yes
3GPP output	Yes	Yes	No
PSP Output	Yes	Yes	No
Plug-ins/Features			
On2 VP6 Pro Encoder	No	Yes	$100 upgrade
Flip4Mac WMV9 Encoder	No	Yes	No
Squeeze 4.5 Training DVD	No	Yes	No
Command-line control	No	Yes	No
Real-time HD encoding	No	No	No
Unlimited monthly encoding volume (via Watch folders)**	No	No	No

  * Real Media available only for Windows and non-Intel Mac users.

** For transcoding more than 1,500 files via Watch folder per month, users must upgrade to Squeeze Suite Unlimited ($2,500 per year per CPU).

What Does It Look Like?

As mentioned, Squeeze's interface is easy to follow and fairly attractive. It is also one of the most organized UIs we have looked at so far. It's divided into the following panes: Input, Filters, Format & Compression Settings, Details, Preview, and Batch (**Figure 5.38**).

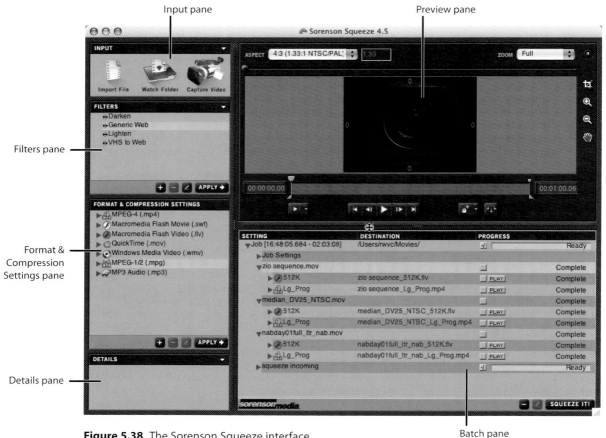

Figure 5.38 The Sorenson Squeeze interface.

Starting in the upper-left corner, you'll see the following:

Input: Use this pane as a quick shortcut to import files, to set up a Watch folder, or to capture live video from supported FireWire device. You can also drag files into the Batch pane to import them into Squeeze.

Filters: Filters are the preprocessing options available in Squeeze, including settings such as brightness, contrast, deinterlacing, cropping, and fade in/out. The separation of filter presets from compression settings makes it easy to apply them in combination, saving time and requiring fewer templates (10 filter templates and 10 format templates would create 100 possible configurations in other transcoding tools, for example). The notion of separate templates is unique to Sorenson, and it is very useful when you need to achieve certain looks quickly. That said, Squeeze's image preprocessing is a little lacking in comparison to the competition, so this mitigates some of the effectiveness of the feature.

Format & Compression Settings: This contains all the formats and various specific templates (targeting specific uses) available to the user. This list may vary depending on the version of Squeeze you are using.

Details: This is a small information box indicating contextually specific data (similar to the tool tips that appear in applications when you hover over an object).

Preview: The window where your video preview will appear. There are standard playback controls as well as the ability to crop, mark in/out points, and add chapter markers to your video. The Preview pane has clear playback, zoom, and—new in Squeeze 4.5—aspect ratio controls. The Quick Preview button encodes one to five seconds to spot-check your settings before starting a long batch. The preview slider also shows the effect of applied filters and allows you to alter crops visually.

Batch: This is the primary work location in Squeeze. This is where you will add content and then apply filters and format settings. Work is also submitted here (using the hilarious "Squeeze It!" button), and this window is where you'll see the progress of your encodes, making this a combination of batch and queue all at once. Once a job has completed, a Play button appears that, if clicked, will launch the content in your system's default player for that file type.

How Does It Work?

The batch setup process has a job-related orientation that allows the user to manage complex groups of jobs. A job can consist of as little as one source video with settings, multiple sources with the same settings, or multiple sources with unique settings. You can also set up multiple jobs in the Batch pane simultaneously, allowing you to continue adding and working on compression while the batch is being processed (though once a job is being processed, its settings are locked out of further editing).

Watch folders are also handled as their own jobs. By clicking the Watch Folder button in the Input pane, you can select a designated Watch folder on your system. Once it has settings applied (Squeeze allows you to apply an unlimited number of settings to a given Watch folder) and it is active (known as *watching*) in the Batch window, any content copied to it will be processed against the assigned templates.

Files are automatically moved when finished to subfolders. Finished source videos are moved to a folder called CompletedSource, and finished encoded files are located in a folder named CompressedOutput.

Squeeze has additional workflow automation with the Optional Tasks feature (select Batch > Modify Optional Tasks) such as copying output files to multiple destinations—including FTP servers—or sending output to other applications such as iTunes (**Figure 5.39**).

Figure 5.39 The Optional Tasks window allows you to set up post-encode processes such as FTPing finished files to remote locations.

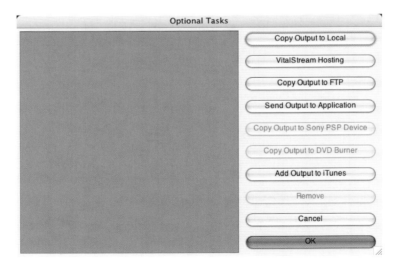

To see the batch capabilities of Squeeze, let's assign multiple settings and source files to the same job. For this scenario, we want to create both an iPod video and a broadband Flash clip for each source video we add to the Batch window from our example DV-NTSC footage. Since both are headed toward progressive playback destinations, we'll need to deinterlace our source video as well.

1. Locate the two source movies on your computer, and drag them into the Squeeze Batch window. If no job has already been started, a new one will be added that includes your two files (**Figure 5.40**).

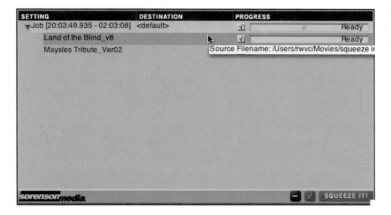

Figure 5.40 Files have been added to the Batch window, creating a new Job.

2. Click the job name to make sure all settings you apply in the next steps are applied globally. If an individual movie is selected, the setting will be applied to that one clip, not to all movies in the job.

3. In the Format & Compression Settings pane, click the arrow next to the MPEG-4 collection to display all the templates available for that format. Locate and click the iPod_Hi setting. Click Apply. The setting will be added to the job and both source files.

4. Now open the Flash Video (.flv) collection in the Settings pane, locate and select the setting VP6_512K, and click Apply. This setting will also be added to the job and all movies in the job (**Figure 5.41**).

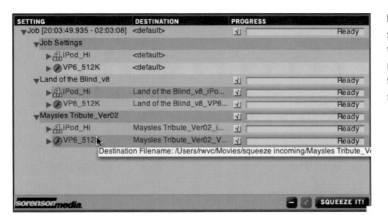

Figure 5.41 Two movies settings have been applied to the job, meaning four movies in all will be created from this job (two for each source file).

5. In the Filters pane, click the Generic Web filter. This filter already includes deinterlacing and some simple image adjustments that Sorenson recommends for Web-bound media. Click Apply to add it to the job and movies.

Note that when it is added to each setting, both in the job and in the individual movies, it expands the pop-up tabs for each so that you can confirm the filter has been applied (**Figure 5.42**). After confirming that it has been added, you can collapse the tabs again in order to conserve real estate in your Batch pane if desired, though Filter will now be hidden.

Figure 5.42 The filter has been applied to the job and is visible in each movie in the expanded view.

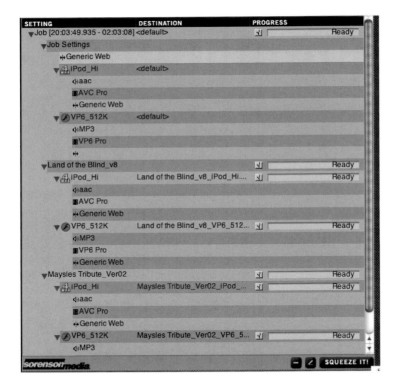

6. If desired, click the individual settings applied to your source movies in the Batch pane to preview them in the pane above. Dragging the small circle above the playback area across the frame will show you the difference between the source and encoded image, with the encoded clip on the right and the original source footage on the left (**Figure 5.43**).

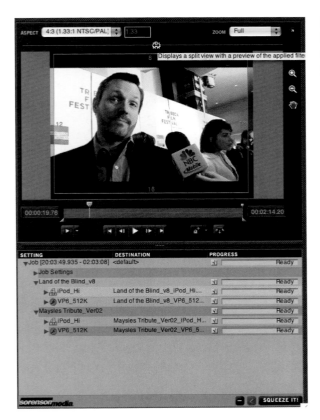

Figure 5.43 By clicking an individual movie to be encoded, you can preview it.

7. Click Squeeze It! to begin encoding your content. A number of different progress bars appear, alerting you to the percentage and time estimate to encode the overall job, each group of source files, and individual encodes, respectively (**Figure 5.44**).

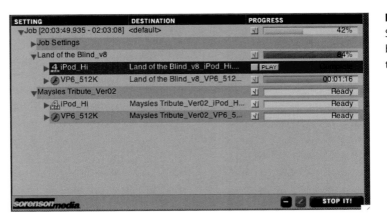

Figure 5.44 After you click Squeeze It!, your movies will begin being processed in top-down order.

NOTE By default, encoded movies are saved in the location of the source material.

Figure 5.45 After a particular file is encoded, you can preview it in the default player for its file type.

8. When files are finished, you'll see the word *Complete* in its row of the Batch pane, and you'll see a Play button. Clicking the Play button will launch the default player for that file format to preview the results of your encode (**Figure 5.45**).

What Makes It Special?

Squeeze's most noteworthy characteristic is its easy-to-use interface. Even novice compressionists will be able to run this application like pros after just a few uses. Performance is also fairly good, though Mac users should make sure they have the updated Universal Binary version on the Intel platform (4.5 and later)—the previous version performs incredibly slowly.

Squeeze also does a fairly good job of serving up a variety of formats for the compressionist who wants to experiment with different deliverables.

However, other products may handle different specific formats better (Expression Encoder, for example, will create much better-quality VC-1 files). Though there is deep integration with Flash, including player templates, Silverlight is not mentioned, primarily because the software hasn't updated since Silverlight was launched. That said, Windows Media files created with Squeeze would be compatible with Silverlight developments you may be supporting.

What Should You Watch Out For?

Although Squeeze's interface shines, its image processing proves to be subpar. The basic deinterlacing filter produces results with less detail than other tools we have discussed. Also, the inverse telecine filter discards fields even on progressive frames, visibly reducing detail and causing ugly aliasing on high-contrast diagonal edges. Saturation and audio volume filters are missing completely.

As a result, Squeeze performs poorly in subjective quality tests when presented with poor-quality source files but works fine with pristine, high-quality sources.

What Should You Remember?

Sorenson Squeeze is a great tool for novice compressionists who need something to cut their teeth with and who require support for a variety of formats and deliverable options. Less-than-perfect preprocessing options, however, may force more advanced users to seek an alternative, more feature-rich application.

Squeeze is available on both the Mac and PC, and both share identical interfaces, making it a further bonus for those working in cross-platform production workflows. Interestingly enough, the same serial numbers work on both platforms (albeit only one at a time). This is a great bonus for users who might upgrade or change platforms—purchasing the same software again for a different system would be unnecessary.

EPISODE PRO

Episode and Episode Pro (**Table 5.7**) make up part of a Mac-centric transcoding product family from Telestream (makers of FlipFactory and Flip4Mac). Formerly known as Popwire Compression Master, the product was rebranded as Episode after Telestream acquired the Swedish company Popwire in 2006. The other main element of the Episode family is Engine, a grid-based encoding service for enterprise customers that allows multiple Episode stations to share and distribute work.

Table 5.7 Episode Pro Specs

Price	$395 (Episode) to $995 (Episode Pro with Flash 8)
Developer	Telestream
Current Version	4.4.1
OS	Mac OS X 10.4.9 or later
Formats	Episode supports dozens of formats—check their Web site for a complete list.
Link	*http://flip4mac.com/episode.htm*

Episode differs from Episode Pro only in the formats its supports. Episode is focused on Web, disc, and mobile media formats such as QuickTime, MPEG-4, and Windows Media, while Episode Pro adds support for professional production formats such as MXF and GXF. Flash 8 (On2's VP6 codec) comes with an additional plug-in cost for each product.

Episode Pro is a favorite amongst Mac-based compressionists for all the controls provided in terms of video and audio preprocessing. Although a great option, it's hampered by a slightly overcomplicated interface.

What Does It Look Like?

Much like Squeeze, Episode is a single-interface product that incorporates a Batch/Queue window and your predefined templates. Unlike Squeeze, Episode has a preview monitor that can be summoned by right-clicking a clip in the queue and selecting Preview. A separate window opens and allows you to select between viewing the source video and viewing the encoded video (if a template has been applied).

Although it is disappointing to have to manage another window for previewing work, Telestream assumes you won't really need to preview every video you load, and this approach also frees up that interface real estate to devote more workspace to your templates and videos—a valid and worthy trade-off.

Figure 5.46 shows the Episode interface.

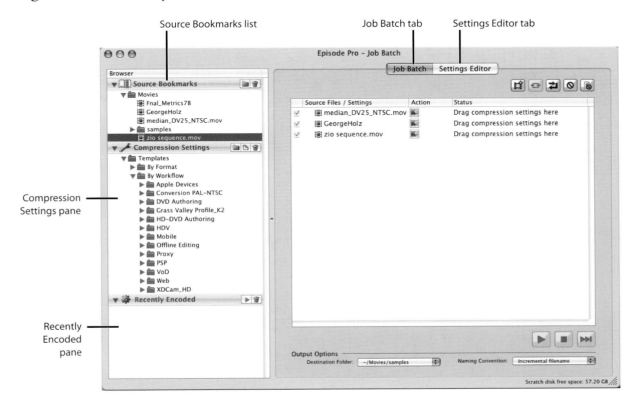

Figure 5.46 The Episode/Episode Pro interface.

Starting in the upper left of the interface, you'll see the following:

Source Bookmarks list: This is a list of bookmarks for folders containing your source material. The Movies folder in your system becomes the default bookmark folder when installing Episode. Any media files Episode understands that are in that folder will appear in the Episode interface and can be dragged quickly to the Job Batch tab to begin working.

Compression Settings pane: This is where your settings are stored. Settings are files that determine how your input files will be encoded. Episode comes with a large number of setting templates to get you started. They are divided into two subfolders, By Format and By Workflow. The By Format folder contains templates organized according to output format so that you find templates for MPEG output, QuickTime output, Windows Media output, and so on. The By Workflow folder organizes the templates according to the output medium instead so that you can find templates for creating DVDs, videos for mobile phones, Web video, and so on. You can use the templates as they are, edit them to fit your particular needs, or create all new custom templates that will be stored in a new Custom Templates folder.

Recently Encoded: This contains clips that have been encoded during this session. You can click the Play button to play a selected clip. It will be cleared out when you quit the application.

Job Batch tab: This is where the actual encoding is done. Combine your source files with the settings you intend to use in this area. At the bottom of this window you'll also find tools to set default encoding locations and naming configurations. Both have pop-up menus providing some predefined settings, but the compressionist can edit and create new ones that will then be available via these menus.

Settings Editor tab: The Settings Editor tab is used to adjust the existing encoding templates or create entirely new ones.

How Does It Work?

As mentioned, Episode comes with an incredibly thorough set of templates that will satisfy most compressionists' needs (or at least get them close enough to start customizing for specific uses). It can be a little unclear when you are working with template settings whether you are editing a stored template or a setting that has been applied to a specific file. Take care when editing settings to note where and what you are saving. It's quite easy to make a great deal of custom settings that disappear once you delete a given job because they were specific to that source's setting, rather than the template.

To better understand the Episode workflow, let's quickly encode some content. Let's assume we have a 1080i60 YV12 source file (uncompressed HD content) that is a 2-minute clip comprising a collection of 30-second sports promos. Episode is one of the few encoders on the Mac platform that can decode and work with this format. Let's create a 720p clip that will play back on Apple TV set-top boxes and other devices that support HD H.264 files, but let's encode only one of the 30-second spots rather than all four (requiring marking in/out points in our settings).

1. In the Episode interface, select the HD clip to be encoded, and drag it to the Job Batch tab (**Figure 5.47**).

Figure 5.47 Dragging files into the Batch window from the Source Bookmarks panel is the fastest way to start a job in Episode.

2. Next, in the Compression Settings area, locate the appropriate Apple TV setting by navigating to By Workflow > Apple Devices > 720p (**Figure 5.48**).

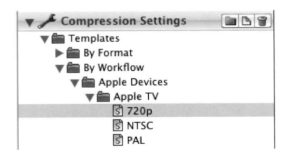

Figure 5.48 Select the correct setting from the Compression Settings list.

3. Drag this setting onto your clip in the Batch window. The status of your movie will now change to Pending, meaning it is ready to be encoded but hasn't been submitted yet (**Figure 5.49**).

Source Files / Settings	Action	Status
▼ 📼 wral_1080i_yv12.avi	🖼	Pending...
🗟 720p		Pending...

Figure 5.49 The status is now Pending for your movie.

4. Double-click the setting 720p that has been applied to your movie, and a window opens allowing you to edit the compression settings for this specific file (leaving the template intact).

NOTE The output for-
mat (wrapper) is set to
iPod Video compatibility. If
desired, you can select
another wrapper such as MP4
that would still work with the
Apple TV but expand compatibility to other platforms as
well. Since we are targeting
the Apple TV in the setting, I
will not make that change.

5. Episode settings are divided into several tabs, with similar settings
grouped together. In the Output tab (the first one), locate and click
the buttons next to the In and Out settings in the In/Out Points section. Keep the In point set to 00:00:00.0, and change the out setting
to 00:00:30.0 (**Figure 5.50**). The first 30 seconds of the video will now
be encoded.

Figure 5.50 The Output settings tab allows you to make changes to the overall
file you are creating, such as the muxer (wrapper) mark in/out points, and allows
you to insert an image or movie as a bumper or trailer to the encoded video.

6. Click Apply to close this window and return to the Job Batch tab.

7. Click the Play button at the bottom of the Job Batch window. The
video begins the encode process, and a status bar indicates its progress
(**Figure 5.51**).

NOTE The small clock
icon in the settings row
indicates that only part of the
source clip will be encoded.
The numbers in brackets next
to the setting name indicate
the starting and stopping
times for the encode.

Figure 5.51 Monitor the progress of your encode directly in the Batch Job tab,
both through a progress bar and through an estimate of time remaining.

8. When the encode is complete, locate the file in your destination folder, and double-click it. Because it is an MP4 file, it should open by default in iTunes and play (**Figure 5.52**). It would now be possible to sync the movie with Apple TV for playback on an HD display. Note that the finished encode is only 30 seconds in length, rather than the length of the entire source content.

Figure 5.52 The completed encoded clip plays back successfully in iTunes and on an Apple TV set-top box.

What Makes It Special?

No other transcoding tool on the Mac can compare to the sheer volume of format support that Episode offers, both for ingest and export. It is also the only Mac encoder that makes Windows Media MBR files for streaming. Although there is a great deal of support for the Web and mobile formats, there is a good amount of disc-based and even broadcast video on demand (VOD) support built in.

It's easy to set up new templates once you have mastered the application, though all the options available can be daunting to the new compressionist. Very useful contextual help menus break down virtually every tab and button in the interface, providing a way to learn all the options that are available.

Versions running on modern Intel Macs shine when it comes to performance. Though it runs well on the PowerPC G5s as well, it has been optimized for the Intel chipset, making it a very fast transcoder on the latest Mac systems.

NOTE Features like file stitching are also fairly unique to Episode (though not exclusive). Stitching allows you to select a header or tail video, combine it with the primary source video, and encode them as one. This is very useful for adding reoccurring title slates or credits or other information to a video.

NOTE As mentioned, Episode also has a plug-in that now allows users of Compressor to combine both applications into their workflow. This is a very handy feature for compressionists looking to take advantage of the flexibility of the Episode templates and encoder while staying inside the Final Cut Studio workflow.

The deep level of control built around Episode's preprocessing tools is perhaps its best feature. Its deinterlace options have no rival—virtually any configuration of motion and fields can be cleanly deinterlaced better than any other application. On the audio side, Episode even includes an option to remap surround sound channels (like Compressor).

What Should You Watch Out For?

With much power comes much responsibility. Episode's powerful interface, which allows for the robust control that I described earlier, can become a land mine for those new to it or trying to set up new templates for the first time. Having so much control can also lead to a desire to overexperiment, constantly tweaking templates trying to get the perfect balance between quality and file size.

For all its control of the settings, however, Episode does lack some of the sophistication of Squeeze in the application. There is no idea of Watch folders built into Episode Pro (though it is part of the more expensive Engine option), and there isn't any of the functionality that Squeeze has in its Optional Tasks panel such as FTPing or moving files around locally. Episode is very much an operator-driven application that you will want to monitor for processing completion before moving on to perform the next tasks.

What Should You Remember?

Episode is a workhorse that would do very well in any Mac-centric production studio. It supports a ton of formats and has a great deal of audio and video preprocessing options. It does, however, lack automation features that less expensive applications have, so be aware of the trade-offs.

HIGHER- AND LOWER-END OPTIONS

Although I have covered several really good encoding applications in this chapter, many, many more exist, and prices range from free to several thousands of dollars. Why is there such a disparity? Some are very cheap, consumer-friendly apps designed to encode video to very specific purposes but offer no advanced features. Others are very expensive enterprise applications designed as high-capacity professional work tools and may be plugged into pretty sophisticated workflows. It's good to at least be aware of the options in these areas; less-expensive apps often have very easy-to-master interfaces and are handy for quick, small projects that may creep up. Enterprise-class applications, meanwhile, often have cutting-edge features that may be useful as your workloads increase.

Less-Expensive Solutions

The video iPod has helped drive the market for low-end encoding apps on both the Mac and PC. Once consumers had the desire to take their movies with them, small tools built on top of the FFmpeg encoder began cropping up. FFmpeg is a command-line tool comprising a collection of free and open source software libraries. Because the command line is not the interface of choice for most consumers, clever developers began creating simple interfaces that would act as a way for users to connect their movies with specific settings and then submit them to the FFmpeg encoder. Perhaps the most popular of the low-end tools on the Mac is Techspansion's VisualHub, found at *www.techspansion.com/visualhub* (**Figure 5.53**).

Figure 5.53 VisualHub is one of the best and simplest inexpensive encoding tools on the market today. Everybody should buy it twice—it's that good.

VisualHub is an advanced version of a free tool called iSquint by the same developer. iSquint was first designed just to allow users to quickly encode iPod videos with one click of a button. People enjoyed it so much and demand was significant enough that Techspansion developed VisualHub as a multiformat encoder. Users can easily queue up and encode video to H.264, Windows Media, DVD-ready MPEG-2, AVI, and Flash. MPEG-specific platforms such as the iPod and PlayStation Portable have their own tabs as well. Files get dropped in, and within a few clicks the user can configure and send their video off to be encoded. There are even advanced settings available, but the user is humorously reminded to proceed with caution right in the Advanced Settings window (**Figure 5.54**).

Figure 5.54 Users daring to change advance settings are warned that their mileage may vary.

All this functionality will set the buyer back an odd price of $23.32, and it's worth every cent plus quite a bit more.

VisualHub isn't the only option, however; see **Table 5.8** for a rundown of some other free or near-free encoding options.

Table 5.8 Inexpensive Encoders

Name	Price	URL
MPlayer/MEncoder	Free	http://sourceforge.net/project/showfiles.php?group_id=62947
Riva FLV Encoder	Free	www.rivavx.com/index.php?downloads&L=3
Super	Free	www.erightsoft.com/Superdc.html
Visual Hub	$23.32	http://visualhub.net
Viddy Up!	$9.95	www.splasm.com/viddyup/
Roxio Crunch	$39.99	www.roxio.com/enu/products/crunch/windows/overview.html

A Note About Enterprise Solutions

Enterprise encoding tools sound incredibly expensive when compared to all of the options described so far. Why do business customers need their own tools? Why don't they just use more of the apps we've discussed in this chapter? Well, the fact is, enterprise encoding tools are business-class solutions designed for customers who either are working with an incredibly large amount of content or have specific industrial needs and requirements that the average user would most likely not face. The consumer and even professional encoders I've talked about in this chapter scale only so far before adding more boxes and operators becomes an inefficient way of trying to increase your capacity.

Ironically, enterprise solutions often have less-sophisticated interfaces than some of the encoders I've already discussed. Since they serve a smaller, more specialized market, the interface and its niceties often take a back seat to pure performance numbers and interconnectivity to existing production infrastructures. Enterprise solutions also often combine the file transcoding functionality I've discussed so far with real-time live encoding from tape or other broadcast sources. Companies that create enterprise solutions include Rhozet (purchased by Harmonic in late 2006), Digital Rapids, Anystream, and Inlet Technologies.

Inlet's Fathom product (**Figure 5.55**) is a combination of file-based transcoding and real-time encoding from live sources for everything from HD quality all the way down to mobile video (and, of course, everything in between). It has some of the same features of the traditional tools I've discussed, such as Watch folders, templates, and status monitoring but also has features such as file analysis (the ability to open a video on a graph and view statistical data about it). Such diagnostic tools are essential for production professionals who are not only worried about high-quality results but who also need quantifiable analysis tools to verify issues.

Figure 5.55 Fathom is an enterprise-level HD and SD encoding tool designed for a variety of professional video environments. It combines high-speed performance with diagnostic tools.

Although the average user may not run out and buy these tools, or even be aware of them, they offer important features and capabilities required by industries that deal with high-quality and high-volume video content. It's not uncommon for such companies to need the capacity to encode upwards of 150 hours or more of HD-quality video, and that takes specialized enterprise tools.

CONCLUSION

Encoding tools run the gamut from free to hundreds of thousands of dollars, and they service diverse industries that all want to use video and audio to communicate their message better or simply entertain. Even hobbyists have become savvy and are starting to use compression tools to manage their video consumption.

The information in this chapter is an excellent jumping-off point to get anyone started using a specific application for their compression needs, but you still need a little more knowledge to encode video efficiently. The remaining chapters of this book will divide the various delivery platforms you are likely to encounter in your work—specifically, the areas of disc-based media (both HD and SD), the Web, mobile video, and set-top boxes. I'll cover the fundamentals of each platform, identifying the unique issues you are likely to encounter, and I'll incorporate more recipes for applications I've already covered to create specifically targeted content.

Interview with a Compressionist

Name: Nico Puertollano

Location: Quezon City, Philippines

Title/Role: Designer and Director

Company: 27+20

URL: *www.2720.tv*

How did you get involved in video compression?

Back in college I would make videos for interactive CD-ROMs and for the Web. I also did a lot for my own portfolio. I wanted to know how to get the best quality of video in a small amount of space or fast downloads.

What was your biggest project?

I'd say in terms of compression projects, it would have to be the site of rhinofx.tv. This was a time when DSL started to be the norm. As a visual effects company, it was imperative to be able to show our work online and be able to see the details of the work but at the same time keep the file size to a minimum where the quality did not start to break. There was a lot of trial and error in seeing what the best compression to use was. At the time, since they were just 30-second spots, we opted for Photo JPEG. Our average file sizes were 4 MB to 5 MB at 400 by 300.

What was your favorite project?

In terms of compression, I would have to say my own site. For some reason even though I've come up with a formula to compress, I still play around and get surprised when I try something different and I get the result I want. I guess since there is no pressure, it's still fun. And I get to say whether a 45 MB file is OK or not.

What's your format of choice?

This is a toss-up for me. A lot of my work deals with heavy motion graphics or special effects. For live footage only, I like H.264, .mp4, or .divx, but it depends what I'm using it for. There are some blogs that really work well with .divx or .mp4 but are not H.264 friendly. With graphics I like Sorenson or Photo JPEG.

What does your average workday look like?

It really depends. When I do have a project, I compress and upload work in progress to my clients for approval. This can also take time because sometimes the clients can't read certain formats. They seem to love MPEGs, at least here in the Philippines. But for graphics and VFX, you lose the details. And when a project is done, I compress it to upload to my site.

What does your encoding hardware look like?

I have a 2.5 GHz quad G5 with 8 GB of RAM, but don't let the RAM fool you; most apps max out at 2 GB, and OS X prefers virtual RAM—I don't know why.

What's your encoding software of choice?

I really want to be able to use Compressor, but it doesn't seem to like my style. So, I use either Squeeze or QuickTime Pro.

What role does compression play in your work?

Compression is a big part; I use it to show clients the work in progress and to update my site with new QuickTime files.

What surprises you most about video compression today?

How much the porn industry takes advantage of every new compression technology. Also it seems like companies like Apple and Amazon are really trying to push a certain standard, but we'll see. iTunes has made a big impact on downloadable media. Places like Stage 6 and YouTube and video blogs have made compression seem to be a normal part of the Internet lifestyle of the masses. Because of video compression, who needs cable when you have the Net?

CHAPTER SIX

Compressing for DVDs

For many compressionists, optical media, whether standard-definition DVD or Blu-ray Disc, will be the sole, or certainly primary, delivery medium for their compressed content. In this regard, it's an exciting time, and also kind of a scary time, to be a video producer.

Though many of us have had a high-definition TV set in our living rooms for years and perhaps even an HDV or AVCHD camcorder, the ability to deliver in a useful HD optical format is relatively new. Even as recently as November 2006, there were no optical formats that you or your clients could use to play back high-definition video on your living room TV.

Then, the first "hybrid" disc technology appeared, which allowed producers to record high-definition video footage onto standard-definition (SD) DVDs. You got only about 20 to 30 minutes of video per disc (double that for dual-layer DVDs), but that sufficed for many applications. Of course, you still needed either a Blu-ray or HD DVD player to play the results.

Soon thereafter, Pioneer shipped its first Blu-ray recorder, the BDR-101, and Sonic Solutions shipped the first Blu-ray authoring software, DVDit HD, designed for use by consumers and small-shop producers outside major studios specializing in the Blu-ray format. Though the BDR-101 produced only single-sided Blu-ray Discs, this still gave prosumer videographers 25 GB to play with. (Note: Blu-ray Disc's one-time rival for HD disc supremacy, HD DVD, bowed out shortly before this book went to press. For details, see sidebar, "Rumors of HD DVD's Demise *Not* Exaggerated.")

But, once again, I'm getting ahead of myself. Clearly, most producers will still be targeting good old standard-definition DVDs today, so that's where we'll start, after covering some preliminary concepts.

WHAT'S A DVD?

At a high level, DVDs are incredibly simple, whether standard definition or high definition. All DVDs have two components: content, which consists of video, slide shows, and audio; and menus, which are used by the viewers to access the content. In the age of such Internet savviness, a DVD is not that different from a very simple, super media-rich Web site about one particular topic (that is, a movie).

In the old days (meaning, pre-2000), you created your content in one application and "authored," or created, your DVD in another. Since then, programs have become more integrated. Still, DVD authoring—whether for SD or HD—is simple in concept: you create your menus and then link to your content.

What gets complicated are the specific requirements necessary to ensure that your DVD plays on your target player. Although most authoring programs shield you from many of these technical details (because in theory, all players should be standardized against one set of specifications), it helps to understand these requirements before starting production.

PRODUCING SD DVDS

Let's begin at the beginning, which is producing for standard-definition DVD players. As you might have guessed, Blu-ray players can play SD DVD discs (so can the legacy HD DVD players already in consumers' living rooms), but you obviously have to produce for the lowest common denominator. Interestingly, Blu-ray recorders can also record SD DVD discs, though you'll obviously need to use the parameters discussed here for SD playback.

So if you're producing a disc to play on an end user's $19.95 Wal-Mart DVD player, you'll have to use a certain kind of media and a limited set of compression technologies.

SD Media

Back in the early days of SD DVD recordable media, there was a format war between –R/RW (pronounced "dash R" or "dash RW") and +R/RW (pronounced "plus R" or "plus RW") media and their respective recorders.

As you probably know, in either dash or plus versions, R stands for recordable, and RW stands for rewritable.

Though both –R and +R played on standard DVD players, which avoided any confusion on the playback side, DVD-R recorders required DVD-R media, and DVD+R recorders required DVD+R media. Since different vendors supported different standards (like HP and +R, and Apple and –R), producers with different computers often needed to stock multiple standards of recordable media. Add rewritable and dual-layer media to the mix, which are also standard-specific, and your shelves could easily look like those at Office Depot.

Fortunately, after a few years of that chaos, affordable "dual RW" recorders appeared that could record to media of both formats. If you have a dual RW recorder, you can use both media standards; otherwise, you'll need either +R or –R recordable media.

Note that both +R and –R are available in both single and dual layer, with the capacities shown in **Table 6.1**. If you're producing a single-layer disc in either format, you have a capacity of 4.7 GB, which adds up to about 74 minutes of audio/video at a combined 8 Mbps, which is the highest recommended rate.

Table 6.1 Standard Disc Types and Their Characteristics

Standard options	DVD±R/RW	DVD±R/RW Dual-Layer
Number of layers	1	2
Capacity	4.7 GB	8.5 GB
Video at 8 Mpbs (in minutes)	74	135

Dual-layer discs in both formats can hold up to 8.5 GB, sufficient for about 135 minutes of audio/video at 8 Mbps. Note that dual-layer discs have two layers on a single side, so you don't have to turn the disc over to either record or play the disc. There are some dual-sided media around (mostly from Ritek), which you have to turn over to record and play, though I haven't seen these used much.

One final caveat before moving onto the format side: not all recordable discs will play on all DVD players. See the sidebar "Compatibility Risks of Recordable Media" for more details.

Compatibility Risks of Recordable Media

Virtually all Hollywood DVDs are produced using a different process than DVD recordable, often called *replication*. Playback compatibility for these replicated discs on the wide variety of DVD players is near 100 percent, since the raison d'être for these players is to play Hollywood DVDs, and their manufacturers test accordingly.

Unfortunately, recordable media didn't become widely available until long after DVD players started selling, so lots of players were on the market before most recordable media brands became available for compatibility testing. As a result, many early DVD players can't play recordable discs, though most newer players can. Playback incompatibilities can be absolute, or can relate to recorder, media brand, or even recording parameters.

If you're producing for your own use, you can use a combination of media and recorder that plays on your player—no big deal. When producing for wider distribution, however, the risk of playback incompatibilities becomes much more significant. For example, the last time I looked, incompatibility rates were down to about 5 percent or so, which still means 5 unhappy customers out of 100.

You can minimize (but not eliminate) the risk by doing the following:

- Use name-brand premium media. I use Ridata and Verbatim exclusively. Once you find a media brand that works for you, don't switch.

- Use recordable, rather than rewritable media, and use single-layer rather than dual-layer media, which has significant compatibility problems.

- Record at a combined audio/video data rate of less than 8 Mbps, or even 7 Mbps if serving a broad base of customers who may have older players, which will choke and sputter on recordable media with video encoded at high data rates.

When delivering content on recordable media, it never hurts to include a note in your documentation to the effect that not all recordable media plays on all players. That way, the customer knows that it's not your fault that the DVD won't play. You might encourage them to try a different player before returning the disc or try playing it on their computer.

These same principles apply to high-definition recorders and recordable media. That is, early Blu-ray players couldn't be tested for compatibility with recordable media, because it didn't exist when they shipped, which obviously increases the risk of compatibility issues. Fortunately, you're producing for a much smaller target audience, so you can and should test compatibility early in the process. Expect incompatibilities, test to minimize the risk, and warn your customers and clients that issues may occur.

SD Codecs

Now that you have the media side down, I'll address the codec side of this DVD you're producing for your end user's $19.95 Wal-Mart DVD player, which involves much less guesswork. The only video codec you can use is MPEG-2, and all assets containing visual images will be compressed to MPEG-2.

For example, if you use your DVD authoring program to create a slide show, which is a very common feature, the authoring program will encode the slide show into MPEG-2 video during the authoring process. If you create motion menus for your DVD, these will also be encoded into MPEG-2.

You probably won't need to actually *do* anything to choose MPEG-2. As you can see in **Figure 6.1**, a screen from Roxio's DVDitHD, you really don't have a video codec option, just an audio codec option.

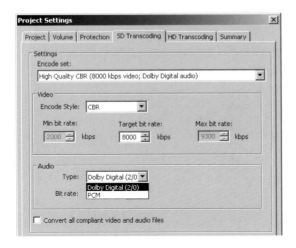

Figure 6.1 All SD DVDs use the MPEG-2 video codec and either Dolby Digital, PCM, or MPEG (not shown) audio compression.

You have a bit more flexibility on the audio side, where you can choose Dolby Digital or PCM compression and sometimes MPEG-1 Layer II audio compression. All DVD players sold in U.S. markets *must* support the first two formats, while support for MPEG audio compression is *optional* (although most players do support it).

Most prosumer and professional authoring programs offer Dolby Digital, and when it's available, it's the best option. Some consumer programs offer only MPEG and PCM, and typically I'll choose MPEG in that instance. If

NOTE There are two versions of the Dolby Digital encoder—Standard and Professional. Dolby Digital Professional offers better quality encoding, but not all applications will offer both, so if audio quality is extremely important, you may want to investigate which version you are using.

you choose PCM, it has a data rate of about 1.5 Mbps. To meet your 8 Mbps total target, you'll have to drop your video data rate to 6.5 Mbps.

In contrast, both MPEG and Dolby Digital have configurable data rates that usually go as high as 400 Kbps or so, though most producers stick to 192 Kbps or less. At this rate, you have 7.8 Mbps to devote to video, which is about 20 percent higher than the 6.5 Mbps you'll have with uncompressed audio. For this reason, it almost always makes sense to use some form of compressed audio, with Dolby being the best choice when available.

What the Heck Is a VOB?

As you probably know, if you produce an MPEG-2 file on your computer, it typically has an .mpg, .mp2, or .mpv extension. Yet if you scan the contents of a DVD in Windows Explorer or Finder, you won't find any files with that extension. Rather, as you can see in **Figure 6.2**, you'll see that all the really big files have .vob extensions.

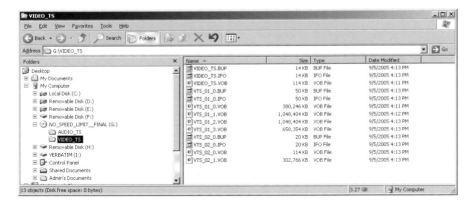

Figure 6.2 During the rendering stage, the authoring program combines menus and content into VOB files that DVD players know how to read.

Technically, a video object (VOB) file is a "container format" for the menus and content. If you copy a .vob file to your hard drive and change the extension to .mpg, your default MPEG player will probably play the video, though you'll likely lose any interactivity.

More important, you should know that you can extract the original MPEG-2 files from a DVD using most consumer authoring and editing programs such as Adobe Premiere Elements or Pinnacle Studio, assuming the DVD isn't copy-protected. This is often useful when you need to access videos that you've previously produced to DVD but have since deleted the source files from your production station.

In addition, if you do see a bunch of MPEG-2 files on the DVD, it probably won't play on a desktop DVD player. Instead, you'll need the VOB files in the proper Video_TS folder for the DVD to play. That's why you need to go through the authoring stage to produce a DVD that will work on a TV-attached player.

WHAT'S A BLU-RAY DISC?

Until recently, there were two hi-def DVD formats, HD DVD and Blu-ray Disc, and the prospects for delivering high-def content on disc were decidedly muddled. In mid-February 2008, after a "format war" that seemed to drag on interminably, Toshiba withdrew the HD DVD format (see sidebar, "Rumors of HD DVD's Demise *Not* Exaggerated"), industry harmony was restored, and the so-called format war ended fairly quietly, leaving Blu-ray Disc as the consumer standard for HD delivery on optical disc.

As Blu-ray Disc (BD) emerges as the HDTV-ready successor to DVD, what will content producers and compressionists need to know to be prepared to deliver in the BD format? The first thing we'll need to do it is to get familiar with the basic specs, such as capacities (which directly affects bit budgeting), video resolution and frame rate support, and—most importantly—codec support, which is a little more complicated with DVD. **Table 6.2** provides the low-down on Blu-ray Disc.

> **NOTE** I mentioned transport streams as they relate to MPEG-2 back in Chapter 2, but that is not the only way that codec gets bundled and used. Two more common stream formats exist known as program streams (PS) and elementary streams (ES). Program streams, also referred to as MPEG-2 PS, are the standard format for storing MPEG-2 video muxed with other streams (like audio or subtitles). Elementary streams on the other hand are the individual audio and video files that haven't been muxed together. Each channel of the audio would be an individual file, so a surround sound export would include 6 individual files.

Table 6.2 Desktop producer's view of Blu-ray Disc Features

Features	Blu-ray details
Capacity: single/double layers	25/50 GB
Video formats	AVC/VC1/MPEG-2
Video resolution (maximum)	1920x1080 24p or 50/60i HDTV
Maximum video bit rate	40 Mbps
Audio formats	Dolby Digital/DTS/PCM
Interactivity	Blu-ray Disc Java (BD-J)
Recorders availability in the United States	Since January 2007

Rumors of HD DVD's Demise *Not* Exaggerated

Up until recently, there were two physically distinct and mutually incompatible formats, HD DVD and Blu-ray Disc, battling to succeed DVD as the standard for HD content delivery on optical disc. On the manufacturing and patent side, HD DVD was essentially a Toshiba format, while Blu-ray Disc was backed by Sony, Pioneer, Panasonic, and roughly 150 other companies. That said, HD DVD did carry the endorsement of the DVD Forum, which had been the leading industry advocacy group for DVD (including many DVD patent holders), and the support of some major movie studios, which many felt would be a key factor in determining which format would win out. Other advantages of HD DVD included its manufacturing similarities to DVD, which meant that the replication plants that crank out DVD movies could adapt their existing lines to HD DVD production with less effort and cost than it would take to migrate to Blu-ray Disc.

Blu-ray Disc, meanwhile, offered greater capacity per layer on each disc (25 GB versus 15 GB for HD DVD), and arguably more opportunities for adding interactivity and web connectivity on the authoring side, although most of those haven't been explored yet. And it had a lot more companies behind it. But as far as consumers were concerned, the formats were functionally the same: both could deliver full 1080p HD movies on disc, with some nice additional improvements over DVD like pop-up menus. But what was frustrating was that the presence of two formats meant a kind of stalemate that was keeping manufacturing and sales volumes low, player and disc prices high, and most consumers wary of choosing one or another format lest they get burned as Beta users did in the late '70s when VHS doomed their format of choice to instant obsolescence. And that went double for content producers who needed the consumer market to stabilize before they could confidently start developing for one format or another with assurance that their end users could play the discs they produced.

The stalemate broke in January 2008 at the annual Consumer Electronics Show (CES) in Las Vegas when Warner Bros. announced that they would exclusively back the Blu-ray format and deliver their high-def movies only on Blu-ray Disc. With several other key players having already jumped ship, Warner's defection tipped the scales decidedly in Blu-ray's favor. The HD DVD camp's immediate response was to cancel the HD DVD party they'd planned for the first night of the show, and initiate a fire sale on all the HD DVD players in the channel. In rapid succession, similar announcements followed from Netflix, Best Buy, Walmart, and others, and by mid-February, rumors were circulating that Toshiba would be announcing the death of HD DVD very soon. That announcement came on February 19, and HD DVD was history.

So now it's a one-horse race, at least on the optical disc side, leaving Blu-ray Disc the de facto, HD-capable successor to DVD.

I didn't list all supported audio codecs, but Dolby Digital should clearly be the codec of choice for most desktop producers. The Blu-ray format enables interactivity beyond that offered by SD DVDs, although no prosumer program that I'm aware of supports these features. Rather, they simply extend current SD DVD features to the higher-capacity discs (and higher-quality video codecs).

Blu-ray Discs require dedicated set-top players for playback; the format is not backward-compatible, so the discs can't play on SD DVD players. Currently, Blu-ray players cost around $300, and movie titles sell for around $30. Blu-ray burners are available on the Web for around $400, with media pricing around $15. As adoption of the format (both on the consumer playback and production side) grows with the end of the format war, expect those prices to drop significantly, although it may still be a couple of years until we're buying Blu-ray players, movies, burners, and blank discs for the same prices as their DVD counterparts.

Though there are levels of Blu-ray authoring that I'll discuss, from the viewpoint of the desktop developer, there's very little difference between producing SD DVDs and high-definition Blu-ray Discs. That is, your menu and interactivity options are identical to those offered for SD DVD; though you may want to choose a different video codec and a larger disc capacity when recording to your BD recorder, there's no real learning curve for SD producers moving to desktop high-definition production.

So with all of this in mind, let's take a quick, high-level look at some of the issues related to producing in each format; then we'll dig in and actually produce an SD DVD and a Blu-ray Disc.

PRODUCING BLU-RAY DISCS

To produce Blu-ray Discs, you have to understand the different types of Blu-ray Discs produced by the different authoring programs and how their differences might affect playback compatibility. In addition, some programs, such as Adobe Encore, can format and write full-length Blu-ray Discs (BD) only to BD recorders. In contrast, some consumer authoring programs can produce Blu-ray-compatible discs on SD media, allowing producers to produce discs with about 20 to 25 minutes of HD video *without* a BD recorder.

Is It Clear Sailing Now for Blu-ray?

As the format war dragged on, many journalists and technologists speculated that if it went on long enough, digital downloads could easily overtake and kill both formats. Digital downloading is the notion of purchasing electronic movies through services such as Amazon Unbox or the iTunes Music Store and then downloading them for consumption on a TV (through some sort of set-top box or bridge device), computer, or portable device (such as an iPod, Apple TV, or Zune). Although digital downloads have certainly picked up steam in the past year, they are far from being the winner in the format war right now for several reasons. It's true that digital consumption of music has heavily impacted sales of music on physical media, but even that has taken nearly a decade to move from the realm of techie college kids into the full consumer market.

Even aside from the natural tendency for the average consumer to adopt new technologies like this, there are still two very closely related issues that will continue to keep digital downloads as a slower second option in the video consumption realm: file size and consumer bandwidth. Music files are often only a few megabytes in size, so downloading an entire album over even a modest broadband connection can take only a few minutes. By comparison, even a standard-definition one-hour TV show (or even slightly "sub-SD" show, as iTunes has billed it) is right at 1 GB! This can take quite a bit longer to download—often half an hour or more on modern broadband connections (sorry, dial-up users—when it comes to TV shows, you're out of the game altogether).

Feature-length movies take even longer, and we still haven't broached the subject of HD downloads. Even a fairly low-resolution HD digital download today (through services such as the Xbox marketplace) is going to run around 8 GB or more. Consumers wanting to be early adopters now suddenly have two major challenges ahead of themselves: patiently downloading these very large files and then organizing and managing the storage of them.

In the digital realm, an average DVD owner's collection could easily be a couple of hundred gigabytes of stored media. Although hard drive capacities have increased exponentially, that is still a big chunk of data to maintain. On top of all of these issues, you still need to figure out how to pair that large drive of digital files with your TV, which remains the preferred vehicle for video consumption today, despite inroads by computers and mobile devices. A number of IP video-savvy set-top boxes are coming onto the market, but no particular product or service has completely claimed consumer mind share as yet.

So, what does that mean for Blu-ray Disc going forward? Well, it means that disc-based media still has a big role in the industry and in our consumption of video. With the large leap in storage capacity that it offers over SD DVD discs, BD easily outstrips the capacity (and patience) of nearly every digital downloader in the world—I can't even imagine trying to download a 30 GB movie, and I love this technology! So, disc-based media is still an important, even dominant player in this industry. But digital downloads will continue to gain popularity and market share as we move forward. And who knows—in 10 years, maybe my super-fast mega-high-speed broadband and the multiterabyte video jukebox home entertainment system that interconnects my TV, computers, and portable devices will make delivering movies on optical disc obsolete—at least I secretly hope it does.

Blu-ray Overview

There are three types of Blu-ray Discs. The richest set of authoring functionality is available with the HDMV (Movie Mode) specification, which includes pop-up menus, interactive graphics, and other content. To access this level of functionality, you'll need a professional authoring program such as Sonic Scenarist, which are priced several times higher than prosumer programs such as Adobe Encore, Sonic DVDit Pro HD, and Sony's Blu-print.

For the most part, only Hollywood producers use HDMV to author and then replicate their discs for mass-market consumption. Again, from a compatibility perspective, this type of disc is safest in terms of both media and format, since replicated media is the most reliable and all consumer Blu-ray Disc players have been tested for compatibility with replicated HDMV discs.

Next is the BDMV (Blu-ray Disc Movie) specification, which offers the same level of authoring functionality as current DVDs but can include Blu-ray content and can write to Blu-ray media. This is the level of functionality provided by Adobe Encore and Sonic DVDit HD, which essentially extend their current DVD authoring capabilities to Blu-ray.

The least functional specification is BDAV (Blu-ray Disc Audio/Visual), which is offered by consumer-level programs such as Sonic's Easy Media Creator, Corel's MovieFactory, CyberLink's PowerProducer, and the like. BDAV discs don't have menus, and viewers choose videos via a file manager available in all Blu-ray players. This can make playback comparatively primitive (**Figure 6.3**) compared to BDMV options, at least until the video starts playing, at which point the quality of the high-definition video should be identical.

Figure 6.3 This is an example of the type of menu viewers will use to choose videos from Blu-ray Discs authored to the BDAV specification.

Note that not all versions of all set-top players support BDMV playback, though I'm guessing that the situation will improve over time. Since Blu-ray isn't yet a mass-market technology, you're probably producing for a limited number of devices. If you're in a position to recommend a Blu-ray player to a customer, make sure it's one that will play your discs.

Recording Blu-ray Discs

With this as background, you can record discs that play on Blu-ray players in three ways:

- Record a BDMV-formatted project to a full-capacity disc on a Blu-ray recorder. This is *probably* what most readers want to do, and it's what I'll demonstrate with Adobe Encore in this chapter.

- Record a BDAV-formatted disc to a full-capacity Blu-ray Disc on a BD recorder, which is the level of Blu-ray support afforded by most consumer video production programs, including CyberLink PowerProducer, which is shown in **Figure 6.4**.

Figure 6.4 Producing a BDAV disc in CyberLink's PowerProducer. This is a full-capacity single-layer Blu-ray Disc; it doesn't have a menu, and videos selected as shown in Figure 6.3.

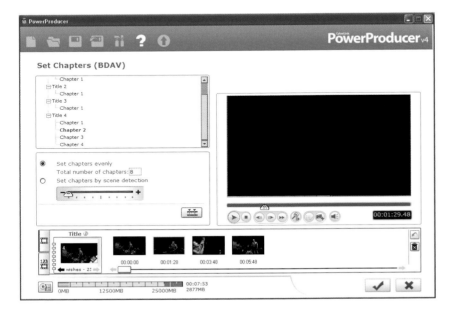

- Record a BDMV-formatted disc to an SD DVD, which is a fairly common feature found in Pinnacle Studio, shown in **Figure 6.5**. Though recorded on SD media, this disc will play back only on Blu-ray players. Note that I'm recording to a dual-layer disc that will provide up to 63 minutes of Blu-ray video at the default 17,000 Kbps. This "hybrid" approach has the advantage of enabling HD production on SD drives.

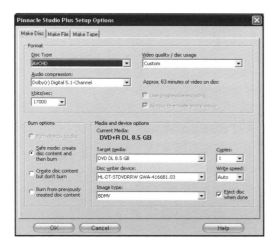

Figure 6.5 Producing a BDMV disc on SD media in Pinnacle Studio. This is a dual-layer SD disc with an 8.5 GB capacity that can hold about 63 minutes of video.

Obviously, you, as the producer, need to choose the type of disc that best suits your needs and budget.

With this technical information as background, let's look at the different workflows you'll deploy to actually produce your DVDs.

DVD WORKFLOWS

As discussed earlier, DVDs have two high-level components, content and menus. In the early days of DVD production, you created your content in one program, typically a video editor; created your menus in another, typically an image editor such as Photoshop; and then merged them into a DVD in another, typically an authoring program.

Since then, these functions have become more integrated. Most prosumer suites, such as Adobe Production Premium CS3 and Apple Final Cut Studio, still have separate programs for editing (Premiere Pro/Final Cut Pro) and authoring (Encore/DVD Studio Pro), and both authoring programs can create menus, though they can also use menus created in a separate program such as Photoshop. Interestingly, both programs can also create slide shows, a feature that bubbled up from consumer authoring programs.

Some programs take this integration one step further and edit *and* author in a single interface. Most integrated are Pinnacle Studio and Avid Liquid, which actually include menus in the video timeline (that's Studio shown in **Figure 6.6**).

Figure 6.6 Pinnacle Studio includes menus and video on the same timeline for a highly integrated editing/authoring environment.

What's nice about this approach is that it eliminates the risk of multiple compression generations in your footage, which is the most significant compression-related risk in authoring. More specifically, because you edit and author in the same environment, you don't encode your video until you actually produce the DVD.

In contrast, when you edit and author in separate programs, you may have to render your footage in your editor and then input it into your authoring program. I call this the *handoff*. For example, suppose you've edited your video in Premiere Pro. You're producing your video for SD DVD authoring, so when it's time to render from Premiere Pro, you output MPEG-2 files at a combined data rate of 8 Mbps or less.

Then you author in Encore, but when it's time to produce your DVD, you have a whopping 100 minutes of content, which means you need a combined data rate of less than 6.3 Mbps. To fit your content onto the DVD, Encore has to reencode down to the lower rate, which means another generation of lossy compression, which isn't tragic but certainly isn't best practice. Or, you can go back to Premiere Pro and reencode the original video footage, which takes a whole lot of unnecessary time.

To avoid this hassle, when working with most separate editing and authoring programs, you have to "mind the handoff." This means you have to manage the transition between your editing and authoring programs to ensure that you don't compress the video twice. In most instances, this means rendering the video to a format and data rate that ensures that all your content will fit on the DVD. To accomplish this, you have to know how to bit budget, which I cover in the next section.

Note that you can avoid this issue when producing in Final Cut Studio by outputting a QuickTime reference movie from Final Cut Pro and inputting that into DVD Studio Pro. Briefly, a QuickTime reference file contains the entire uncompressed audio file and "pointers" to the video that's on your disc, as well as instructions from Final Cut Pro about how to edit the video. Since you're not actually rendering the video when you create a QuickTime reference movie, you can create the video in only a few seconds, and then you can import it into DVD Studio Pro like any other file. This avoids the handoff problem and delays the final rendering until you're ready to produce the final DVD, rather than inserting it between the editing and authoring stages.

On the other hand, Apple Compressor, the rendering program for Final Cut Pro, offers much more control over video and especially audio encoding and has a range of useful presets. You can also render your audio into Dolby Digital format in Compressor, while you can't in DVD Studio Pro.

For these reasons, I recommend exporting DVD-ready files from Final Cut Pro via Compressor, and *not* using QuickTime reference movies. This is the workflow that I demonstrate later in this chapter, after describing how to bit budget your projects.

THAT WHOLE BIT BUDGET THING

For those of you jumping in at this section, *bit budgeting* refers to assigning audio and video bit rates to your source footage to make sure the compressed footage fits on your selected media. If you're working with an integrated editing/authoring solution, you probably have to bit budget only when you're ready to produce your DVD. With most programs, you'll have some kind of meter showing disc capacity as your guide.

On the other hand, when working with separate programs such as Adobe Premiere Pro and Adobe Encore, you'll want to perform your bit budgeting before rendering from your editor to avoid double compression. Fortunately, bit budgeting is pretty simple. Each disc has a known capacity, and you have a certain number of minutes of content, so divide the latter into the former to figure out the data rate you need to fit the content on disc.

Complicating this equation is that capacity is measured in giga*bytes*, while data rate is measured in mega or kilo*bits*; in addition, you probably care more about *minutes* of content on the disc, rather than *seconds*. To simplify things, I've illustrated the math in **Table 6.3** and **Table 6.4**.

Specifically, Table 6.3 answers the initial question you should always ask when producing a DVD: "Do I have to care?" That is, if you encode at the maximum data rate supported by the device, do you have sufficient disc capacity for the video in your project?

Table 6.3 Bit Budgeting for DVDs at Maximum Capacity

Measurement	Blu-ray	Standard DVD
Capacity (in bytes)	25,000,000,000	4,700,000,000
In bits (times 8)	200,000,000,000	37,600,000,000
Per sec max	40,256,000	8,000,000
Seconds	4,968	4,700
Minutes (divide by 60)	83 (79)	78 (74)

For Blu-ray devices, if you encode at the maximum bit rate, which probably isn't necessary, you still have 83 minutes of capacity, though I always round the calculated number down by 5 percent to be safe, which brings me to the number in parentheses, 79. For DVD, where I recommend you stay below 8 Mbps combined data rate, the number is 74 minutes. If you have less content than any of these numbers, you're safe.

If you're exceeding that number, you have to compute the bit budget for each second of compressed video, which I illustrate how to do for a project with 100 minutes in Table 6.4. Briefly, you use the same capacity divided by the seconds of video in your production. Again, the computed rate for 100 minutes is shown first, and then 95 percent of that is in parentheses.

Table 6.4 Bit Budgeting for Projects with 100 Minutes

Measurement	Blu-ray	Standard DVD
Capacity (in bytes)	25,000,000,000	4,700,000,000
In bits (times 8)	200,000,000,000	37,600,000,000
Minutes of content	100	100
Seconds of content (times 60)	6,000	6,000
Per second data rate	33.33 (31.67) Mbps	6.27 (5.95) Mbps

Remember to include the capacity needs of motion menus, slideshows, and first-play videos in your computation of total minutes of video. If you have unusually lengthy audio menus, you should subtract the total bit rate for that audio from the available capacity before dividing the balance by the number of minutes of video.

Once you have the total data rate, you're in charge of divvying up that bit rate between audio and video. I typically use 192 Kbps for stereo audio and allocate the rest to video. If you're producing in six-channel, 5.1 surround sound, you might go as high as 448 Kbps.

As they say in the construction business, when you calculate bit budget, "Measure twice, cut once." Encoding video, particularly HDV, can take quite a long time. For example, I recently encoded 84 minutes of HDV source video into SD MPEG-2-compatible video on a Dell Precision 390 workstation running a dual-core 3.0 GHz Core 2 Duo processor. I produced the video in Premiere Pro, bound for authoring in Encore, and used 2-pass VBR. Encoding took almost exactly five hours.

The result fit quite neatly on a single-layer DVD, thank you very much. Had I blown the computation, which is not totally unheard of, I admit, I would have lost pretty much a complete day on the project. Note that there are several online sites with bit-rate calculators, including www.videohelp.com/calc.htm, which even lets you download the calculator for desktop use when not online.

Whew! That's enough background—let's produce some DVDs. I'll start by showing how to produce an SD DVD in Final Cut Studio, and I'll conclude with a look at Blu-ray production in Adobe Production Premium CS3.

RECIPES FOR PRODUCING SD DVDs

Here's the high-level workflow I'll use in Final Cut Studio to produce my SD and HD DVDs. I'll edit in Final Cut Pro and, before rendering my file, take some DVD- and compression-specific steps in Final Cut Pro to improve compression quality and simplify the authoring task. Next I'll export DVD-ready assets using Compressor and then import those assets into DVD Studio Pro and produce my DVD.

Let's begin.

Compression and DVD Studio Pro Markers

As you learned in Chapter 2, "The Language of Compression," most codecs use a group of pictures (GOP) structure to encode, with each GOP starting with an I-frame. As you recall, I-frames are totally self-contained, which makes them the largest frame type but also the highest-quality frame type, particularly in a dynamic setting involving a scene change or high motion. I-frames are particularly useful at the start of new scenes because they provide a high-quality base for subsequent B- and P-frames.

To produce the best available compressed quality, Final Cut Pro automatically inserts compression markers at each cut point and at the first and last frame of each transition between two clips, ensuring that Compressor inserts an I-frame at those locations. Usually, this is sufficient to ensure optimal quality.

However, sometimes, when you have particularly dynamic footage, you may want to tell Compressor to insert I-frames at specific locations, which you do by inserting a compression marker. I show this in **Figure 6.7**, where I'm encoding a scene from an amusement park ride. The ride swirls around pretty quickly, and I want to make sure that the short scenes containing the three young lasses in the figure look their best. So, I'll insert a compression marker in the first frame of each brief appearance.

The process is simple. Navigate to the target frame, and then press the M key on your keyboard. This inserts the marker. Make sure you don't have a clip selected in the sequence, because this will create a marker in the clip, not in the sequence.

To define the marker, press M again, which opens the Edit Marker window shown in Figure 6.7. Then click Add Compression Marker, which tells Final Cut Pro to make this a compression marker and helpfully inserts "<COMPRESSION>" in the Comment field.

Figure 6.7 Adding compression markers in Final Cut Pro.

You use the same procedure to add chapter markers to the clip, clicking Add Chapter Marker rather than Add Compression Marker. You should also name your marker, since this will assist your linking buttons to chapter points in DVD Studio Pro. As you probably know, chapter markers are frames in the video that you can link to directly via a button on your menu or jump to directly using your menu remote.

Although you can insert chapter markers in DVD Studio Pro or Compressor, I recommend you insert them in Final Cut Pro for two reasons. First, Final Cut Pro offers superior navigation controls, and you can also see the audio waveform, which for many productions, such as concerts, plays, and other events, is the fastest way to identify where you want to insert a chapter market.

Second, in Final Cut Pro, you can insert a chapter marker on any frame in the sequence, while in DVD Studio Pro, you can insert markers only on I-frames, which limits your precision to one frame in each 15. Often this is enough to force you to start at a visually or auditory awkward moment, such as halfway through an audio or video fade-in or fade-out.

Rendering a DVD-Compatible File in Compressor

OK, you've edited your video in Final Cut Pro and set compression and chapter markers. For this example, producing an SD DVD, let's assume you have 90 minutes of video in your project, which could be either SD or HD source. You've already done your bit budget calculations and know that you need to produce at a combined data rate of about 6.6 Mbps. You'll allocate 192 Kbps for your stereo audio, leaving about 6.4 Mbps for video.

If you're unfamiliar with Compressor, refer to Chapter 5, "Compression Tools," for more details on the interface and high-level workflow.

To render DVD-ready assets in Compressor, follow these steps:

1. From Final Cut Pro, choose File > Export > Using Compressor. Compressor opens.

2. Compressor has 10 DVD-related folders of presets; the first six are the most appropriate for SD DVDs. Choose the preset closest to your target settings, which in this case are those contained in DVD: Best Quality 90 Minutes. Drag those into the Batch window (**Figure 6.8**).

Figure 6.8 Get started in Compressor by dragging the preset closest to your target onto the job in the Batch window, in this case DVD: Best Quality 90 minutes.

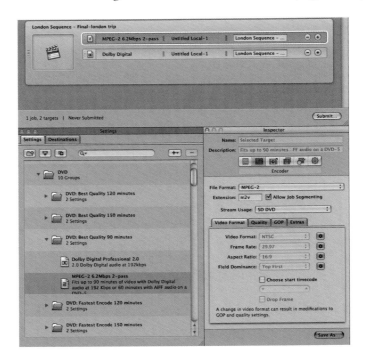

3. Let's start with a look at the MPEG-2 video-related settings. Click that setting in the Batch window, and then in the Inspector, click the Encoder button (second from the left) to open the Encoder pane. Note that the Stream Usage setting in the Inspector should be set to SD DVD; otherwise, you've chosen the wrong preset. All other settings, including Field Dominance, should map directly from your project settings, which is why they are grayed out.

4. Select the Quality tab in the Inspector (**Figure 6.9**). The following are the settings to consider in this tab:

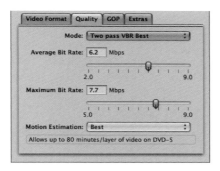

Figure 6.9 Quality settings for your SD DVD encode. The screen says 80 minutes; I say 90. Who's right? (See Figure 6.21 later in the chapter for the answer.)

Mode: Under Mode options, choose the mode that best suits your quality requirements and time budget. The Compressor help screen has excellent (if somewhat self-laudatory) descriptions of the trade-offs associated with all modes. Basically, as you learned in Chapter 2, VBR will deliver better quality than CBR with challenging clips, and two-pass VBR will deliver better quality than single-pass VBR. To this, Compressor adds "Best" modes that take even longer but deliver "outstanding quality" at 3.5 Mbps and faster. If you have the time, choose Two Pass VBR Best.

Average Bit Rate: Insert your target bit rate here. To be conservative, I'll just go with the 6.2 Mbps shown in Figure 6.9, rather than the 6.4 we calculated earlier.

Maximum Bit Rate: As you know, when using variable bit rate encoding, the bit rate will vary with scene complexity. To ensure that the video streams smoothly off the DVD, choose 7.7 Mbps here, which, when combined with 192 Kbps audio, gives you 7.9 Mbps, just less than the 8 Mbps target.

Motion Estimation: Choose between Good, Better, and Best, keeping in mind that higher-quality settings take longer to calculate. With low-motion (talking head) footage, you probably won't see much difference between these settings, but with high-motion footage, you should. Note that your choice here should map to your choice of encoding modes, with Good for CBR, Better for one- and two-pass VBR, and Best for "Best" modes.

5. Select the GOP tab (**Figure 6.10**). The settings on this tab allow you to change the number of B-frames in the GOP, choose whether your GOP is open (and refers to frames in previous GOPs) or closed (refers solely to frames within the GOP), and change the GOP size. In general, unless you really know what you're doing, you should accept the default settings here.

Figure 6.10 GOP settings for your SD DVD encode.

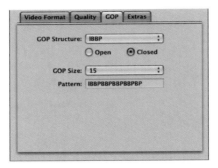

6. Select the Extras tab (**Figure 6.11**). Here are the settings to consider in this tab:

Figure 6.11 Extra settings to consider for your SD DVD encode.

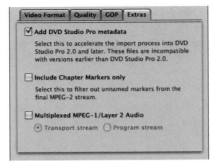

Add DVD Studio Pro metadata: The default is checked; the only reason to deselect this option is if you're encoding for DVD Studio Pro versions earlier than 2.0.

Include Chapter Markers only: Selecting this check box will parse out compression markers. I can't think of any reason why you would enable this.

Multiplexed MPEG-2/Layer 2 Audio: DVD Studio Pro wants what are called *elementary* streams, which is one stream for audio and one for video. When producing MPEG-2 files for DVD Studio Pro, as we are here, leave this box unchecked.

7. Now let's check the audio-related settings. Click the audio setting in the Batch window (the Dolby Digital setting in Figure 6.8) and then click the Encoding button in the Inspector. You should see the screen shown in **Figure 6.12**.

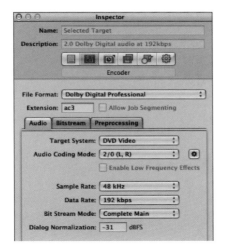

Figure 6.12 Compressor's Dolby Digital audio settings.

Note that many of the controls in this Dolby Digital Professional setting are very technical settings that are critical for Hollywood producers seeking to optimize their Dolby-related settings. If this defines your activities, note that Dolby has an online PDF titled "Dolby Digital Professional Encoding Guidelines" that you can access for more information on these parameters:

www.dolby.com/assets/pdf/tech_library/46_DDEncodingGuidelines.pdf

For most event, business, and casual producers, the default values work just fine. In this screen, here are the options:

Target System: Choose DVD Video when producing for DVD Studio Pro.

Audio Coding Mode: Stereo is shown; if you have multiple audio tracks, select the mode that matches your source files.

Sample Rate: Use 48 kHz.

Data Rate: Choose the target audio data rate; I'm using 192 Kbps for this stereo audio.

Bit Stream Mode: Use Complete Main, as shown, when producing the main audio track for the video. If you're producing for specific playback devices, such as karaoke or commentary dialogue for the director's cut of a DVD, choose that.

Dialog Normalization: This setting normalizes audio volume between different tracks of audio on your DVD. Using -31 (Decibels Full Scale) as the target, Compressor will add metadata in the audio bit stream that tells the playback device to boost audio volume by the difference between -31 and the value input into the Dialogue Normalization field. For example, if you insert the default value of -27, Compressor will tell the playback device to boost playback volume by 4 dB. If you're comfortable that you have the appropriate audio levels and don't want the player device to adjust them, enter **-31dBFS**, and choose None in the Compression Preset menu in the Preprocessing tab, discussed in a moment.

8. Select the Bitstream tab (**Figure 6.13**). Leave these settings at their default values unless you have a good reason for changing them.

 **Figure 6.13** Compressor's Dolby Bitstream settings.

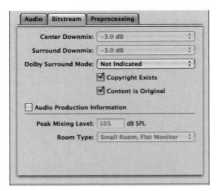

9. Select the Preprocessing tab (**Figure 6.14**). On this tab, note the following settings:

Compression Preset: Make sure this is set to None unless you're producing specifically for one of the presets in this pop-up menu. Note that the default setting is Film Standard Compression, which could distort your audio.

LFE Channel: This will be grayed out unless you choose an audio coding mode that contains an effects channel and select the Enable Low Frequency Effects check box in Figure 6.12. If grayed out, leave it alone; if active, disable the filter if the digital signal fed to the LFE's input does not contain input greater than 120 Hz.

Full Bandwidth Channels: Selecting these check boxes will apply these filters to your audio. They probably will do no harm, but I prefer to apply these filters, if necessary, in my audio editor, so I recommend disabling them here.

Surround Channels: These settings will become active for any surround sound configuration. The 90-degree Phase-shift produces a stream that sounds better when played on stereo systems and should always be enabled. The 3 dB Attenuation should be enabled only if you're mastering audio in a studio calibrated for 5.1 surround channels.

Figure 6.14 Compressor's Dolby Preprocessing settings.

10. We're done with the compression-related settings. Remember to choose a destination for the two files you're about to produce, and rename them if necessary. Then click Submit, and then click Submit again to begin encoding.

Creating an SD DVD in DVD Studio Pro

You probably know your way around DVD Studio Pro; if not, consider picking up a copy of *Apple Pro Training Series: DVD Studio Pro 4* by Martin Sitter and Adrian Ramseier, because authoring a DVD falls outside the scope of this book. Here, however, are the format- and compression-related steps for creating the SD DVD:

1. Set your project preferences. DVD Studio Pro 4 has a setting for creating DVDs in the now-defunct HD DVD format, which is no longer especially advisable to do since sales of HD DVD players have been discontinued. If you're producing an SD DVD and started work using the HD DVD preset, you have to create a new project file and start over. So, check this preference first.

Figure 6.15 Compressor's Project preferences screen, which you should check at the start of each project and make sure you're working in a still-viable format.

2. Now it's time to set your general preferences. Click the General icon in the Project preferences screen, which opens the window shown in **Figure 6.16**. In this screen, set the Display Mode preference for your SD DVD menus, tracks, and slide shows—I'm using 16:9 Letterbox.

Figure 6.16 Compressor's General preferences screen.

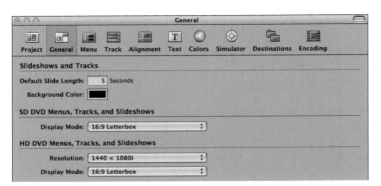

3. Now it's time to set your simulator preferences. Click the Simulator icon in the Project preferences screen, which opens the window shown in **Figure 6.17**. In the Playback Output section, set Resolution to SD, and set Display Mode to the appropriate mode for your source footage.

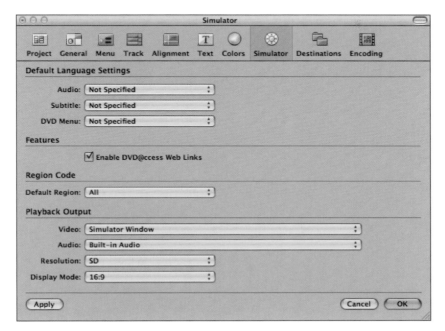

Figure 6.17 Compressor's Simulator preferences screen.

4. Not it's time to set your encoding preferences. Click the Encoding button to view the Encoding window (**Figure 6.18** on the next page). This is where you'll set your video-encoding options for any uncompressed assets that you import into the project or for assets created during authoring, such as motion menus or slide shows. As you can see, the controls are much simpler than those in Compressor and lack some of the more advanced settings.

Again, set your targets based upon your bit budgeting as I've done in the figure. (All the controls are defined earlier in the Compressor discussion.) Note that there are no settings for audio; that's because DVD Studio Pro automatically converts the audio you insert into the project into a standard 48/16 two-channel AIFF file en route to the DVD and can't apply AC3 compression. Note that you can set both SD and HD preferences, but you'll want to stick with the SD preferences for authoring SD DVDs.

Figure 6.18 Compressor's Encoding preferences screen, where you set video-encoding preferences.

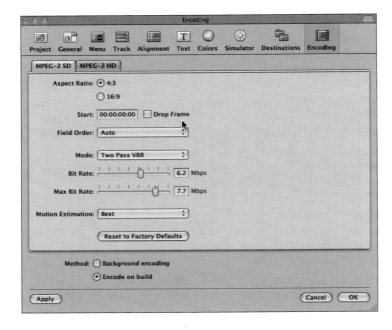

Note the Method option on the bottom of **Figure 6.18**, which allows you to select Encode on build, which encodes all content when you push the magic button to create the DVD, or Background Encoding, which starts encoding when you insert or create the asset.

I suggest trying Background encoding to see whether it makes your computer feel sluggish during editing, which will relate to both the processor speed and the amount of content being encoded. If you either don't notice or don't mind the sluggishness, keep the Background encoding setting enabled. If it gets irritating, disable it.

5. Now it's time to set the disc parameters. Typically, you'll want to set these parameters right before you're about to build. To open the Build & Format window shown in **Figure 6.19**, click the Build/Format hammer above the preview window, and select the Disc/Volume tab of the Build & Format window. In this window, here are the settings:

   Disc Media: Choose Red Laser for all projects unless you have an HD DVD recorder.

   Layer Options: Choose the number of layers in your target media.

Dual-Layer Break Point: This will become active only for dual-layer discs. Automatic is the default option. Note that if you check Seamless, you'll see an error message warning you that this option may cause inconsistent playback behavior at the break point. For this reason, I recommend not checking this option.

Direction: These radio buttons will become active only when you select Dual Layer. Choose the default OTP, which minimizes the delay between playback of the first and second layers.

Number of Sides: Choose the number of sides in your target media.

Disc Size: Choose 8 cm or 12 cm.

Note that after you complete the information in this window, DVD Studio Pro will show the maximum data size, 4.7 GB in the figure, which will correspond with the maximum capacity in the disc meter shown later in Figure 6.21.

TIP If you first build the project, you can manually set the break point. Once you do a build, the Dual-Layer Break Point pop-up menu is not dimmed and you can choose from the possible layer break points available for that disc.

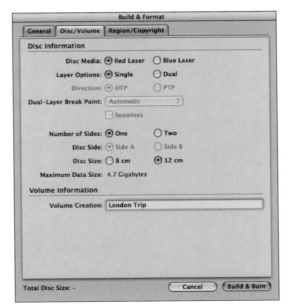

Figure 6.19 Setting disc and volume information.

Figure 6.20 DVD Studio Pro's Assets tab.

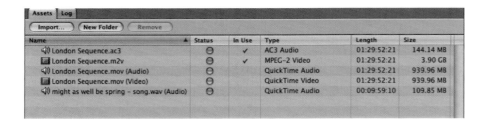

6. Import and deploy your content. This is standard stuff; I just want to make sure you understand what the little color-coded balls in the Status column of the Assets window (**Figure 6.20**) are telling you and mention a few other details. Here are the key points to take away from this screen:

- I produced the first two assets, London Sequence.ac3 and London Sequence.m2v, in Compressor, as shown earlier in "Rendering a DVD-Compatible File in Compressor." Though you can't see the colors in the grayscale picture, the status balls are green, which means the assets are encoded and ready for use. The check marks in the next column, In Use, tell you that I've deployed the assets in the project, and you can see the formats in the next column to the right.

- The third and fourth assets, London Sequence.mov, are the two components of the QuickTime reference movie I created from Final Cut Pro. The little status balls are yellow, meaning that the file hasn't yet been encoded. It also means that DVD Studio Pro can encode them (otherwise the balls would be red), and if you turned on background encoding, you'd see little progress bars in the window, indicating that they were being encoded.

- The fifth asset, a song titled "Might As Well be Spring," also has a green ball but is QuickTime Audio (full rate PCM) rather than AC3 audio. This makes the point that DVD Studio Pro considers PCM audio ready for encoding onto your DVD and doesn't convert PCM to AC3 during the encoding process. If you want to use AC3 audio, you'll have to encode to AC3 audio prior to inputting into DVD Studio Pro.

7. Check the disc meter. **Figure 6.21** shows the disc meter located above Menu Editor. I'm working with a single-layer DVD, which contains up to 4.7 GB, and the meter shows that my content equals 4.5 GB, which confirms that the bit budget calculations implemented in Figure 6.9 actually support 90 minutes of video, not 80 as shown in the screen. I know you've been holding your breath (and applause) since Figure 6.9, so now you can let loose with both.

NOTE Ok, so I actually haven't done any magic here. DVD Studio Pro is designed to pad the minute count slightly to account for menus and audio on the disc. They are protecting us users from not having enough room on the DVD, and I for one am glad it's there.

Figure 6.21 DVD Studio Pro's Assets window includes the Disc Meter, which shows how close you are to exhausting DVD capacity.

OK, let's get back on task. You now know all your content should fit, so produce the disc as normal.

RECIPES FOR PRODUCING BLU-RAY DISCS

Blu-ray was the feature I coveted most in Adobe Production Premium CS3, and Adobe didn't disappoint, though as you'll see, the Premiere Pro/Encore handoff could use some work. Still, you get HDMV authoring, basically the same feature set you get with SD DVDs, and you can burn single-layer Blu-ray Discs with a whopping 25 GB of data.

Adobe keeps promising to include a list of compatible Blu-ray recorders on its Web site (*www.adobe.com/encore*) but hasn't as of this writing. I had very good luck with the LaCie d2 Blu-ray drive but problems with the Pioneer BDR-101. Before buying a Blu-ray drive, check to see whether Adobe has published a list of known compatible drives, and if not, check its support forums, which generally have messages identifying drives that work well and those that don't. I prefer external drives because it simplifies working on multiple systems.

I've successfully used both Ridata and Verbatim media with the LaCie unit but can't vouch for any other brands. Find one that works for you, and stick with it.

From a bit budget perspective, let's keep it simple. Let's say that I have 80 minutes of video, which, according to Table 6.3, I can encode at the maximum data rate of 40 Mbps and still fit the video on disc.

Working in Premiere Pro

As with Final Cut Pro, you can and should insert chapter markers in Premiere Pro, since this gives you frame-accurate placement and the ability to view the audio waveforms, which makes it simple to find periods of quiet and/or applause that mark many chapter points.

To set a chapter marker, move Premiere Pro's Current Time Indicator to the target frame, right-click, and choose Set Encore Chapter Marker (**Figure 6.22**). This opens the dialog shown on the right of the figure. Type the desired name in the Encore Chapter Marker Name field, and click OK. As you probably know, Encore can use this field to name buttons that you link to when creating your menus, so I always name my chapter markers precisely, including the capitalization I want for that button in my menu.

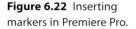

Figure 6.22 Inserting markers in Premiere Pro.

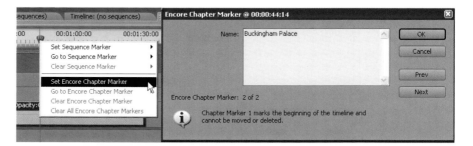

Managing the Handoff

You can export video from Premiere Pro to Encore in two ways. The first is to choose File > Export > Export to Encore, which sounds good but opens a series of compression presets that don't match those offered by Encore, which I find confusing. In addition, Encore opens a project that matches the previous project, not the target project, so even if you export using a Blu-ray preset, if your last project was SD, Encore will open an SD project. You can change it, but again, I find this confusing.

Until these issues get resolved, I find it conceptually simpler to export using Adobe Media Encoder and then create the desired Encore project manually. That's the workflow I'll demonstrate here.

Premiere Pro can output both MPEG-2 and H.264-compatible files, and I'll describe both.

Producing an MPEG-2 Blu-ray-Compatible File in Adobe Media Encoder

To export an MPEG-2-compatible Blu-ray file from Premiere Pro using the Adobe Media Encoder, follow these steps:

1. Choose File > Export > Adobe Media Encoder. In the Export Settings window (**Figure 6.23**), choose the following:

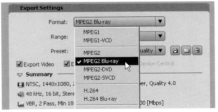

Figure 6.23 Initial export settings in Adobe Media Encoder.

Format: Choose MPEG2 Blu-ray.

Range: Choose either Entire Sequence or Work Area.

Preset: Choose a preset that matches your source footage and quality goals (**Figure 6.24**). For example, use 1440x1080i for HDV and HDTV for 1920x1080 formats. Note that High Quality uses two-pass VBR encoding, while Medium Quality is one-pass VBR.

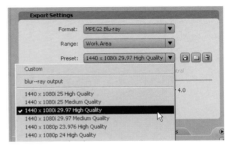

Figure 6.24 Choose your preset.

Export Video/Export Audio: Choose which content types to include in the final stream.

TIP In general, H.264 should deliver higher quality than MPEG-2, but it should also take longer to encode. How much longer? During tests on a dual-processor 3.0 GHz dual-core Mac, it took 11:10 (min:seconds) to render a 3:15-length video into MPEG-2, and it took 24:17 to produce an H.264 file with similar parameters. So, figure it takes a bit more than twice as long to produce in MPEG-2. Overall, when you're seeking optimal quality, choose H.264; when pressed for time, use MPEG-2.

2. Customize your video settings (**Figure 6.25**). Start with MPEG-2 video by selecting the Video tab. In this window, choose the following:

Figure 6.25 Encore's MPEG-2 Blu-ray configuration options.

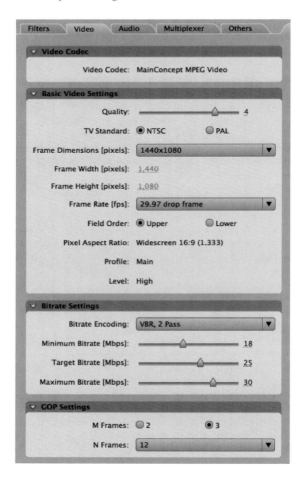

Quality: Set this to 5.

TV Standard: Choose the appropriate standard.

Frame Dimensions [pixels]: This should follow your choice of preset. If incorrect, change it to match your source footage.

Frame Width/Height [pixels]: This should follow your choice of presets. If incorrect, change it to match your source footage.

Frame Rate [fps]: This should follow your choice of presets. If incorrect, change it to match your source footage.

Field Order: This should be Upper.

Pixel Aspect Ratio/Profile/Level: These are hard-coded to the resolution and in some instances not configurable (as shown). If configurable (as with 720x480), accept the default values.

Bitrate Encoding: CBR, 1 Pass, and 2 Pass encoding are available. Choose the desired method.

Minimum/Target/Maximum Bitrate [Mbps]: We could fit our 80 minutes of video at Blu-ray's maximum bit rate of 40 MB/sec, but this increases the risk of playback problems. Use the presets here unless the footage is very challenging.

GOP settings: Leave these at their default settings.

3. Now configure your audio settings. Select the Audio tab, and under Audio Format Settings (**Figure 6.26**), choose PCM. (We'll encode to Dolby Digital in Encore.) Leave all other encoding options at their defaults.

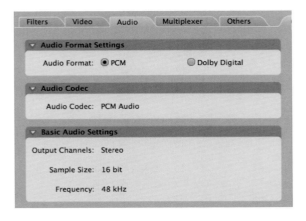

Figure 6.26 Adobe Media Encoder's audio configuration options.

Producing an H.264 Blu-ray-Compatible File in the Adobe Media Encoder

To create an H.264 Blu-ray-compatible file from Premiere Pro using the Adobe Media Encoder, follow these steps:

1. Choose File > Export > Adobe Media Encoder. In the Export Settings window (**Figure 6.27**), choose the following:

Figure 6.27 Initial export settings in the Adobe Media Encoder.

Format: Choose H.264 Blu-ray.

Range: Choose either Entire Sequence or Work Area.

Preset: Choose a preset that matches your source footage and quality goals (**Figure 6.28**). For example, use 1440x1080i for HDV and HDTV 1080 for 1920x1080 formats. Note that High Quality uses two-pass VBR encoding, while Medium Quality is one-pass VBR.

Export Video/Export Audio: Choose which content types to include in the final stream.

Figure 6.28 Choose your preset.

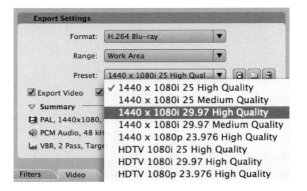

2. Customize your video settings (**Figure 6.29**). Start with H.264 video by selecting the Video tab. In this window, choose the following:

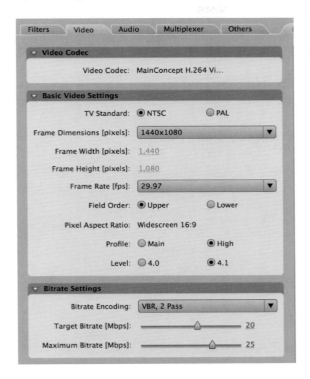

Figure 6.29 Encore's H.264 Blu-ray configuration options.

TV Standard: Choose the appropriate standard.

Frame Dimensions [pixels]: This should follow your choice of preset. If incorrect, change to match your source footage.

Frame Width/Height [pixels]: This should follow your choice of preset. If incorrect, change to match your source footage.

Frame Rate (fps): This should follow your choice of preset. If incorrect, change to match your source footage.

Field Order: This should be Upper.

Pixel Aspect Ratio/Profile/Level: If configurable (as shown), accept the default values.

Bitrate Encoding: CBR, 1 Pass, and 2 Pass encoding are available. Choose the desired method.

Minimum/Target and Maximum Bitrate [Mbps]: We could fit our 80 minutes of video at Blu-ray's maximum bit rate of 40 MB/second, but this increases the risk of playback problems. I would stick with the presets here unless the footage is very challenging.

3. Configure your audio settings. Select the Audio tab, and on this screen (**Figure 6.26**), choose PCM. We'll encode to Dolby Digital in Encore. Leave all other encoding options at their defaults.

Creating a Blu-ray DVD in Encore

Now that you have your assets encoded, it's time to start work in Encore. Here are the steps:

1. Run Encore, and choose New Project in the Encore splash screen (or choose File > New Project in Encore). On the Basic tab of the New Project window (**Figure 6.30**), choose the following:

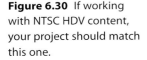

Figure 6.30 If working with NTSC HDV content, your project should match this one.

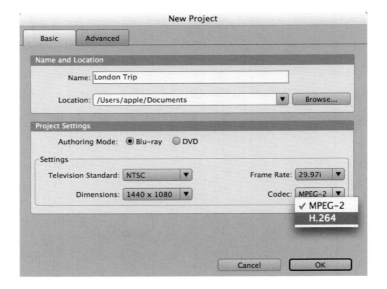

Authoring Mode: Choose Blu-ray.

Settings: Conform these to match your encoded assets, particularly the Codec setting.

2. Select the Advanced tab (**Figure 6.31**) and choose the following:

Automatic Transcoding: Choose the desired maximum.

Audio Transcoding: Choose Dolby Digital.

Then click OK to close the dialog, and start the new project.

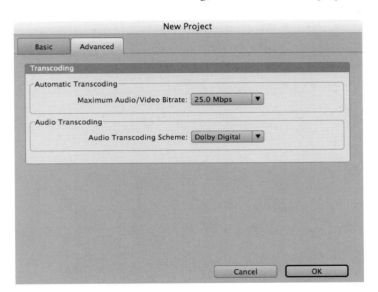

Figure 6.31 Advanced encoding options.

3. Import your content as normal.

Now you have your project setup and assets imported. My concerns at this point are to make sure that I don't reencode my video and that I encode my audio to the correct format. I can resolve both issues on the Project tab (**Figure 6.32**).

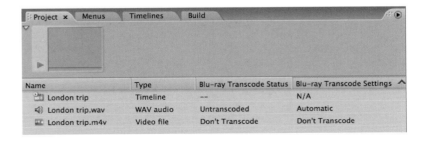

Figure 6.32 The status of the content on the Project tab.

For example, you can see that the H.264 file London trip.m4v has Don't Transcode in both the Blu-ray Transcode Status and Blu-ray Transcode

Settings columns. This means that Encore finds the asset Blu-ray Disc-compliant and won't reencode when recording the DVD; it will simply copy the content to the disc. If you see Untranscoded for video files that you've attempted to encode into Blu-ray format, you have a problem.

4. Before you panic, check to make sure you're looking at the right column and are looking at the Blu-ray Transcode Status column, not DVD Trancode Status, which precedes Blu-ray status in the window (you can adjust which columns display by right-clicking the label area, choosing Columns, and then choosing the desired column). If you're looking at the Blu-ray Transcode columns and the video columns say Untranscoded, you have to review your encoding settings in the Adobe Media Encoder.

5. Since we produced PCM audio in the Adobe Media Encoder, its status should be Untranscoded. To check the settings, right-click the audio file on the Project tab, and choose Transcode Settings and then Edit Quality Presets. This will open the Project Transcode Presets window, which looks like the Adobe Media Encoder but has different settings.

6. Select the Audio tab (**Figure 6.33**). Select the Dolby Digital option, and choose the desired bit rate, 192 Kbps in the figure.

Figure 6.33 Audio transcoding settings in Encore.

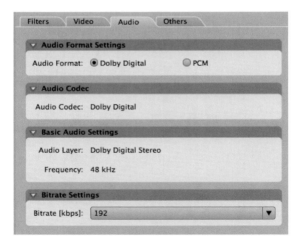

If you have extensive motion menus or slide shows, it may pay to root through the Video tab and conform your settings to those chosen in the Adobe Media Encoder, but be prepared for different labels and settings.

7. When you're ready to produce your disc, click File > Build > Disc (**Figure 6.34**).

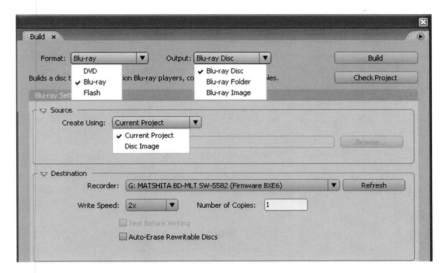

Figure 6.34 Building your Blu-ray Disc.

Figure 6.34 Building your Blu-ray Disc.

NOTE Notice the Format pop-up menu in Figure 6.34? Encore allows its users to export not only SD- and BD-formatted DVDs, but also an Adobe Flash version of the project. This is very cool for those looking to create interactive CDs and non-disc based interactive video.

8. Choose the Blu-ray format option and the Blu-ray Disc output option, and then click Build. If you have problems, first try creating a Blu-ray Image, storing that to your hard drive, and then using it as your source for the next attempted burn. If you can create the image but can't successfully record it to Blu-ray Disc, try a third-party recording program, or try copying the image to a different computer and recording to disc there.

CONCLUSION

As mentioned at the beginning of the chapter, video on physical media may be the most traditional form of video we discuss in this book. It's exciting that the HD format war is coming to a close because now the tools and workflows needed to create those projects will filter into the hands of non-studio content creators.

But then again, you may very well not care about DVD and Blu-ray distribution, and you wouldn't be alone. Many people are skipping the traditional route altogether and going straight to the Internet with their content. Compared to DVD encoding, creating and encoding video for the Web is the wild west—nearly anything is possible. While that may seem liberating, it actually makes optimizing the video more difficult because you have almost too many options. The next chapter will explore the ins and outs of Web-based video and offer some suggestions for improving the content you publish there.

Interview with a Compressionist

Name: Ben Waggoner

Location: Portland, OR

Title/role: Principal Video Strategist, Silverlight

Company: Microsoft

URL: *http://on10.net/blogs/benwagg/Default.aspx*

How did you get involved in video compression?

I was oddly obsessed with compression for many years before it occurred
to me to make a profession of it. I was taking a 3D animation class at
UMass Amherst in the fall of 1989. This was back in the days of 1.4 MB
floppies, and we needed to figure out a way to move our renders from
machine to machine. I slacked off on the 3D part of the class and spent a
huge amount of time playing around with Macromind Director Accelerator
and using its Run Length Encoding (RLE) compression mode to make our
composites smaller.

At the start of my aspiring screenwriter years (1993), I was collaborating on the requisite post-college H. P. Lovecraft–inspired low-budget miniseries and wrote an unbelievably turgid scene hinging on the compression ratio of Apple Compact Video (later renamed Cinepak).

With some college friends, I started up a postproduction company in 1994 targeting the independent video producers. It was a Radius VideoVision system running on the first-gen PowerMacs, and it wasn't capable of keeping sync for more than two to three minutes. We scrambled desperately to find a market where we could use that boat anchor and avoid defaulting on the loans from our grandparents. One day, someone called us up and asked if we could do CD-ROM video. Turns out the clips were only about five minutes, and 15 fps 320 by 240 was a lot more forgiving of sync problems! The rest is history.

What was your biggest project?

The big projects I've worked on have mainly been around industrial-scale encoding. In terms of number of clips, the biggest was probably the Getty Images stock library. In terms of capacity and budget, probably the Iam.com workflow, which was capable of ingesting 5,000 photos, 20 hours of video, and 50 hours of audio each day, back in 2000. The company vanished in the dot-com meltdown before it got really stress tested. But it probably remains one of the most expensive compression installations ever, with a budget of more than $1 million, including more than a dozen of the hardware-accelerated Media Cleaner Power Suite systems.

What was your favorite project?

My first really big consulting project was for LEGO, developing the workflow for the Mindstorms launch CD-ROM. They flew me out to Denmark for a week and put me up in the Hotel Legoland (rather cold in February)! It was a nice, juicy project that was well funded, with high-quality source available, and a team motivated to make the stuff look great. This was in 1998, so our codec technology was primitive; we needed to make a cross-platform title and had over 20 minutes of cut scenes and several hours of instructional videos to fit on a single CD-ROM.

We used QuickTime for the playback API and to get 640x480, which meant Cinepak was the only codec with enough performance for playback on the computers of the day. We encoded everything in both the "original flavor" Cinepak and the beta of "Cinepak Pro" and picked whichever looked best. For the instructional video, we built a custom DeBabelizer workflow driven by AppleScript that would take the animations of the assembly video and convert them to a custom 16-bit RGB palette and then export it to the Apple Graphics codec (about two times as efficient as Animation). We had to use a keyframe every four frames in order to preserve full-speed forward/ backward playback. It took several days to tweak everything until we got a perfect, flattened 16-bit palette without dithering for optimal compression.

The runner-up would be building the Silverlight demo kit for NAB 2007. I had compelling content in uncompressed HD source, support from the codec team to help tune the settings, and for once enough time to really tweak the clips to perfection. The final deliverable was more than 200 clips, all among the finest work I'd ever done and demonstrating what VC-1 was really capable of.

What's your format of choice?

Windows Media, of course. One thing I've noticed is that as codecs get better, the real thing that matters for a format is the systems layer—how the format handles stuff like scalability, metadata, and DRM.

Windows Media 9 Series really introduced the first complete, end-to-end format to address all the important scenarios for a digital media format. It defined a base level of interoperability that we've been able to extend with improved, backward-compatible video and audio codecs, and it added new players such as Silverlight, Flip4Mac, and others.

I'm often asked about H.264 versus WMV, which is really the wrong question. H.264 versus VC-1 is an ongoing conversation. Overall, I'd say the best H.264 implementations are slightly more efficient at low bit rates, but VC-1 is able to transparently encode film content at lower bit rates due to the less-aggressive loop filter and more variable block sizes. And when both are encoded at maximum compression efficiency, H.264 takes about two times the MIPS per pixel to play back. But really, the differences between different H.264 and VC-1 implementations are bigger than the differences between the codecs themselves.

Going forward, I think the bigger differences are going to be a higher level yet, really focusing on how interactivity can be deployed well across a broad range of playback environments, which is where stuff like Silverlight comes in. While Silverlight isn't a media format itself, similar technologies are going to be where the next-generation innovation in media formats comes about.

What does your encoding hardware look like?

Since I travel a lot, I wind up doing a disturbing amount of my encoding on my Toshiba Qosmio G35 laptop. It's a Core 2 Duo with dual hard drives and a 1920 by 1200 display, so it's quite a bit more capable than my best workstation of a couple of years ago. Not so great for battery life on the airplane, though. I've been yelled at by airport security more than once for having too many electronics in my bag between the Toshiba, a PowerBook for Silverlight demos, and a couple of external HD drives.

What's your encoding software of choice?

I long for the days of Media Cleaner Pro 3.1, when it was really the only tool you needed to use. The good news is that I spend a lot of time working with the compression tool vendors helping them improve their implementations, particularly around WMV and VC-1, so the stuff that annoys me tends to get fixed over time.

Today, the products I use the most are Rhozet Carbon Coder (best batch encoder, with good preprocessing) and Inlet Fathom (first offline tool supporting the VC-1 Encoder SDK, with nice segment reencoding facilities). I also recommend Sorenson Squeeze (easiest-to-learn encoder) and Episode (best Mac encoder) a lot. The new Expression Encoder version 2, which is about to enter beta as I write this, is also shaping up to be an extremely nice product for encoding for Silverlight delivery.

Outside of compression itself, I use AVISynth, VirtualDub, and After Effects for preprocessing and controlling source decode.

What role does compression play in your work?

Pretty much everything I do is about compression, although I can't say that I spend that much of my average day doing compression per se anymore.

And the compression I do is much more often about defining a workflow than actually delivering the final goods. I've got a number of projects right now for internal customers like Xbox Live Marketplace, Zune, Soapbox, etc., helping them refine their encoding workflows, and I do that for a wide variety of partner companies publishing in Windows Media for Silverlight. So, I might spend a couple of days iterating on a few hard clips to figure out the optimal settings and workflow and then get them set up to apply the same encoding in high volumes. A lot of that winds up turning into postproduction consulting, since the ingest workflow is often where quality problems start.

I'm involved with the beta versions of various compression tools, helping vendors make presets for our formats and I hope offering other useful suggestions for refinement.

I also spend a lot of time working on long-term strategy around digital media—how we support partners in making it, how we support it better in our own products and platforms—so we make sure that Silverlight and Windows are able to do the right things involving media in the appropriate business contexts.

What surprises you most about video compression today?

How good the results are is huge. A decade ago, we were doing streaming targeting 28 Kbps modems with H.263-derived codecs, and much of anything beyond a talking head and voice content was essentially incomprehensible. Today, we can do 700 Kbps using modern codecs to most consumers, and the experience is a lot better than VHS. And for downloads, we're delivering 720p today with 1080p coming soon. And playback off optical discs, which was the core of my business the first five years, has become almost boringly easy—it's been a long time since there was an excuse for an artifact to appear.

It's also amazing how much compression has become something people actually do and talk about—tons of consumers are compressing their own video and particularly audio today and getting pretty good results.

It's also fast and easy compared to what it was. My first big encoding workstation was an 80 MHz PowerMac 8100/80, with 4 GB of RAID that cost $6,000. We budgeted 80 minutes to encode each minute of video, at only

320 by 240 15 fps Cinepak. I can do HD with the much more high-quality VC-1 codec today many times faster than that, on cheaper hardware.

It's also amazing what hasn't changed. Preprocessing remains the hard part, and I'm *still* waiting to get high-quality scaling and reliable inverse telecine in all products. I never would have guessed a decade ago I'd still be spending as much time in After Effects as I do.

CHAPTER SEVEN

Compressing for the Web

Let me just get it out of the way—I heart the Web. There, I said it. My wife is continually fascinated by my ability to surf an unending string of obscurely connected topics for hours (and I can do it too, believe me). So, a love of video on the Web for me is almost a no-brainer. I love the idea that video has started to become an integrated part of the user experience. And the era of video on the Web really has just started—we're at the beginning of a great deal of technology potential when it comes to Web video.

But forget the future of Web video for the moment—that's practically a book itself. Instead, let's begin with a quick review of the history of Web video, including where its roots are and what has made it popular, and then move on to the tools modern Web video producers are using. After that, I'll present you with some Web-specific recipes to help you get your content online.

The Early Days of Web Video

The early days of Web video were dominated by the question of streaming video versus progressive download (refer to Chapter 2, "The Language of Compression," for more information about the differences). In many ways, today's mobile Web video is what streaming video was like on the Web a decade ago: small-resolution, low-data-rate, low-frame-per-second video that was closer to a blurry animated GIF than a watchable video "experience." The World Wide Web, when it was introduced, was a graphical interface for the Internet that made pictures and text pretty, but video wasn't really part of the equation. In fact, consumer PCs and Macs were just getting powerful enough to play video locally, and the idea of connecting to remote content and "streaming" it seemed a long ways away.

Why Web Video Didn't Grow Faster

There are several reasons for Web video's stunted growth in the '90s. Here are the most significant:

- **Lack of broadband:** Broadband Internet was in its infancy, and most users were on varying speeds of dial-up connections. Some companies and techies had expensive ISDN or DSL modems, but modems were not yet a commonplace home appliance.

- **The multimedia unfriendliness of PCs:** These were the days of Mac OS 8 and Windows 98, and earlier. Though both would play video, it wasn't a core service either performed very well. Video was still the province of the television, the VCR, and the DVD player.

- **The dot-com crash:** The bubble popped, and when it did, online video stalled. The wild amounts of money being thrown at half-baked ideas slowed down. It wasn't until end users and venture capitalists alike regained confidence in the Internet technology sector that we once again saw real development in this space.

- **No clear player choice:** There were three players back then: QuickTime, Real, and Windows Media Player. Each was fairly proprietary in terms of what it played.

- **Small audience:** For all the other reasons I've cited, the number of people trying to regularly consume video online in the '90s was just very small, period. Video on the Web then was seen as a very small slice of the experience—maybe a demo reel here and there or some news-related or training content, but that was all.

When video did come to the Web, it was more or less just animating the pictures on the page. A user had to perform several steps to make it work. You needed the right player/plug-in installed; in fact, you often had to select the right player and resolution after selecting a video—not a great user experience. But user experience wasn't the only reason Web video wasn't a bigger deal in the '90s. See the sidebar "Why Web Video Didn't Grow Faster" for a laundry list of obstacles Web video faced in the '90s that kept its growth far short of initial expectations.

The dearth of decent-quality content was the final major problem plaguing online video in the '90s. The toolsets a content producer needed to master just to post content were quite intimidating. Not only did you need to be a good filmmaker, but you also needed to know compression, understand Web design, be capable at coding, arrange hosting, and so on. It was a real commitment to attempt to post content, and given the relatively low penetration of video-capable broadband at the time, you were doing all that for a fairly small audience.

Modern Web Video

Online video technology has come a long way from the early days. The slow growth and market stagnation caused by the dot-com crash had been resolved by early 2003, and Web-based video was once again being talked about seriously. What suddenly revived Web-based video? It's not just one thing that led to an increase in online video consumption—as with all things, it was a growing groundswell of interlocking reasons.

The Rise of Short-Form Video

Short-form content and segments of longer shows and movies became the most popular sharable content. Short-form content naturally lends itself to viewing on the Internet, because viewers are typically viewing as part of other ongoing activities (versus watching TV on your couch). These clips are typically shorter than 10 minutes (with many shorter than a minute) and are designed to be sharable; and if popular enough, they become viral video success stories. The phenomenon of video clips started as soon as broadband networks developed popularity, but it became very mainstream starting in 2005 with the emergence of Web sites for uploading clips, including

YouTube, Google Video, Yahoo! Video, and other smaller sites such as collegehumor.com and ebaumsworld.com. These videos often show moments of significance, humor, or oddity. Sources for video clips include news, movies, music video, and amateur video. In addition to the clips coming from high-quality broadcast sources ("mainstream video"), these sites showcase clips from DV cameras, Webcams, and mobile phones to be uploaded and shared.

By mid-2006, tens of millions of video clips were available online, with new Web sites springing up that focused entirely on offering free video clips to users. Meanwhile, many established and corporate sites had begun adding video clip content to their Web sites as well.

More Broadband Penetration

The speeds of home broadband connections increased and prices dropped, so consumers began switching from their slower dial-up connections to faster, always-on DSL and cable modems. A 2006 Pew Internet & American Life Project report (**Figure 7.1**) stated that 42 percent of all Americans had broadband at home. That figure represented a 40 percent increase from the previous year, and many of those people were first-time home Internet users who had skipped dial-up altogether and chosen broadband.

Figure 7.1 A Pew report on broadband shows a steady growth of broadband penetration for the first half of this decade. The numbers on the left represent the percentage of adult Americans with high-speed broadband.

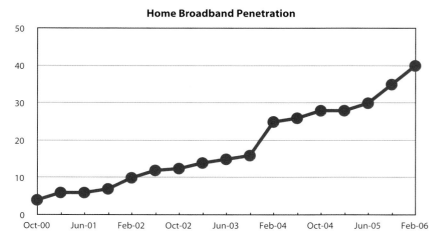

Better Tools

The tools content creators were using just plain got better. Posting video to the Web in the late '90s meant knowing a lot about HTML embedding, plug-ins, FTPing, and other non-video-related tasks. These extra steps have gone away in the past several years. Posting video has become as easy as filling out a form on a Web page. Sites emerged such as YouTube where users could post video for viewing, and these types of sites also created tools that allowed the content creator (or anyone) to cut and paste a piece of code that would embed the video in any Web page or blog of their choice. Suddenly it was much easier to post and share videos, thanks to YouTube and a range of other sites dedicated to video sharing and user-generated content such as those listed in **Table 7.1**.

Table 7.1 Eight of the Most Common Video Upload Sites

Service	Creator	Launched	Ads	Max Video Size (MB)	Max Video Length (min)	Video Codec
blip.tv	blip.tv	May 2005	Opt-in	1,024	No limit	Flash (On2 VP6)
Break.com	Break.com	1998	Yes	60	n/a	Flash (On2 VP6)
Dailymotion	Dailymotion	March 2005	No	150	20	Flash (Sorenson)
imeem	Imeem	October 2004	Yes	No limit	n/a	Flash (Sorenson)
Metacafe	Metacafe	July 2003	Yes	100	n/a	Flash (On2 VP6)
Veoh	Veoh Networks	September 2006	Yes	No limit	n/a	Flash (On2 VP6)
Vimeo	Connected Ventures	November 2004	Text	500	n/a	Flash (On2 VP6)
YouTube	Three ex-PayPal employees; acquired by Google	February 2005	Yes	1,024	10	Flash (Sorenson)

And it's not just the video-sharing tools that got easier and better. It became much easier for nontechnical, non-Web-savvy users to publish and manage their own Web sites. Often these sites take the form of a Weblog, or *blog*, or a simple online journal. Such tools suddenly meant that viewers were also publishers.

What Did YouTube Mean to Online Video?

One of the surprising benefits of the rising popularity of online video was YouTube. YouTube was founded by Chad Hurley, Steve Chen, and Jawed Karim, who were all early employees of PayPal. Prior to PayPal, Hurley studied design at Indiana University of Pennsylvania. Chen and Karim studied computer science together at the University of Illinois at Urbana-Champaign. The domain name YouTube.com was activated on February 15, 2005, and the Web site made its public preview in May 2005, six months before its official debut.

During the summer of 2006, YouTube was one of the fastest-growing Web sites on the Web and was ranked the fifth most popular Web site on Alexa, far outpacing even MySpace's rate-of-growth. According to a July 16, 2006, survey, 100 million video clips are viewed daily on YouTube, with an additional 65,000 new videos uploaded every 24 hours. The Web site averages nearly 20 million visitors per month, according to Nielsen/NetRatings. On October 9, 2006, it was announced that the company would be purchased by Google for $1.65 billion (U.S.) in stock.

Nobody goes to YouTube for the quality of the video. Instead, it was the ease of use with which someone could first publish and then share their video. YouTube continues to be one of the most dominant names in online video today.

Audience and Creator Are the Same Thing

Tools for creating and distributing online video isn't the only thing that got better—content creators and viewers alike became more accustomed to online video and willing to create and consume it. Demand for online video was going up, and as it did, the source of the new content wasn't traditional movie studios or production companies; instead, it was the users themselves. A 2007 Advertising.com survey of trends (**Figure 7.2**) estimated that 20 percent of all content viewed online is user-generated. Additionally, viewing content online isn't a passive event. Users are both contributing and forwarding content to others.

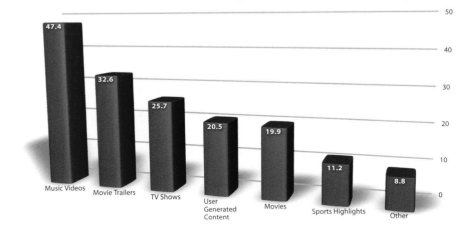

Figure 7.2 Types of online content users are likely to consume, by percentage of survey respondents (data from Advertising.com).

Everybody Is a Star

In 2005, two Chinese students, Huang Yixin and Wei Wei, now known as the "Back Dorm Boys," showcased their lip-syncing talent in a home-produced video of a Backstreet Boys song that was uploaded to a few Web sites and became one of the first viral online videos (http://www.youtube.com/watch?v=YBlCtqsat-w). Not only did they appear on television shows and perform "concerts," but they were also given a contract by a media company in Beijing for lip-syncing for cash.

Humans weren't the only ones cashing in on the craze either; videos of animals doing funny things always seem to please us. Tyson the skateboarding dog was already popular before YouTube but became even bigger there and now even has his own Web site at www.skateboardingbulldog.com.

Citizen Journalism

Posting video to the Web doesn't have to mean being funny or famous, though. Online video has allowed an increase of citizen journalism, the act of the public reporting the news. Citizen video reporting dates back as early as the development of camcorders, but all videos were still screened and published by the local media outlets of the time. (Remember news clips of "amateur" video? The 1990 clip of Rodney King being beaten by L.A. police officers was probably the most famous, or infamous, example.)

In the age of online video, everything from elections to natural and human-made disasters find their way onto the Web in the form of amateur journalism. In December 2004, the images the world saw of the earthquake and tsunami that damaged many countries on the Indian Ocean were shot by tourists on vacation. In the United States, students on the Virginia Tech campus used their cell phones to capture footage as a disturbed student went on a killing rampage. Broadcasters such as CNN now regularly incorporate user-contributed video in their ongoing coverage of major events.

Traditional Media Catches On

Traditional media entities, such as the major broadcast networks, have struggled with the best way to leverage the popularity of online video. Many were plain afraid of how the business model would change. Initially, clips of shows were used as marketing, trying to drive viewers back to the television, a domain the media entities were much more comfortable with.

By spring 2006, however, the major networks were beginning to experiment in earnest with online video, making many of their primetime shows available online immediately after airing (usually with some sort of advertising associated with them). Web sites such as Hulu (www.hulu.com), which represent collaborations between large media companies, are also emerging. Hulu is a mix of Fox News Corporation and NBC/Universal content, available both as full-length episodes and as short clips.

Online content isn't just being given away, however. Distributors are also partnering with the likes of Apple and Amazon to make TV shows and movies available for purchase and rental. It's unclear right now whether online video purchases have cut into the DVD market, but it's obvious that at least some of the public is willing to buy and download their content (and, in fact, some prefer it).

Though it's heartening to see traditional media companies offer their content online, they are still ultimately just packaging and offering familiar product in a new form. Some production companies have taken a step further and used the new medium as a way to offer viewers unique content designed specifically for the Web that ties directly to the shows. *Battlestar Galactica* is a perfect example of using original online content effectively. In addition to having a wildly popular weekly podcast by the show's creator and executive producer Ronald D. Moore, offering commentary on each week's show (similar to a director's commentary track on a DVD), the show created a special, Web-only series known as *Battlestar Galactica: The Resistance*. The series is the collective title of 10 two-to-ten-minute "Webisodes" released exclusively through the Sci Fi Channel's Web site. The storyline follows events that occurred between the close of season 2 and the beginning of season 3 of the TV series. The Webisodes were released weekly in the lead-up to the third season and were an effective way to both market the show and fill in storylines.

Modern Web Tools and Formats

As I alluded to earlier in the chapter, the tools we now use to publish video for the Web have also contributed greatly to the rise in popularity of online video. Simply making video easier to publish on the Web was immensely useful in driving adoption. Additionally, the viral tools these sites make available, such as embedding tags and scripts for e-mailing videos to friends, give video additional features that consumers have come to expect and rely on as they share this content and increase its distribution to potentially exponential levels.

The compression tools we use continue to evolve to feed the Web video phenomenon as well. Compressing video is often only one of their features. Many have built-in capabilities such as FTP to allow you to quickly and easily publish your content in addition to encoding it. Apple's Compressor has becomes a podcaster's friend, allowing for the addition of chapters and other enhancements (see Chapter 8 for an explanation of how to make a chaptered video podcast using Compressor). It would be great to see software makers like Apple continue to incorporate interactive authoring and publishing capabilities in the compression tools we used today.

Even the codecs and formats we are using in our modern online video are smarter and better. Of course, the quality has improved over time, but the innovation hasn't stopped there. Adobe Flash and Microsoft Silverlight have both brought a new level of interactivity and enhanced user experience to online video. Video has moved from a postage stamp embedded on the page to an integral part of the page, incorporating interactive links and alpha channels to make it hard to tell where the video ends and the rest of the page begins.

Silverlight and Flash: The Blu-ray/HD DVD War of the Web (Except This One Isn't Over)

As mentioned in Chapter 6, the HD DVD and Blu-ray battle that officially ended just before this book went to press really proves that competition is a good thing and can drive innovation. Though Flash is the established plug-in of choice, Silverlight is a technology that can catch up and gain momentum. It has the backing of one very big, very will-driven company and the attractiveness of offering traditional IT environments features that Microsoft never had for its .NET sites in the past. Adobe, not one to stand down from the fight, has been very smart about extending support to H.264 video, a format of choice for content creators. We'll see both these companies work on the way their technologies function both in browsers and as stand-alone online experiences (also known as *rich Internet applications*). Though this innovation won't focus solely on video, video will no doubt continue to play a huge part in both their offerings. I, for one, hope both continue to challenge each other and provide their users with a wealth of interactive and online video innovations.

RECIPES FOR COMPRESSING VIDEO FOR THE WEB

Now that you've learned about some of the options for uploading video to the Internet and what the common supported video types are for delivery on the Web, let's look at some video compression recipes for specific applications.

Encoding for YouTube from Episode Pro

YouTube, although known for making it easy to both view and publish video, has never been known as a high-quality source of content. This is because all the video uploaded was transcoded by its system to Flash 7 Video (Sorenson Spark codec). YouTube went with Flash 7 instead of Flash 8 because it was both more ubiquitous and a faster transcode. It does, however, have a poorer resolution. So, lots of people want to know how to export video in such a way that it looks as good as it can on YouTube.

So, let's take a sample DV clip—this one happens to be one of the Zoom In Online documentaries (www.zoom-in.com). It's a 4:3 clip that is letter-boxed, so we'll need to crop it in addition to making the other changes.

1. Starting in Episode Pro, select the video in the Source Bookmarks pane of the Browser, and drag it to the Job Batch window.

2. In the Compression Settings pane, navigate to Templates > By Format > H264 > Download, and select H264_High Quality. Drag it onto the source clip in the Job Batch window (**Figure 7.3**).

NOTE What are we doing to the clip? We're using the preprocessing filters to oversaturate the video, as well as to tweak the black-and-white levels, the brightness, and the contrast.

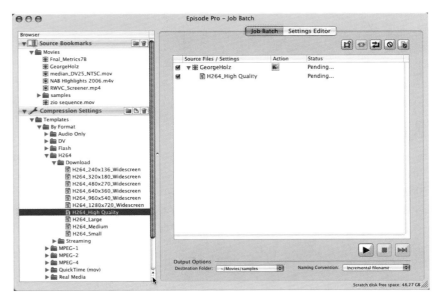

Figure 7.3 Episode's Browser and Job Batch window.

NOTE As YouTube moves away from Flash 7 Video toward H.264 as a delivery option, extra effort like this may be completely unnecessary.

3. In the Job Batch window, double-click the setting to edit it.

4. Under H264, change Bandwidth control to Peak Rate, change the Peak rate setting to 2400, and change Average rate to 2000 (**Figure 7.4**).

Figure 7.4 Choosing H264 bandwidth settings in Episode.

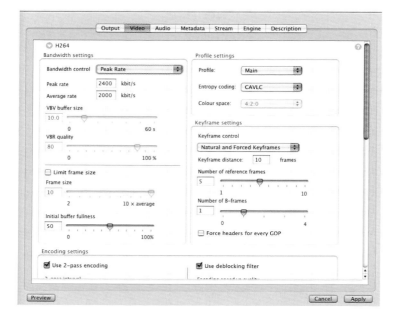

5. Under Frame Rate, change the rate to Fixed, 15 fps (**Figure 7.5**).

Figure 7.5 Selecting the frame rate settings.

6. The video is letterboxed and needs cropping, so under Resize, select Custom, and change Image Proportions to 16:9 (**Figure 7.6**). Now change Image Size to 320 by 180. Choose Cut from the Maintain proportion with pop-up menu. Use the Initial Crop area to remove the black bars (in this instance, it's 45 from the top and 40 from the bottom, but this can vary slightly from video to video). In Advanced options, choose Derive From Source from the Source display aspect ratio pop-up menu.

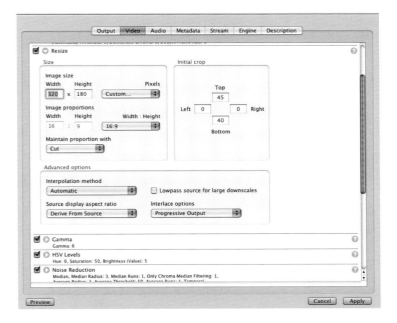

Figure 7.6 The Resize settings. This is where you adjust the letterboxing of the source video.

7. Under the Gamma options, adjust the setting to 6.

8. Under the HSV Levels options, change the Saturation setting to 50 and the Brightness setting to 5 (**Figure 7.7**).

Figure 7.7 The Gamma and HSV Levels settings.

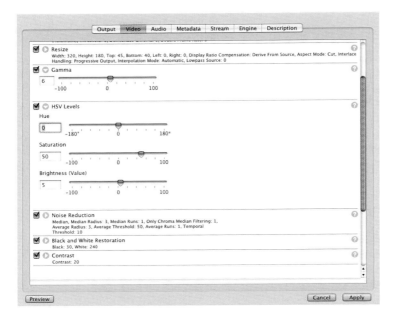

9. Under the Noise Reduction settings, set Median Radius to 3, and select the Only Filter Chroma check box (**Figure 7.8**).

> **NOTE** Remember earlier when I cautioned against going overboard on preprocessing? Well this is the one place where I break my own rules. We're stepping pretty heavy on the content in an effort to boost the quality. Do I think this is the best thing to do to the content? Nah, not really, but then many people do want a way to get a better looking YouTube clip, so it's worth exploring how to go about it.

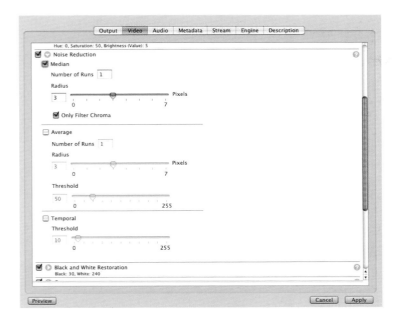

Figure 7.8 The Noise Reduction settings.

10. Under the Black and White Restoration settings, change the Black level to 30 and the White level to 240.

11. Change the contrast to 20 (**Figure 7.9**).

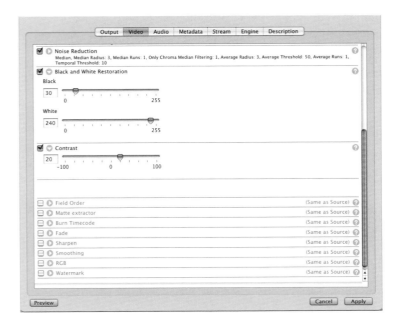

Figure 7.9 Adjusting Black and White Restoration and Contrast settings on the Video tab.

12. Click Preview to see whether the new image settings look correct (**Figure 7.10**). If you're satisfied with what you see, click Apply to save the settings changes and return to the Job Batch window.

Figure 7.10 In the Preview window, compare the videos before and after your settings changes.

13. Click the arrow at the bottom of the Job Batch window to encode the video. After the video finishes, check it in QuickTime to confirm that the results are correct. The file is ready to upload to YouTube.

14. If you're happy with the results and want to reuse this setting, click the Save icon in the Job Batch window next to the setting. Give it a unique name in the dialog that appears (**Figure 7.11**). It will now be saved in your Settings folder for future use.

Figure 7.11 If you like your settings enough to save them, be sure to give them a name you'll remember when the time comes to reuse them.

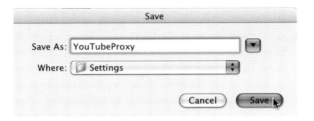

This process isn't a cure-all for all the shortcomings of YouTube video, but it will improve your video quality some when uploading to YouTube. Want proof? I encoded and uploaded samples of the same video via QuickTime Pro and Compressor. Although the results aren't earth-shatteringly brilliant, the video does look better (**Figure 7.12**). Notice that with QuickTime Pro, I didn't crop to correct the image aspect ratio, though I did in Compressor. Both are very light in comparison to the original. The Episode clip has fewer bits, meaning a smaller file size, yet is better-looking. That will allow you to have longer clips and still adhere to the 100 MB upload cap.

Compressor Test - ZIO

QuickTime Pro Test - ZIO

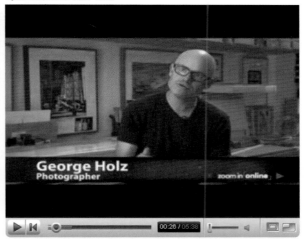

Visual Hub Test - ZIO

Episode Pro Test - ZIO

Figure 7.12 Comparisons of the same frame uploaded to YouTube. Only the Compressor and Episode clips have the pixel and image aspect ratio adjusted correctly, and only the Episode Pro clip has decent chroma and luma values. Which one would you want to watch online? You can see the difference for yourself at *http://youtube.com/profile_videos?user=andybeach*.

Streaming Windows Media from Compressor

Next, let's make Windows Media clips suitable for use with a streaming server. For this scenario, let's assume my video was edited on a Mac in Final Cut Pro. The source is 4:3 DV-NTSC, but the clip was letterboxed during the edit process. If there was cropping needed, you could just use the Flip-4Mac plug-in with QuickTime Pro to export, but since we want to perform some image adjustments, let's use the QuickTime component plug-in with Compressor to allow us to create a cropped 16:9 streaming WMV 9 file. We want as wide an audience as possible with our clip, so let's create both a high- and a low-resolution streaming file so users can pick. To perform this encode, you need Final Cut Pro Studio 2 and the Flip4Mac WMV Studio Pro or Studio Pro HD.

1. Starting in Final Cut Pro, make sure the sequence you want to export is selected, and choose File > Export > Using Compressor (**Figure 7.13**). Compressor automatically launches and adds your sequence.

Figure 7.13 Exporting using Compressor.

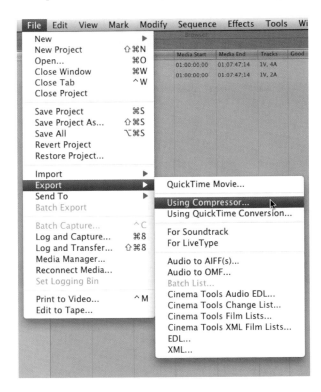

2. In the Settings window, click the + button, and choose QuickTime Export Components to create a new blank setting (**Figure 7.14**).

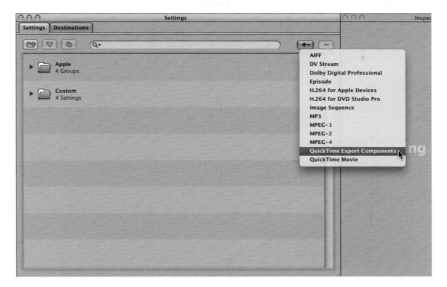

Figure 7.14 Creating a New QuickTime Export Components setting.

3. In the Encoder tab of the Inspector, name the setting WMV streaming – hi. In the Encoder Type pop-up menu, select Windows Media (**Figure 7.15**). The extension automatically updates to WMV.

Figure 7.15 Changing to Windows Media in the Inspector.

4. Select the Options tab. A separate window opens and presents the standard Flip4Mac interface (the same windows available via QuickTime Pro and other encoders). If you open the Profiles pop-up menu, you can see a wide variety of templates based on usage (**Figure 7.16**).

Figure 7.16 A wide array of template options from which to choose.

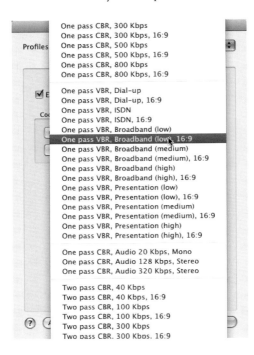

5. At the bottom of this list, select New Profile (**Figure 7.17**).

Figure 7.17 Scroll to the end of the profiles, and select New Profile.

6. In the dialog that appears, type a memorable name for the template. Mine is 16:9 2-pass CBR 800kbps (**Figure 7.18**). Click OK to save the name.

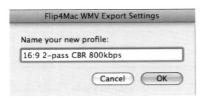

Figure 7.18 Giving the new profile a descriptive name.

7. On the Video tab of Flip4Mac, select the Export Using check box, and choose WMV 9 Standard in the menu options. Set the coding method to Two pass, constant bit rate (CBR). Set the Quality slider to 50 percent and the Bit rate to 736 kbps/second. Finally, set the size to 640x360 and the Frame Format to Current (**Figure 7.19**).

Figure 7.19 Choose your settings on the Video tab of the Flip4Mac's Export Settings dialog.

8. Click the Advanced button on the Video tab. In the dialog that appears, select the Main profile if it is not already selected. Change Input Type to Interlace – Upper Field First, and make sure Output Type is set to Progressive (**Figure 7.20**). Click OK.

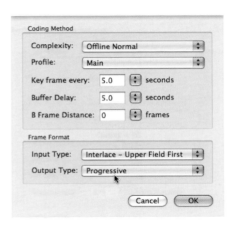

Figure 7.20 The Advanced area of the Video tab is where you tell Flip4Mac to deinterlace the video before outputting it.

9. In the Export Settings dialog, select the Audio tab (**Figure 7.21**). Select the Export using check box, and choose WMA 9 Standard in the pop-up menu. Under Coding Method, choose One pass, constant bit rate (CBR) and 64 kbps, 44.1 khz, Stereo. Click OK.

Figure 7.21 Choose audio compression settings on the Audio tab.

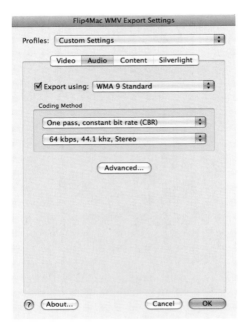

⊕ **TIP** Notice the Content and Silverlight tabs? Flip4Mac allows you to add metadata to the file from here, as well as select a template to create for the file in Silverlight, much the way Expression Encoder does.

10. In Compressor, select the Geometry tab in the Inspector pane. Change the crop to 16x9 1.78:1 (**Figure 7.22**).

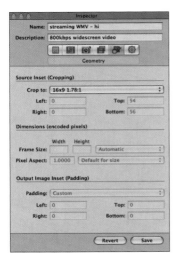

Figure 7.22 Set up your crop in the Geometry tab of the Inspector.

11. In the Preview monitor, use the pointer to drag the red line to the appropriate crop (**Figure 7.23**). Click Save in the Inspector.

Figure 7.23 Preview the crop in the Preview monitor.

12. Perform steps 2 and 3 again to create a new, blank setting. Name the new setting WMV streaming – low.

13. Click the Options button in the Inspector. Once again, create a new profile setting, and name it 16:9 2-pass CBR 200kbps.

14. Use the same settings as before, except change the data rate to 168 Kbps, the size to 320x180, and the Frame Rate to 15 frames/second (**Figure 7.24**).

Figure 7.24 The new profile setting for the second movie.

15. Click the Advanced button on the Video tab. In the dialog that appears, select the Main profile if it is not already selected. Change Input Type to Interlace – Upper Field First, and make sure Output type is set to Progressive. Click OK.

16. Select the Audio tab (**Figure 7.25**). Select the Export using check box, and choose WMA 9 Standard in the pop-up menu. Under Coding Method, choose One pass, constant bit rate (CBR) and 32 kbps, 44.1 khz, Mono. Click OK.

Figure 7.25 Back on the Audio tab.

17. Once again, in Compressor, select the Geometry tab in the Inspector. Change the crop to 16x9 1.78:1.

18. In the Preview monitor, use the pointer to drag the red line down to the appropriate crop. Click Save in the Inspector.

19. Now drag your two settings onto your sequence (**Figure 7.26**).

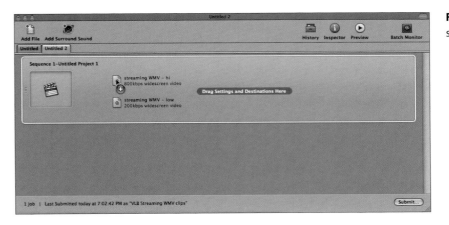

Figure 7.26 Drag the new settings onto the source.

20. Choose User Movie Folder for the destination. Change each name to something descriptive. Here I've chosen VLF_hi.wmv and VLB_low.wmv (**Figure 7.27**).

Figure 7.27 Assigning destination and names for the files.

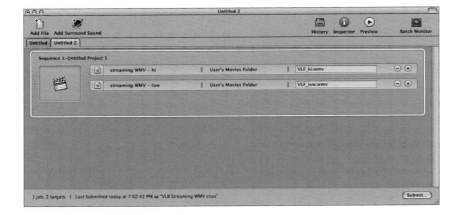

21. Click Submit. Assign a unique name to the batch as it is submitted, and click OK. The files will begin encoding, and you can track the progress in the Batch Monitor or the History window (**Figure 7.28**).

Figure 7.28 The progress bar in the History window.

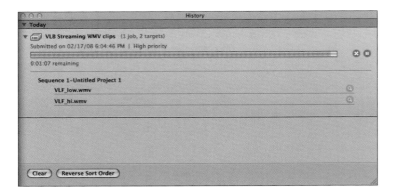

22. When the output files are completed, locate the files, and play them in QuickTime to confirm they're correct (**Figure 7.29**). Assuming all is well, they are ready to be uploaded to your streaming server.

Figure 7.29 Previewing the finished results in QuickTime.

Progressive Download Flash Video

Rather than focusing on a step-by-step recipe for a progressively downloaded Flash Video file, I'll list a variety of settings that may be applicable to the various scenarios you may face with Flash Video encoding. Given the popularity of Flash, you will no doubt be encoding video to it at some point and may not be happy with the results unless you stick to these tips.

Remember that unless you specifically have a Flash streaming server, then you should be using VBR encoding to get the best quality possible for your progressive download video files. Unless you specifically need to support users of older Flash versions, you should also be using the VP6 codec.

By now I think you've gotten the idea that the data rate and frame size will certainly impact the quality and file size of your output (if you haven't, please reread Chapter 2). Since everyone's content varies, you'll need to tweak the settings to best fit your content, but **Table 7.2** is a good starting guideline for Flash Video. I've included both full-screen and wide-screen aspect ratios so you can choose the appropriate type for your content.

TIP Unless you absolutely must, I do not suggest trying to serve 16:9 content to dial-up users. As you can see, the resolution is so small that is not a very good viewing experience. Instead, crop the video on the left and right, and change the aspect ratio to the 4:3 standard. The image is still small, but not quite as small as it was before.

Table 7.2 Flash VBR Settings for Various Target Connection Speeds

Target Connection Speed	Video Bit Rate	Peak Rate	Audio Bit Rate	4:3 Video	16:9 Video	FPS	Keyframe Interval
High motion (lots of zooms, fades, and/or camera motion)							
1.5 Mbps	1.2 Mbps	2 Mbps	128 Kbps	480x360	480x272	30	60
800 Kbps	675 Kbps	1 Mbps	96 Kbps	400x300	224	30	60
400 Kbps	329 Kbps	700 Kbps	64 Kbps	320x240	320x180	15	30
56k Dial Up	60 Kbps	120 Kbps	16 Kbps	192x144	192x108	10	20
Low motion (static shots, talking heads)							
1.5 Mbps	950 Kbps	1.2 Mbps	128 Kbps	480x360	480x272	30	60
800 Kbps	500 Kbps	1 Mbps	96 Kbps	400x300	224	15	30
400 Kbps	178 Kbps	550 Kbps	64 Kbps	320x240	320x180	10	30
56k Dial Up	50 Kbps	100 Kbps	16 Kbps	192x144	192x108	10	40

If you still aren't sure what to do, Adobe has a handy tool in its Developer Center (*www.adobe.com/devnet/flash/apps/flv_bitrate_calculator/index.html*). Created by Rob Reinhardt, the FLV bit rate calculator (**Figure 7.30**) allows you to punch in a variety of parameters about your video (including the motion type, aspect ratio, and quality of audio) and identify the suggested encoding method and video and audio data rates to use for good results. The only downside to the calculator is it doesn't suggest a peak data rate if you are doing two-pass VBR encoding, but it is a valuable tool regardless.

Figure 7.30 Not sure what settings to use? Try Robert Reinhardt's bit rate calculator in Adobe's Developer Center.

Embedding Flash Video

Also remember that if you are working with Flash and creating FLV files, you will typically not be posting these files directly for your viewers to consume. Although it's true the Adobe Media Player can directly play FLV files, Web browsers do not. If you're planning to embed your Flash FLV video in a Web browser for your viewers, you will need to create a SWF player in Flash CS3. For more information on creating SWF players for your video and to learn more about Flash video in general, check out Robert Reinhardt's book, *Adobe Flash CS3 Professional Video Studio Techniques* (Adobe Press, 2007).

CONCLUSION

As much as I enjoy finding new ways to use video online, it's far from the final frontier of video distribution these days. Although video has only recently gained popularity with the masses online, it has already leap-frogged into other delivery platforms.

Mobile is perhaps one of the most popular new areas for video distribution and consumption and while it may seem like the iPod and iPhone are the only forms of mobile video, that's far from the truth. A myriad of cell phones and other portable devices are letting us view video on the go; and of course, they each have their own special quirks. The next chapter will discuss the variety of mobile video options, the formats that are popular, and identify the devices you may be targeting.

Interview with a Compressionist

Name: Jim Rohner

Title/Role: Associate Producer/Editor

Company: Zoom In Online flagship of Magnet Media

URL: *www.zoom-in.com*

How did you get involved in video compression?

When I first started at Magnet Media as an intern two years ago, their primary focus was on video-based training. I often used uncompressed exports of screen-captured video out of Final Cut Pro to compress H.264 and Flash video for interactive DVD-ROMs and the Web. I have also worked on videos for Zoom In Online, Magnet's site dedicated to creative professionals.

What was your biggest project?

The biggest project in terms of time was probably video training I did on Premiere Pro CS3 to complement the book published by Peachpit Press. When it came to screen capturing, editing, exporting, and compressing, the ball was entirely in my court. I had to ensure that a proper codec was used for the screen capturing that would keep the file size low but the quality high and would be acceptable for editing in Final Cut Pro. Once the lessons were cut, I had to choose an export compression that would once again not sacrifice quality for file size (thank God for H.264!). From screen capture to edit to revisions to final delivery, the entire process was a shade under a month.

What was your favorite project?

One of my favorite projects was also, ironically, one of the most frustrating projects. A few months back, we produced video training for Apple Color as part of our Final Cut Studio 2 bundle. The screen captures were done at a few different sessions and then handed off to me for editing. Any previous training we captured in a 16:9 ratio was typically captured around 1360 by 768, but Color, with its wide-open layout, had to be captured on a Cinema Display monitor at a 16:10 aspect ratio of 1680 by 1050 using the TechSmith Ensharpen codec. The file sizes for the screen captures were understandably huge, and it wasn't until we developed a picture-in-picture feature for the massive training that we realized how processor-intensive two video tracks of uncompressed video were for my editing station. There was a lot of freezing, skipping, and curses thrown at the pinwheel during the editing process. But after throwing the uncompressed exports into Compressor and applying an H.264 compression on them, they were *much* more manageable and still looked terrific. I guess it doesn't seem like such a frustrating project should be my favorite, but lessons learned the hard way are some of the best lessons learned—I know I won't forget it!

What's your format of choice?

It should be no surprise that I say H.264, seeing as how that's the only compression I've mentioned so far. Truth be told, I'm far from an expert when it comes to compression, but so far a vast majority of what I've needed has been satisfied by the relatively low file size and high quality that H.264 provides.

What does your average workday look like?

When the focus is on video-based training, the tasks (after editing) often revolve around compressing the uncompressed Final Cut to FLV (Flash 8 Video) in order to plug into Magnet's DVD-ROM interface. Recently a few of us at Magnet Media attended the Sundance Film Festival, where our task was to record audio for a certain number of the panel discussions and turn them into enhanced podcasts suitable for viewing/listening on our Web site and through iTunes. I learned very quickly that exporting an hour-long panel discussion with images from Final Cut to an MPEG-4 and changing it to an M4V is far from optimal conditions when something has to be uploaded to three separate locations in a 24-hour time frame—the file size ended up being close to 200 MB. Through working in GarageBand and exporting as an M4A, the file sizes were often 10 percent of the M4V size.

What does your encoding hardware look like?

I typically work on a PowerPC G5 with 4 GB DDR SDRAM and dual 2.5 GHz processor. There is about 500 GB of internal storage for small projects, but we have a variety of FireWire RAIDs used for the big projects.

What's your encoding software of choice?

Oftentimes I'll encode video-based training directly out of Final Cut Pro using QuickTime conversion. In order to encode those exports to FLV format for DVD usage, I'll export out of Final Cut using Compressor and the Flip4Mac plug-in. We've recently expanded our outreach to include You-Tube, BlipTV, and iMeme, and for those compressions our saving grace is VisualHub, believe it or not.

What role does compression play in your work?

While I'm not expected to be a master of compression, I probably would be currently seeking other employment if I were completely clueless about it. Since big-name clients like Apple and Adobe support our video-based training, we're under pressure to nail our deadlines with a quality product. Using the wrong codec or compression scheme could easily slow down the process for days and delay the delivery to the client and to the customer who has paid for a quality product.

What surprises you most about video compression today?

Everything. It amazes me that I'm able to sit down with a friend who has an external hard drive connected to his Xbox 360 and watch HD-quality movies that are barely 2GB in size. On top of that, there's so many compressions for so many uses that just thinking about all the MOVs, VCDs, SWFs, and

DWIs (just kidding about that one) makes me really appreciate and respect those who know this stuff like the back of their hands. With new media on the rise and more content shifting to the Internet, the person who can master compression is on the frontline to cash in on the movement.

CHAPTER EIGHT

Compressing for Mobile

For some content creators, mobile video is an afterthought—just another way to repurpose their content. For others, it is a groundbreaking distribution platform that allows them to connect directly to their viewers more than was ever possible. More than any other delivery option discussed in this book, however, producing for mobile delivery means dealing with a morass of nuanced format-, network-, and device-specific quirks. It's easy to get confused or, worse, flat-out screw up something and cut off your audience from viewing your content.

So, in this chapter, you'll learn the basics of mobile video, including types of distribution, content models, and devices your viewers are likely to be using. Then you'll see some recipes that target some specific uses.

How Little Video Became Big

It seems just as everyone started clamoring for bigger, higher-resolution HD video that they also went in the opposite direction, looking for smaller mobile-friendly content. This is not really all that surprising when you consider that mobile devices have gotten more powerful and can now handle audio and video playback much better than they did before. Modern cell phones such as the HTC Kaiser (aka the AT&T Tilt or 8925) have more processing power, storage, and connectivity than my laptop did just a few years ago.

Also, our existing SD production techniques and workflows scale down to small screens better than trying to shift up to HD. Don't believe me? Go watch your DV-quality home movie on your video iPod and your 60-inch plasma TV, and tell me which looks better. Small screens will forgive quality issues that large ones make all too obvious.

Little Can Be Big, Too

Not all mobile video is substandard definition. Some podcast producers have been experimenting with 720p and 1080p content delivered as a video podcast. San Francisco–based media developers guild The Pixel Corps (www. pixelcorps.com) has done an amazing job of creating short-form HD content that users can subscribe to and consume through devices such as the Apple TV. In fact, podcasters like this were providing the first HD content you could really use with the Apple TV, because all the iTunes Music Store video was still SD when it launched.

I see this as a great advancement of distribution and hope more producers begin trying this method for reaching audiences.

Generally speaking, consumers are going to be viewing content on the go in one of two ways that should be pretty familiar by now: streaming and download. That's because mobile distribution is closely tied to the IP network it shares with the Internet. Most mobile delivery is either identical to or at least mirrors Internet options as well. Internet distribution often differs by the interactive functionality associated with the video player (such as the tools YouTube and others offer its viewers). For more about online delivery, see Chapter 7, "Compressing for the Web."

Live Streaming to Mobile Devices

By now you should be familiar with the basic tenets of streaming technology. When mobile video was first introduced, streaming was an obvious choice; the devices were fairly simple, with no large storage abilities and slow network connections. Streaming video often looked a little more like an animated postage stamp than a video "experience."

Wireless data networks have increased speed, albeit quite slowly, and the devices playing them have increased both in processing speed and in storage. Of course, the quality of the video has improved (and lest I forget, codecs have also gotten better). Data speed varies greatly among the technologies that are implemented, all the way from a very meager 10 Kbps up to a potential 2 Mbps.

These speeds are only what is theoretically possible, however—local conditions, deployment issues, and both transmission hardware and cellular handsets can all affect the actual connection speed, so if you are planning to deliver streaming video to mobile customers in a wide audience, choose your data rates wisely. Consumers can easily get confused by the marketing names applied to these technologies as well, so confirm the type of service offered by the mobile carrier that your target audience will use to receive your content (**Table 8.1**). Remember that mobile viewers streaming video may be paying per kilobyte they download, because unlimited plans aren't the norm yet in the United States (though the iPhone is changing this), so the quality and the content need to be engaging enough to get viewers to buy in (literally). Since the content is designed to be consumed immediately by end users on the go, the technology lends itself to multiple short clips instead of one longer clip.

Table 8.1 Theoretical Data Rates for Wireless Technologies

Technology	Speed
GSM mobile telephone service	9.6 to 14.4 Kbps
High-Speed Circuit-Switched Data (HSCSD) service	Up to 56 Kbps
General Packet Radio System (GPRS, aka 2G)	56 to 114 Kbps
Enhanced Data GSM Environment (EDGE, aka 2.5G)	384 Kbps
Universal Mobile Telecommunications Service (UMTS, aka 3G)	Up to 2 Mbps

Most experiments in this area have involved individual broadcasters or other content distributors streaming live encodes of their content. But some companies have popped up that bundle groups of channels in a model similar to cable TV. MobiTV (www.mobitv.com) has been fairly successful in this space. The company says it has more than 3 million subscribers (adding 1 million alone in about 6 months in 2007), and it offers many popular TV channels from content providers such as MSNBC, ABC News Now, CNN, Fox News, Fox Sports, ESPN 3GTV, NBC Mobile, CNBC, CSPAN, The Discovery Channel, TLC, The Weather Channel, and others that deliver cartoons, music videos, and comedy. MobiTV is available through AT&T, Sprint, Alltel, and several smaller U.S. carriers.

Download and (Maybe) Sync

The other method for viewing mobile content is downloading. Although many sites can also make video available in a similar manner as streaming—as a file connected to on the go for immediate consumption—there is another way that downloaded files get used in the mobile realm. Perhaps unique to mobile devices is the idea that you can download the content at home from your broadband connection and then move or synchronize it to a mobile device for entertainment on the go. By no means the first device to do this, the iPod was nonetheless the first to make the process consumer-friendly to engender mass consumption. Thanks to the iPod, it was suddenly no big deal to carry your entire music library with you because it would sync to your portable device.

Since video files are so much larger than audio files, it simply makes sense to download a high-quality movie on the faster home connection and then move it to your portable storage device for viewing on the go. You lose the immediacy and timeliness of streaming and progressive downloading, but you gain several things. The quality is better, and since the entire file is already cached locally, there is no need to worry that your end user will catch up to the downloaded section before completing the viewing. This also makes it practical to consume long-form content, such as TV shows and even movies. Instead of packing a paperback for the flight, it's easy to drop a couple of movies on your portable player.

Business models are popping up all over the place to provide users with digital copies of movies and TV shows for their computers and (almost always) their portable devices. Because this download-and-sync process is still so new, it's rare to see either a perfect or all-encompassing model, although buying and watching videos from the iTunes Music Store is pretty close. Instead, an individual site will most likely cater to one device (or device family) and offer catalog and new content from a few studios. These download services also include digital rights management (DRM) to protect the content distributors from having their buyers share content with others easily. The two that are garnering the most attention for their use of DRM are iTunes Music Store (ITMS) and Amazon Unbox.

iTunes Music Store

iTunes Music Store (ITMS) is built right into the iTunes interface and does not require a Web browser for transactions (though you do, of course, need to be connected to the Internet). Users can browse an electronic catalog of current and back titles. In ITMS, all TV shows are $1.99 and can be purchased separately or bundled into seasons (called a *season pass*), though there is no price incentive to buy a whole season because it still costs $1.99 per episode. Movies range in price, with new releases costing $14.99 and back catalog items ranging from $4.99 to $9.99. Once a show is downloaded, the user owns the right to view it indefinitely.

In January 2008, Apple also added movie rentals as a feature to the ITMS (**Figure 8.1**). Users can now rent a movie for up to 30 days or 24 hours from the first time they begin watching. Prices are split between SD and HD content and range from $2.99 to $4.99, depending on resolution and newness. Content available in the ITMS includes proprietary DRM technology called FairPlay. FairPlay allows users to watch a movie on authorized

Figure 8.1 The iTunes Music Store's Movies home page.

Macs and PCs (validated by logging into iTunes on that machine), but limits it to a total number of five machines at any one time. Files can be moved to other devices and burned to disc as data for storage, but they cannot be re-encoded or burned to DVD for playback in a standard DVD player.

ITMS content is H.264 video and AAC audio (AC-3 for AppleTV 2.0, 5.1). It can be played in iTunes, on Apple TV, and on iPods that support video playback (more or less 5G iPods and later, though 5G iPods can play only download-to-own purchases, not rentals). Since Apple makes deals only with studios and other similar distributors, average users won't be upload-ing their content for sale in this venue (users can sell iPod-compatible video outside the ITMS, but without DRM limitations). See the sidebar "Apple Video Settings" later in this chapter for details on the iPod and iPhone-supported formats and rates.

Amazon Unbox

Amazon Unbox (**Figure 8.2**), which launched in September 2006, is part of the greater Amazon Web site, not a self-contained application. It sells a vari-ety of movies and TV shows from a variety of studios. TV shows are $1.99, though there is a discount for purchasing an entire season. Movies range from $3.99 for rentals (and there are always specials for less) and $14.99 or $9.99 for owning. A nice feature not available in ITMS is that the media you purchase is stored in an online electronic library that allows you to redown-load things you have purchased but perhaps deleted. (In ITMS, on the other hand, if you delete it without backing it up, it's gone forever.) Unbox content

Figure 8.2 Download selected Amazon Unbox videos directly to your TiVo Now Playing List.

can be viewed on your PC (though not your Mac), on a Tivo connected to your TV, or on approved portable devices. The devices must support a special Windows Media DRM called Play for Sure. Confusingly, not all devices that play Windows Media support Play for Sure (including, ironically, the Zune), so users need to verify that their device is supported before purchasing content. Supported devices include the Archos and Creative Zen series of products.

Cruxy

Sadly, neither of these options leaves a way for nonstudio types to sell content to consumers. Fortunately, the Internet, being the Wild West that it is, allows anyone who wants to create a new business model to launch a site and try. Cruxy (*www.cruxy.com*) is one such site. It launched in late 2006 as a way for individuals to create digital stores on the Web to sell audio and video. Formats are at the discretion of the creator—a quick look at the site shows content in everything from iPod-friendly MPEG-4 to Windows Media to DiVX video formats. In return for creating a virtual stall on the Web for artists, Cruxy takes a small percentage of each sale. It's free to start an account, so any content owners looking to start their own download store should consider Cruxy.

MOBILE DEVICES AND THEIR FORMATS OF CHOICE

All this little content sounds great, doesn't it? But how is Joe Mobile consuming it on the move? I've already alluded to several players throughout this chapter and at other points in the book, but when I refer to mobile devices for media playback, what am I really talking about?

Cell Phones

According to the CTIA wireless association, there are 250 million U.S. cell phone subscribers as of November 2007. That's just more than 80 percent of U.S. residents using cell phones. Most phones made within the past four years have at least some limited video playback capabilities. Most have small cameras for capturing low-resolution stills and video, as well as screens designed primarily to play back the content the phones have recorded. However, cell phone providers have experimented with services that would allow these users to consume video if their phone supports it in some respect. The devices that do support video are most often optimized for 3GP video.

Each cell phone manufacturer has multiple models available, and all those various handsets tend to have slightly different needs when it comes to targeted settings. How well a cell phone is suited for video playback—based on screen resolution and aspect ratio, as well as how it performs as a streaming device—depends on the hardware and software limitations of the phone and tends to reflect how important video is to the product's intended customer base (**Figure 8.3**). Obviously, some customers just don't want to consume video on their phones, so they don't want to have to pay extra for a device that is powerful enough to play it.

Figure 8.3 The Motorola Razr V3 is one of many models of traditional cell phones that have some streaming video capabilities but is not primarily meant to be a video playback device like the iPhone.

Adobe has developed a great product for content creators who want to support the range of phones out there and encode video with specific phones in mind. Called Device Central (**Figure 8.4**), it is a software program that makes it easy for content creators to preview and test video content for mobile devices. It is bundled with Adobe Creative Suite 3 Production Premium as well as several of the company's stand-alone applications. Device Central includes a comprehensive testing facility that approximates how pages, graphics, and video will look on different cell phones that have different screen resolutions, color depths, memory constraints, and other performance characteristics. It even provides a simulation mode allowing you to test what it would be like to download your video over different network conditions. Device Central shipped with profiles for 200 of the most popular mobile devices, and its profiles are updated regularly via the Internet.

Figure 8.4 Adobe Device Central CS3 allows you to tailor your encoding parameters for phones like this Motorola Razr V3m.

Mobile Delivery Compression Tips

The size of video files compressed for mobile delivery is crucial, because it affects the download cost for the user and the time it takes to download. The latter also affects the likelihood of a successful download. Large videos are more prone to failure.

Accurate video file size device data is critical. Unfortunately, it can differ by firmware. For example, many Sony Ericsson K750i phones have the RC1A firmware version that can handle only about 320 KB of video. The K750i R1A firmware and others can handle up to 512 KB. If you are creating content for mobile phones, know your customer!

It's reasonable to apply a hard limit of 512 KB to any GPRS phone regardless of its memory size for three reasons: anything bigger is too expensive, takes too long to download, and has a high risk of download failure. It's also reasonable to limit 3G phones to just more than 1 MB because of cost.

Try to keep the content to less than 30 seconds wherever possible.

Smart Phones and Pocket PCs

The next class of phone, smart phones and Pocket PCs (**Figure 8.5**), includes more powerful cell phones that augment basic telephone functions with PDA functionality. The term *smart phone* typically describes a more phone-like device where the user interacts through hardware buttons exclusively, while Pocket PCs have larger touch-screen interfaces and are more like tiny computers built into phones. There are a few different smart phone/Pocket PC operating systems out there, but two of the most popular are Symbian and Microsoft's Windows Mobile. As you would imagine, Windows Mobile is closely tied to the Window Media format and includes a built-in Windows Mobile Media player that handles WMA, MP3, and WAV audio files, as well as WMV Simple profile video.

Figure 8.5 The AT&T Tilt is a one of many models of smart phones and Pocket PCs on the market that allow users to view both locally stored video and content streamed to it live over a high-speed data connection.

NOTE Most smart phones that play Windows Media do a fairly good job with video in the 200 Kbps to 500 Kbps data rate range and with resolutions of 320 by 240 or smaller.

Symbian is an open source platform supported by several developers, of which Nokia is one of the largest. Since Symbian is an open source project, many developers have contributed a variety of codecs and video players to the platform. Supported codecs include MPEG-4, DiVX, Xvid, WMV, and Real Video, though individual viewers may need to download and install the appropriate player to view the content.

Some of you are probably wondering whether I forgot the Treo. I know Palm (the Treo's manufacturer) is still around. Though Palm has closed its stores and taken some pretty serious business hits in the past year, the Treo does remain a popular platform for some smart phone users. Unfortunately, for all its other strong PDA features, the Treo has never been the greatest video playback device. I'm not entirely sure whether it's the processor or the displays, but video on the Treo has always looked more like a low-resolution flipbook than true motion video.

TIP A good Symbian combo to try is 120 Kbps Xvid video and 22 kHz mono audio, with resolution set at 192 by 144 for 16:9 or 176 by 144 for 4:3 screens. Try to keep files to about 100 Mb per hour or less.

Apple iPhone

In something of a class of its own is, of course, Apple's iPhone (**Figure 8.6**), a combination media player, telephone, and wireless communication device. It's not quite a PDA, though it more or less has the same functionality as one. Perhaps the most significant difference between an iPhone and a PDA is that a PDA was designed for business users originally with media included as an afterthought, whereas an iPhone is a media device with some business device functionality. Since it is part of the iPod family, the iPhone is primarily an MPEG-4 playback device when it comes to video, supporting MPEG-4 Part 2 and the H.264 (MPEG-4 Part 10) baseline profile.

Just like the other devices discussed in this chapter, the iPod supports specific rates and resolutions. For more detail on supported video formats, see the sidebar "Apple Video Settings."

All these devices rely primarily on your cell phone's data networks to receive video and audio, though the higher-end devices may also have WiFi, which allows them to share local wireless Internet connections when they are available. Cell phone data networks are fairly slow in comparison to broadband Internet, though they have been slowly creeping up in speed. As mentioned at the beginning of this section, the performance of U.S. data networks often falls well below advertised speeds. Edge is fairly well deployed, though most users do not see speeds faster than 100 Kbps (despite a support speed of 384 Kbps). AT&T's 3G network does have speeds that vary from as high as 900 Kbps at times in major urban areas, but from my own personal testing when traveling, I typically get a connection speed somewhere between 300 Kbps to 450 Kbps.

Figure 8.6 The Apple iPhone—part media player, part telephone, part communication device.

NOTE There is an Apple version of the H.264 codec called "Low-Complexity." Basically, it is the Apple version of H.264 that is optimized for Apple devices.

What Happened to the PDA?

Though the *personal digital assistant* has much in common with smart phones and Pocket PCs in terms of basic functionality, it has really disappeared from the map in the past two years. Several manufacturers still make PDAs, but the focus has really shifted to the phone/PDA combo, whether smart phone–style or Pocket PC–style. So, the device itself hasn't gone away, but it has been largely subsumed by another product. Creators can still support PDA users with content, because their specifications typically match that of Pocket PCs, though the users will be reliant on syncing data from a PC or downloading via WiFi.

Media Players

Even smart phones that emphasize video capability more than their smaller cousins are still not the "perfect" mobile video device; first and foremost, they are still phones. Some devices have come to market that are either exclusively designed for content playback or are at least primarily tasked with it while offering some other minor features. There are several names used for these devices: Portable Media Player (PMP) and Portable Video Player (PVP) are the most frequently used. Regardless of what they're called, most share some common traits. They typically have five or more hours of battery life, decent screen size and resolution, and large-capacity storage to allow users to store more than one video at a time on the device.

These devices also have some key differences: some have headphone-only options, while others offer speakers. Some have hard drives built in, while others rely on removable flash drives. Some play video in multiple formats, while others have very narrowly defined playback capabilities. Others are really music players that also happen to play back video; still others are really interactive video players that also happen to play back movies as well.

Apple iPod

Let's go ahead and get the one we all know out of the way. The video iPod was launched in October 2005 and was Apple's first portable video playback device. Because of the popularity of the iPod line, it was quickly adopted, though it has been widely argued that most users bought it for its music features, not as a video player. Although that may be true, it still successfully seeded a very large audience of mobile video players into the market. It was also panned by critics for its lack of external speakers and its very small display screen. With the launch of the iPod touch, many have said that Apple has finally launched a *real* video iPod. The newer player has larger screen positions across the entire face of the iPod, making for a better viewing experience.

Video-capable iPods support both MPEG-4 Part 2 and H.264 at different data rates. The iPod classic (the older model) has a maximum 80GB hard drive, while the iPod Touch ranges from 8 GB to 32 GB of flash storage (**Figure 8.7**).

Figure 8.7 The Apple iPod family (left to right): touch, classic, nano, shuffle (audio only).

Apple Video Settings

Since so much video compressed for use with mobile devices will ultimately be played back on one or another type of iPod (or iPhone), it's important to know what video settings will work with these devices. Here are the supported formats and encoding parameters for iPod/iPhone video:

- **H.264 video, up to 1.5 Mbps:** 640 by 480 pixels, 30 frames per second, Low-Complexity version of the H.264 Baseline profile with AAC-LC audio up to 160 Kbps, 48 kHz, stereo audio in .m4v, .mp4, and .mov file formats.

- **H.264 video, up to 2.5 Mbps:** 640 by 480 pixels, 30 frames per second, Baseline Profile up to Level 3.0 with AAC-LC audio up to 160 Kbps, 48 kHz, stereo audio in .m4v, .mp4, and .mov file formats.

- **MPEG-4 video, up to 2.5 Mbps:** 640 by 480 pixels, 30 frames per second, Simple Profile with AAC-LC audio up to 160 Kbps, 48 kHz, stereo audio in .m4v, .mp4, and .mov file formats.

Zune

Not to be outdone, Microsoft came out with an answer to the iPod in November 2006. Named the Zune, it's similar to the iPod, though it hasn't proven nearly as popular thus far. Zune can play both audio and video, and it supports WMV, MPEG-4, H.264 up to 320 by 240, and unprotected WMA, MP3, and AAC formats. It has a similar design to the other iPod-like media players, as shown in **Figure 8.8**.

Figure 8.8 Microsoft's Zune line—look familiar?

Zune also has its own store, the Zune Marketplace (*www.zune.net*), for purchasing media (**Figure 8.9**). A nice feature of the Zune Marketplace that iTunes doesn't offer is the ability for users to subscribe to music (called a *Zune pass*), giving them access to as much Zune marketplace music as they want to download for a monthly fee.

Figure 8.9 Zune Marketplace users can either purchase content individually or, with a Zune pass, pay a monthly fee and gain access to all the content they want.

Zune Video Settings

Supported video formats and encoding parameters for Zune devices are as follows:

- **Windows Media Video (WMV; .wmv):** Main and Simple profile, CBR or VBR, up to 3.0 Mbps peak video bit rate; 720 pixels by 480 pixels up to 30 frames per second (or 720 by 576 pixels up to 25 frames per second). Zune software will transcode HD WMV files at device sync.

- **MPEG-4 (MP4/M4V; .mp4) Part 2 video[4]:** Simple profile up to 2.5 Mbps peak video bit rate; 720 by 480 pixels up to 30 frames per second (or 720 by 576 pixels up to 25 frames per second). Zune software will transcode HD MPEG-4 files at device sync.

- **H.264 video[4]:** Baseline profile up to 2.5 Mbps peak video bit rate; 720 by 480 pixels up to 30 frames per second (or 720 by 576 pixels up to 25 frames per second). Zune software will transcode HD H.264 files at device sync.

Sony PlayStation Portable

Sony's PlayStation Portable (PSP) is another popular portable media player (**Figure 8.10**). Though its primary function is to play games, it can also function as a video playback device, and it even has its own optical disc format developed by Sony, called Universal Media Disc (UMD). PSP's audio player supports a number of audio codecs, including ATRAC, AAC, MP3, and WMA, and has the option to be played with or without a set of five visualizations. MPEG-4 and AVC video formats are also compatible with PSP.

Figure 8.10 Sony's Playstation Portable—built for games but suitable for video.

NOTE As of firmware update version 3.30, H.264/MPEG-4 AVC Main profile video files of the following sizes can be played: 720 by 480, 352 by 480, and 480 by 272.

With reasonable video and audio bit-rate settings (a resolution of 320 by 240, a video bit rate of 500 Kbps, and an audio sampling rate of 22,050 Hz), a 22-minute video file weighs in at roughly 55 MB, small enough to fit on a 64 MB Memory Stick Duo. Using the same encoding parameters, a 100-minute feature film can fit on a 256 MB Memory Stick.

These popular devices are by no means the only portable ways to watch movies without a cell phone, either. Dozens of makes and models are available, each with it own special set of quirks.

TIP For a very in-depth comparison of PMPs, check out *http://en.wikipedia. org/wiki/Comparison_of_ portable_media_players.* You'll see that MPEG-4 is very popular with the various PMPs. If you are looking to maximize your audience options, an MP4-wrapped MPEG-4 file is a good way to go.

Mobile Video at 65 mph

I've spent most of this chapter discussing personal video devices, but they aren't the only game in this niche market either—video has come to the automobile in a big way. Many car manufacturers are beginning to offer DVD packages as a premium option, and third-party solutions allow any driver to "pimp their ride" with rear-seat and in-dash entertainment options. Almost all these solutions rely on the existing DVD technology and infrastructure, so if you are looking to deliver to this particular area, refer to Chapter 6, "Compressing for DVD," to learn the ins and outs of DVD encoding and delivery.

New systems are beginning to crop up that include elements such as video jukebox players or IP video delivered over the Edge (wireless 2G data) network. For that type of solution, settings similar to broadband Internet video should also deliver good results, but investigate your delivery requirements as much as possible and experiment for the right balance.

Recipes for Compressing Video for Mobile

Now that you've learned about what mobile video is, how it's being used, what the most common mobile video devices are, and what the common supported video types are for mobile delivery, you'll take another step into the real world of mobile video and see some video compression recipes for specific mobile delivery applications.

3GP Files for Those Non–Smart Phones

First, let's create a file designed for playback on cell phones. Since I've talked about the GPRS subscriber base, I'll show how to create a file targeted at them. Let's also make it a streaming file, which assumes you'll be delivering it as true streaming content rather than as a progressive download file (remember, if you don't have a streaming server, don't even try for streaming). The source content is a 60-second commercial for Zoom In Online, a Web site geared toward media professionals (that's you) and is DV-NTSC and 4:3.

I'm specifically going to make sure I choose 4:3 content for sharing with cell phones because the screen is so small that I don't want to waste any of the screen space by letterboxing to correct for aspect ratio. If I absolutely had to start with 16:9 content, I'd probably crop it to the 4:3 aspect ratio, cutting off the two sides. Sure, I'd lose some of the image, but I'd more than make up for it by focusing on the action. In fact, even starting with 4:3, I'm going to crop aggressively as part of creating settings to make sure the action truly gets the focus it needs.

Let's use Episode Pro to create our content. As described in Chapter 5, Episode Pro has a great deal of premade templates, including an entire set dedicated to mobile delivery. But let's start from scratch, just to make sure you get a full sense of what is really going on:

TIP When you are starting compression for mobile devices, feel free to use existing templates, but once you are comfortable with a given application, you should create settings from scratch at least part of the time. This will help you understand the process better overall and gain insight as to just exactly what is occurring to the material during the encode process.

1. Starting in Episode Pro, click the New Setting button. A blank setting is now open in the Settings Editor (**Figure 8.11**). You might also want to adjust the window to make sure you can see as many settings as possible to avoid excess scrolling.

Figure 8.11 Episode Pro's Settings Editor window.

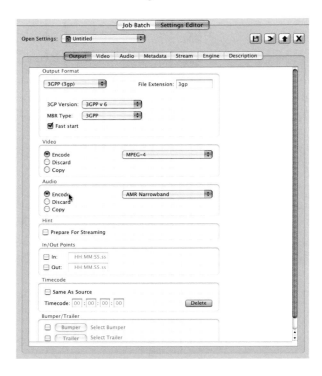

TIP If you want a given setting on any tab to be applied to your video, make sure the check box next to its name is selected and blue. It is possible to open a given section without activating it by clicking the gray arrow icon, but changes you make won't actually be applied to your video. You wouldn't believe how many videos I encoded before I figured that out.

2. On the Output tab, choose 3GPP (3gp) in the first pop-up menu. This will change the Output tab to show some specific 3GP settings. Select 3GPP v6 from the Version pop-up menu and 3GPP from the MBR Type pop-up menu, if those menus are set to something different. Also, make sure the Fast start check box is selected.

3. Next, in the Video section of the Output tab, make sure Encode is selected and then select MPEG-4. In the Audio section, make sure Encode is selected and then select AMR Narrowband. Then select the Prepare for Streaming check box in the Hint section.

4. Select the Video tab. Then click the arrow next to MPEG-4 to expand that section (**Figure 8.12**). In the Bandwidth Settings area, set the average bit rate to 24 Kbps, the Frame skip probability to 0.40, and the VBV buffer size to 0.5.

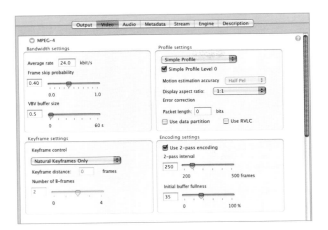

Figure 8.12 The MPEG-4 section of Video tab of the Settings Editor.

5. In the Profile Settings area of the Video tab, select Simple Profile from the pop-up menu, and select the Simple Profile Level 0 check box. Leave the Display aspect ratio set to 1:1, the packet length set to 0 bits, and the remaining boxes unchecked.

6. In the Keyframes setting area of the Video tab, select Natural Keyframes Only.

7. In the Encode settings area, select the Use 2-pass encoding check box. Set the 2-pass interval to 250 frames and the Initial buffer fullness level to 35 percent.

8. In the Frame Rate section of the Video tab (**Figure 8.13**), click the arrow next to Frame Rate. This section opens, and a check mark appears next to it, meaning it is active. Select Fixed, and change the frame rate to 10 fps. Select Fast in the pop-up menu.

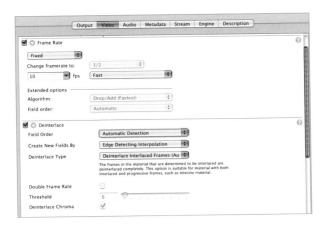

Figure 8.13 The Frame Rate and Deinterlace sections of the Video tab in the Settings Editor.

9. Click the arrow next to Deinterlace to expand this section. Select Automatic Detection in the Field Order pop-up menu, Edge Detection Interpolation in the Create New Fields By pop-up menu, and Deinterlace Interlace Frames (Automatic) in the Deinterlace Type pop-up menu. This group of settings is helpful if you have a mix of progressive and interlace content (as may happen in productions where graphic titles are added or in telecined content).

10. Activate the Resize section of the Video tab (**Figure 8.14**). In the Image size area, choose QCIF 176x144 in the Pixels pop-up menu. Choose Cut in the Maintain proportion with pop-up menu. This allows Episode to crop the image slightly to match the new aspect ratio.

Figure 8.14 The Resize section of the Video tab in the Settings Editor.

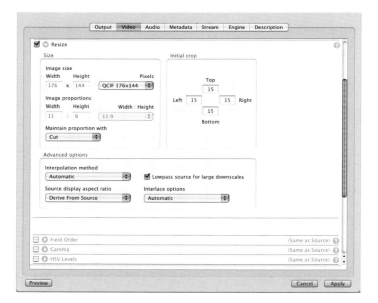

11. In the Initial crop area, crop 15 frames off each side. This is sort of a placeholder, an almost arbitrary amount. It is small enough that it should go unnoticed but significant enough that will help make the action area larger in the final image. Consider changing this to match specific sources if possible. If you can't get that exact, pick a number that generally works with all your content.

12. In the Advanced options section, select Automatic in the Interpolation method pop-up menu, select Derive from Source for Source display aspect ratio, select the Lowpass source for large downscales check box, and select Progressive output for Interlace options.

13. Select the Audio tab in the Settings Editor. Click the arrow next to AMR Narrowband to expand that section (**Figure 8.15**). Select 4.75 kbit/s from the Bit Rate pop-up menu.

NOTE Lowpass Source for Large Downscales is a nice option for making mobile content; it is a preprocessing filter that reduces artifacts when scaling SD and HD video down to such small sizes.

Figure 8.15 The Audio tab in the Settings area.

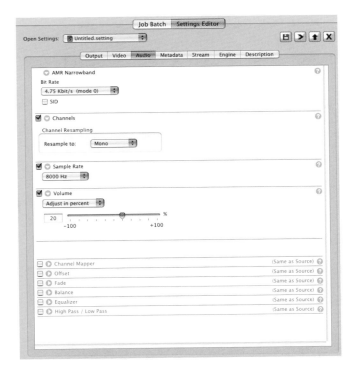

14. Select the Channels check box to activate it. Choose Mono from the Resample To pop-up menu.

15. Select the Sample Rate check box to activate it. Coose 8000 Hz.

16. Select the Volume check box to activate it. Choose Adjust in percent from the pop-up menu, and type **20** in the text box. This boosts the audio slightly, which is useful because most cell phones do not have very high-quality speakers.

TIP Feel free to skip step 16 if you think your volume is adequate.

17. Select the Metadata tab in the Settings Editor. Since some phones can use the embedded metadata to display information about the video, I like to make sure this is specified. Fill out what is appropriate to your content. Since my sample happens to be a 30-second promotional clip for a popular Web site, I've added the appropriate information (**Figure 8.16**).

Figure 8.16 The Metadata tab in the Settings Editor.

 TIP Want to add the copyright symbol to your copyright line like the cool kids do? The keyboard shortcut on the Mac is Option+G.

18. Select the Stream tab in the Settings Editor (**Figure 8.17**). Select the Prepare for Streaming check box. In the MPEG-4 Packetizer section, set the Packet Size Limit to 800 Bytes. In the AMR Narrowband Packetizer area, choose 10 for Frames per Packet, and choose Octet Align from the Packetizing Mode pop-up menu (this is understood by a wider range of phones than Bandwidth Efficient).

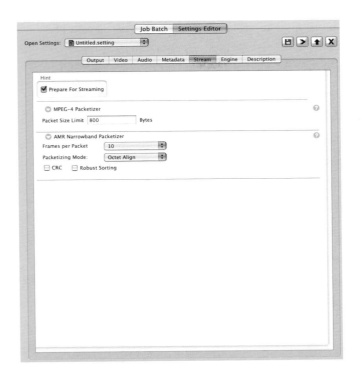

Figure 8.17 The Stream tab in the Settings Editor.

NOTE Since we aren't using the Episode Engine, there is no need to select the Engine tab.

19. Select the Description tab in the Settings Editor (**Figure 8.18**).

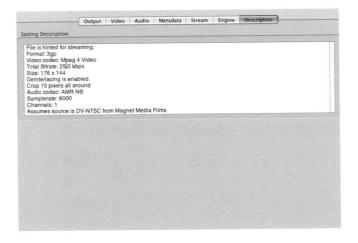

Figure 8.18 The Description tab in the Settings Editor.

20. You are now done applying settings but have not yet saved the file. Click the Save button (the small disc icon) at the top of the Settings Editor window. A small dialog appears where you can choose a name for your file. Try to keep it short and use underscores as spaces because Episode, by default, will append the setting name to the name of the newly encoded file, a handy option when encoding the same source to a number of formats at the same time. The name appears in the Compression Settings window and the file has been saved.

> **TIP** Though completely optional, it is nonetheless useful to make notes about your settings. Sure, you could go through and verify settings, but it's useful to document the basics and perhaps add information such as the specific source file you had in mind for this type of setting or a specific client. Plus, this will allow you to do something really cool in the next step.

21. Hover over the name in the Settings Editor window. After a few seconds, a yellow box known as a *tooltip* appears and displays the summary you wrote on the Description tab (**Figure 8.19**). Now you don't even need to open the setting to refresh your memory of the basic settings and its intended uses.

Figure 8.19 Hover over a saved setting to read the description saved in the Description tab.

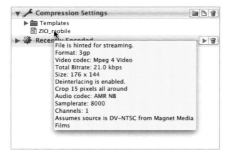

> **TIP** I'm messy in real life, but like to keep my encoding settings organized. Pick a way of organizing, and use the New Folder button in the Compression Settings section to create a folder structure within which you can organize your files. If you encode for a lot of people, categorizing your settings by client is a good way to stay organized. Just pick what works best for you.

Your setting is ready to be applied to your content. So that you can see the results, I've encoded the Zoom In Online commercial (**Figure 8.20**). How does it look? Not great, but it'll stream to a cell phone, and the file size is small. You can tell what's going on in the video, so it does the job.

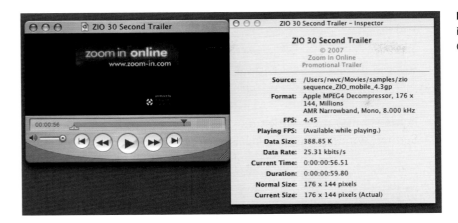

Figure 8.20 Here's the finished movie previewed in QuickTime.

Encoding for Higher-Bandwidth Streaming

Still need to stream, but confident your target device can support higher-quality video and a bigger streaming file? These settings will give you slightly sharper quality and smoother motion, and the file will be only about 200 Kbps larger:

- **Average video bit rate:** 34 Kbps

- **Frame skip probability:** 0.55

- **VBV Buffer size:** 0.5

- **Simple Profile 0:** Yes

- **Keyframe Settings:** Natural Key Frames Only

- **Use 2-pass encoding:** Yes

- **2-pass interval:** 250

- **Initial buffer fullness:** 50%

- **Frame Rate (fixed):** 15 fps (fast)

- **Deinterlace Field Order:** Automatic Detection

- **Create New Fields:** Edge Detecting Interpolation

- **Deinterlace type:** Deinterlace Interlaced Frames (Automatically)

- **Resize:** 176x144

- **Maintain proportion by:** Cut

- **Crop:** 15 on all sides

- **Low-pass Source:** Yes

- **Source display aspect ratio:** Derived from Source

- **Audio bit rate:** 10.2

- **Audio channels:** Mono

- **Audio sample rate:** 8 kHz (8000 Hz)

Note that the total data rate of this video file is still only about 45 Kbps—still well below the rates that GPRS theoretically supports. Technically, you could try boosting the rates to improve quality; however, your viewer will most likely experience buffering because the network is unlikely to maintain a fast enough connection to watch comfortably. If quality is really important but you can't trust the data rates, then switch to progressive download instead of streaming. The quality can be just about anything you want, and your viewer just has to have the patience to download it.

Adding Chapter Markers to a Video Podcast

Adding markers to podcasts is an easy way to allow your viewers to skip quickly to select areas of the video, much like the chapters of a DVD (in fact, in Apple Compressor, you use the same workflow to add markers to podcasts as to create chapter markers for DVDs).

Output File Formats That Support Markers

Not all output file formats support markers. The following is a list of those that do support them:

- MPEG-2
- MPEG-4 when configured for podcasting (audio-only with the Allow Podcasting Information check box selected)
- QuickTime Movies
- H.264 for DVD Studio Pro
- H.264 for Apple devices

You can set and configure markers for other output file formats, but they will not be included in the encoded output file.

What's the Difference Between a Chapter Marker and a Podcast Marker?

A podcast can have both chapter markers and podcast markers. The only difference is that the viewer can navigate directly to a chapter marker but cannot navigate to a podcast marker. If you have an audio podcast that you want to add a slide show to, podcast chapter markers let you assign different images to different parts of the Timeline. Add the file, and it will be present until the next marker with an image to display is reached. Since we're working with a video podcast in this example, we'll use chapter markers instead, which will give us an attractive navigational system in both iTunes and iPods.

Compressor can import and create the following types of markers:

Chapter markers: Chapter markers provide easy access to index points throughout a DVD, QuickTime movie, or podcast. Compressor and DVD Studio Pro can both read chapter markers exported from Final Cut Pro. QuickTime Player can interpret any text track containing time stamps as a chapter track. Chapter markers can also have artwork and a URL assigned to them that appear when playing a podcast.

These markers appear as purple in the Preview window Timeline.

Podcast markers: Like chapter markers, podcast markers can have artwork and a URL assigned to them. Podcast markers cannot be used to access frames within the clip, however, and they do not appear as chapter markers in DVD Studio Pro or QuickTime.

You can use podcast markers to provide a slide show (with URLs) for users to view when playing audio podcasts.

Compression markers: Also known as *manual compression markers*, these are markers you can add to a Final Cut Pro sequence (or in the Compressor Preview window) to indicate when Compressor should generate an MPEG I-frame during compression.

These markers appear in blue in the Preview window Timeline and are the type created when you manually add markers using Compressor. You can convert compression markers into chapter markers using the Edit item of the Markers pop-up menu.

To manually add a chapter or podcast marker to a clip, you first add a compression marker to the Timeline, and then you edit the marker.

To manually add a chapter or podcast marker to a clip, do the following:

1. Drag the playhead to the point in the Timeline where you want to add a marker. Click the Marker button, and choose Add Marker from the menu (or press M). A blue compression marker appears in the Timeline.

2. Open the Markers menu, and choose Edit (or press Command+E) (**Figure 8.21**). A dialog for editing the marker appears.

Figure 8.21 Inserting an edit marker.

3. Choose Chapter from the Type pop-up menu. Enter a name for the marker in the Name field (**Figure 8.22**). This name appears in the output media file where it can be seen with QuickTime Player, in iTunes, and in iPods/iPhones.

Figure 8.22 The Marker Edit dialog.

4. Assign an image to the marker by choosing Frame in Source from the Image pop-up menu. Click OK to close the dialog.

> **NOTE** You selected Frame in Source because the frame comes from the source media file (the default image is the frame 2 seconds to the right of the frame where the marker is at). If there had been no image associated with the marker, you would have selected None. If you'd chosen From File, a file selection dialog would have opened to allow you to select a still image file to assign to the marker.

5. Repeat steps 1–4 to add chapter markers to the beginning of each interview.

6. Add a final marker as the title credits begin. Enter a URL in the URL field (**Figure 8.23**).

> **NOTE** If you select podcast markers, this name does not appear to the viewer, and the user can't navigate to it.

> **NOTE** DVD Studio Pro ignores images assigned to chapter markers.

Figure 8.23 Adding a URL in the Edit window. This URL applies only to podcasts. The marker's name appears over the artwork where the viewer can click it to open a Web browser to the URL in question.

The Timeline now has purple markers for each area you want a chapter to begin (**Figure 8.24**).

7. Submit the video to the batch.

Figure 8.24 Note the purple chapter markers in the Timeline.

8. After it finishes encoding, launch the video in QuickTime. Notice that in the Timeline, there is now a text box that says *start*. This is the chapter menu. If you click this, you will see a list of your chapter markers (**Figure 8.25**). Select one of these chapters, and the playhead jumps to that part of the video.

Figure 8.25 Preview of an enhanced video podcast in QuickTime, with the chapter list menu shown in a menu.

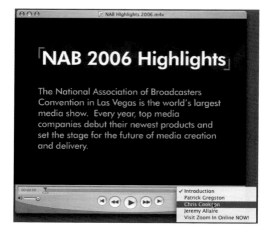

9. Now load the video into iTunes. Click it to begin playing. Notice that as you hover over the video, a book icon appears in the navigation window. If you click it, you will once again see the chapter markers, but this time you also get the image you set in Compressor (**Figure 8.26**).

Figure 8.26 Viewing an enhanced podcast in iTunes.

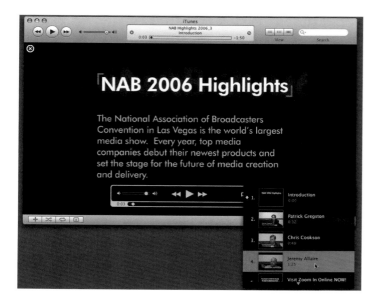

If you navigate to the closing chapter marker, you will see a line of blue text that says Visit Zoom in Online NOW! This is an active hyperlink—clicking it launches your default Web browser and goes to the URL you typed in Compressor for this marker (**Figure 8.27**).

Figure 8.27 An active URL embedded in the video.

NOTE You also have the option of importing a chapter marker list. These lists can use either the QuickTime TeXML format (an XML-based format for constructing 3GPP-compliant timed text tracks in a Quick-Time movie file) or the plain-text chapter list files.

Creating Plain-Text Chapter Marker Lists

You can create a list of timecode points that Compressor can import to create markers.

The timecode values need to match the timecode of the track's video clip. The list of timecode values must be a plain-text file, so you can create the list with TextEdit and save the file as plain text. If you create the list with a more advanced word-processing application, be sure to save the file as a plain ASCII text file with no formatting. The file must follow these rules:

- Each marker must be on a new line that starts with a timecode value in the "00:00:00:00" format. These values identify the marker positions.

- After the timecode value, you can include a name for the marker. You can use a comma, space, or tab character to separate the timecode value from the marker name.

- Any lines that do not begin with a timecode value are ignored. This makes it easy for you to add comments to the list.

- The timecode values do not have to be listed in chronological order.

CONCLUSION

Mobile video isn't going to work for every person or every type of content, but it certainly has a strong position in the future of video distribution. Similar to Web video, as more people grow accustomed to portable video and embrace new ways of using it, new acceptance of it will emerge.

It seems only fitting to wrap up a review of delivery options back where it all started—your television set. IP-based video is finding its way to your regular old TV in a variety of ways. Clever producers have even figured out how to use the video podcast format to distribute HD-quality video via the Internet meant for enjoying in your living room, not on your laptop. So what does all this mean? What's the difference between traditional broadcast and the new options available for distribution? Old and new technologies alike share one common factor—a magic box that serves as the link between video and your TV, whether it's coaxial cable or a broadband connection. So let's explore what this means and identify some methods and settings for putting video back in your living room.

Interview with a Compressionist

Name: Ryanne Hodson

Title/role: Videoblogger, Video Producer

Company: RyanIsHungry.com

URL: *http://ryanishungry.com*, *http://freevlog.org*, *http://ryanedit.com*

How did you get involved in video compression?

My first experience compressing video was in late 2003 when I was trying to get my cable-access show onto the Web. I then started to compress some of my video shorts for a résumé site. Then in late 2004, I found videoblogging, and that's when I really dove into the extreme compression geekiness.

What was your biggest project?

The biggest project, encoding-wise, that I've gotten myself into would have to be Pixelodeon. Pixelodeon (*http://pixelodeonfest.com*) is a videoblogging festival (think film fest but with awesome online video as the content!) produced by my partner, Jay Dedman, myself, and new-media visionaries Zadi Diaz and Steve Woolf, in Hollywood. We screen 30 hours of online video on the big screen for two days straight. We give curators complete freedom to choose what will be screened. Online video + complete freedom = 7 million different formats to be edited onto a screening reel. We had everything from .flv, .swf, .mov, MPEG-1, MPEG-2, VCD, .mp4, .wmv, .avi, and the ever-mysterious-YouTube-secretly-embedded-Flash-with-no-way-of-downloading-it format. I was overseeing (and was one of) a handful of editors gathering and compiling reels for screening. The conversion load was insane. The basic process was to turn everything into digital video to be edited in Final Cut Pro and spit out to both MiniDV and DVD as a backup. It was a monumental task taken on by Web video experts, and I'll tell ya—there were some moments that things looked bleak. But with the amount of conversion tools available now, we were able to convert using MPEG Streamclip, QuickTime Pro, VisualHub, Vixy.net, HandBrake, and pretty much anything we could get our hands on. The event was a huge success, thanks to the encoding wizardry of our editing team!

What was your favorite project?

One of my favorite projects in compression that I've been involved in would have to be FreeVlog.org. Fellow videoblogger Michael Verdi and I started putting video on our blogs in late 2004 (this was pre-YouTube). The most pressing question for the handful of videobloggers at the time was "How do I compress my videos so they look good and can be quickly downloaded?" Independently of one another, Verdi and I began doing compression tests with the 3ivx and Sorenson codecs. We would spend hours and hours changing every combination of bit rate, keyframe, kHz, and so on, until we got a satisfying result. We both published our findings on our sites and on the Videoblogging Yahoo! Group. After months of continuous teaching and sharing settings, we decided to collaborate on a full video tutorial on how to videoblog—the defining step has always been how to compress your video. We put in the hours of testing so you don't have to!

What's your format of choice?

I resisted H.264 for so long because I was set with my 3ivx (a flavor of MPEG-4 codec) settings. I knew the quirks. I knew what worked and what didn't. Plus I was compressing on a G4 PowerBook with 512 MB of RAM, which, for video compression, is like driving your mom's old station wagon in a drag race. Since H.264 was dual-pass (so was 3ivx, but it wasn't as heavy duty), it would take up to eight times as long as the length of the video on my PowerBook, and it was really unbearable even for short videos. Once I upgraded to a faster computer, I switched to H.264 dual-pass for creating mostly .mp4 files. I love it. You can create beautiful files that are a decent downloadable size.

What does your average workday look like?

My partner, Jay Dedman, and I have been editing two videos a week for RyanIsHungry.com, our videoblog about green and sustainable life. We also take on freelance video work for tech companies and nonprofits in the San Francisco Bay Area and beyond. If we're not out shooting, we're editing any number of projects in the queue. As far as compression goes, RyanIsHungry serves up four different formats that all need special attention. We host a high-resolution .mp4, an iPod/iPhone .mp4, Flash, and a free and open source Ogg Theora .ogg file. All can be viewed right on the Web page or downloaded via RSS feed (that's a whole other book!).

What does your encoding hardware look like?

I work on a MacBook Pro with 2 GB of RAM and two 2.33 GHz Intel Core 2 Duo processors. It rocks! It's so much faster than my G4; it's a life-saver for video work and being able to travel with as well. My editing station comes with me wherever I go.

What's your encoding software of choice?

I compress my .mp4 files straight out of Final Cut Pro using QuickTime conversion. This is because the software, Compressor, that came with the Final Cut Pro suite is totally broken for me. It's a well-known bug ("cannot connect to background process"), but for the life of me, I cannot fix it. I make Flash files using Flash 8 Video Encoder. I make the Ogg Theora files in QuickTime Pro using a plug-in called XiphQT. I love QuickTime Pro for most conversions, though. I've found it does the best job at up-resing from smaller .mp4 files to digital video for editing in Final Cut Pro. Another program I also love is MPEG Streamclip, which is free and can pretty much convert anything to anything for Mac or PC.

What role does compression play in your work?

Compression is everything for a videoblogger. It's the final gateway between your computer and the Internet. Good compression is pretty much key to my entire career as a professional Web video producer and videoblogger.

What surprises you most about video compression today?

I'm constantly surprised at how fast the quality of video on the Web has risen. I've seen the videoblogging beginnings start with postage-size MPEGs for pushing from blog to computer. Three years later my cohorts and I are publishing HD versions for people to watch full-screen, on their TVs and in theaters. What's next? I'm hoping that compression will get even better so that folks in developing countries can have good-quality video being uploaded and downloaded even with minimal Internet connections. Cell phone technology is pushing this forward. I hope that it continues.

CHAPTER NINE

Compressing for Set-Top Boxes

By now your head must be spinning with all the possible avenues for compressing and distributing video. I know how you feel. All that tweaking to get the image just right makes you think back to those old days of rabbit ears and tuning in UHF. Fortunately, most of us have put that stuff behind us when it comes to TV tuning, thanks to the ubiquity of cable, satellite, and digital TV. One video delivery device that has become nearly as common in homes, though probably not thought about a lot, is the set-top box.

A set-top box (STB) is a device that connects to a TV and an external source of signal, turning the signal into content that is then displayed on the TV. Before cable-ready TV sets, most of the set-top boxes in use were cable converter boxes used to receive analog cable TV channels and convert them to video that could be seen on a regular TV. Nowadays, cable converter boxes are used to descramble premium cable channels, to receive digital cable channels, and for a variety of other purposes.

But STBs are far more than cable converters. The diversification of video into so many other devices—computers in particular—has invariably led to groups of devices that then bridge this video back to the TV, because that is still consumers' most understood and recognized video playback device. As soon as we stop thinking about video source as just a cable in our house, the use of an STB really opens up. That "signal source" might be an Ethernet cable, a satellite dish, a coaxial cable (such as for cable TV), a telephone line (including DSL connections), broadband over a power line, or even an ordinary VHF or UHF antenna. Content, in this context, could mean any video, audio, Internet Web pages, interactive games, or a combination of several of those elements.

More Than Just Cable

Rather than choosing to narrowly define STBs as the earlier converter tuner boxers, I'm going to really open up the definition of what constitutes an STB and the functionality it brings to our living room. I'll discuss the basic tenets of video delivery to the home, as well as identify how those not in traditional broadcast might seek to share content with viewers right in their living rooms, just like prime-time TV.

Where Do DVRs Fit into This?

Although a digital video recorder (DVR), such as the TiVo series 2 and 3, is certainly an STB, it is still primarily a box that tunes cable channels in and then records them to a hard drive for later playback. Upgrades to the box are providing other options as well, however. The TiVoCast service provides users with select content that is similar in style to a video podcast (though the service offers only select deals with content partners). Amazon Unbox has also brought digital download service to the TiVo line, allowing users to buy shows and movies either online or directly on the TiVo and then download them to the DVR for playback. Though Unbox offers content in only SD formats today, HD will no doubt begin trickling in as an option soon.

Digital TV

Digital TV (DTV) is a telecommunications system for broadcasting by means of a digital signal, rather than the analog transmissions used by traditional TV. DTV uses digital modulation data, which is digitally compressed and requires decoding by newer, specially designed TV sets and older analog TV augmented with a special set-top box. This technology was introduced in the 1990s and has been rolled out in various places around the global. In the United States, all TV broadcasters are slated to switch to DTV broadcasting exclusively by February 2009.

Digital TV is more flexible and efficient than analog TV. When properly utilized by broadcasters, digital TV allows a much clearer picture, better sound quality, and more programming choices than analog. However, where broadcasters do not implement station infrastructure improvements, the DTV signals they send out may not be much better than the analog signals they replaced.

Formats and Bandwidth

DTV versions of high-definition TV (HDTV) use both 720p and 1080i resolutions, both of which are, of course, 16:9 aspect ratios. Some TVs are capable of receiving an HD resolution of 1920 by 1080 at a 60-frame progressive scan frame rate (1080p60), but currently, this is not standard, so today no broadcaster is able to transmit this resolution over the air at acceptable quality.

Standard-definition DTV, by comparison, may use one of several formats taking the form of various aspect ratios, depending on the technology used in the country of broadcast. For 4:3 aspect-ratio broadcasts, the 640 by 480 format is used in NTSC countries, while 720 by 576 (rescaled to 768 by 576) is used in PAL countries. For 16:9 broadcasts, the 704 by 480 (rescaled to 848 by 480) format is used in NTSC countries, while 720 by 576 (rescaled to 1024 by 576) is used in PAL countries. However, broadcasters may choose to reduce these resolutions to save bandwidth (for example, many DTV channels in the United Kingdom use a horizontal resolution of 544 or 704 pixels per line).

Each DTV channel is permitted to broadcast at a data rate up to 19 megabits per second (Mbps), or 2.375 megabytes per second (MB/sec). The video is delivered over a transport stream. The transport stream (TS, TP, MPEG-TS, or M2T) is a communications protocol for audio, video, and data that is specified in MPEG-2 Part 1, Systems (ISO/IEC standard 13818-1). It is designed to allow *multiplexing* (combining multiple signals into a single data stream) of digital video and audio and to then synchronize the output. Using transport streams offers features for error correction for transportation over unreliable media, such as digital TV. Broadcasters do not need to use this entire bandwidth for just one broadcast channel. Instead, the broadcast can be subdivided across several video subchannels of varying quality and compression rates, including nonvideo "datacasting" services that allow one-way high-bandwidth streaming of data to computers.

A broadcaster may opt to use a standard-definition digital signal instead of an HDTV signal, because current convention allows the bandwidth of a DTV channel (or *multiplex*) to be subdivided into multiple subchannels, providing multiple feeds of entirely different programming on the same channel. This ability to provide either a single HDTV feed or multiple lower-resolution feeds is often referred to as distributing one's *bit budget*, or multicasting. This can sometimes be arranged automatically, using a statistical multiplexer (or *stat-mux*).

IPTV

Internet Protocol Television (IPTV) is a system in which DTV is delivered using Internet Protocol (IP) over a data network infrastructure (such as broadband) instead of a traditional broadcast. A general definition of IPTV is TV content that, instead of being delivered through traditional broadcast and cable formats, is received by the viewer through the technologies used for computer networks. Although this delivery can mimic the linear feed of traditional broadcast, it can also take advantage of the interactivity inherent to IP networks to enhance the viewing experience.

For residential users, IPTV is appearing in conjunction with Video on Demand (VOD) and may be bundled with other services such as Web access and Voice over IP (VoIP) telephony. In marketing-speak, the commercial bundling of IPTV, VoIP, and Internet access is referred to as *Triple Play* service. IPTV moves the data using a closed data network managed by the ISP rather than a public Internet connection, allowing the ISP to manage the speeds and packet loss better than relying on the multiple networks meshed into the Internet.

Because IPTV uses standard networking protocols, it promises lower costs for operators and lower prices for users. Using STBs with broadband Internet connections, video can be streamed to households more efficiently than via current coaxial cable. ISPs are upgrading their networks to bring higher speeds and to allow multiple HDTV channels. Because IPTV requires real-time data transmission and uses the Internet Protocol, it is susceptible to packet loss and delays if the IPTV connection is not fast enough and may experience picture breakup or loss if the streamed data is unreliable. This latter problem has proved particularly troublesome when attempting to stream IPTV across wireless links. Improvements in wireless technology are now starting to provide equipment to solve the problem.

In IPTV networks, the STB is, effectively, a small computer providing two-way communications on an IP network and decoding the video streaming media to a TV instead of a computer monitor.

Not Just the Big Guys: Anybody Can Distribute IP Video

Even though major broadcasters will be working directly with ISPs offering IPTV to be part of the closed system described earlier, the fact that these devices do connect to the Internet as well and decode IP video means that there is an opening for nontraditional distributors to offer up content for the viewing public directly to their TVs. The technologies already powering video on the Web can now be leveraged to keep viewers on the couch, watching your content.

Consider RSS feeds and video podcasts. RSS is a simple way for anyone to get updates from a given content creator without repeatedly having to remember to visit their site. That content could be words, images, audio, and video. If you had the ability to subscribe to someone's video podcast on your set-top box like you do in iTunes, how different would that be from having a Season Pass to your favorite show on TiVo? Other than the ability to watch the show as it records on your TiVo (as opposed to waiting for it to download), there is very little difference, particularly if progressive download technology is used, which would allow you to watch the podcast while it's still downloading (this isn't really being done yet as far as I know, but it could be).

Suddenly, airing a show is more an act of publishing it for distribution, but ultimately the effect is the same. In truth, we already have this option—Apple TV and iTunes make it possible to subscribe to high-quality video in podcast form to watch on your TV. There aren't huge budgets behind it yet, but the quality is already amazing; check out the work of the Pixel Corps at *www.pixelcorps. tv*, or search for *Pixel Corps* in the iTunes Music Store. Pixel Corps produces both audio and video podcasts, and its MacBreak program is a popular Mac-centric tech show that is distributed in multiple resolutions, including Apple TV–friendly 720p.

Advertisers get this. They are consistently spending money with podcasters right now looking for a model that gives them the eyeballs they want and a business model that they, the content creators, and the viewing public can all live with. Right now most of this content is nonfiction, but don't be surprised to see serialized fiction shows using the same distribution model—it's just a question of the viewers accepting the medium.

IP-BASED STBs

Let's take a moment to go a bit more in-depth on a few of the types of STBs we've discussed both here and in other chapters. You most likely recognize most of the names already but may not be familiar with the specs you'll need to know to deliver video to them.

Apple TV

Apple TV (**Figure 9.1**) is a digital media receiver designed, marketed, and sold by Apple. It is a network device designed to play digital content originating from the iTunes Music Store or another computer onto an enhanced-definition or high-definition wide-screen TV. Apple TV can store content on an internal hard drive or stream it across a network from another computer running iTunes on either Mac OS X or Windows.

Figure 9.1 Apple's "DVD player for the Internet age," Apple TV.

Apple TV connects to a TV through either High-Definition Multimedia Interface (HDMI) or component video connections. Though it will work with standard-definition TVs, it is really designed with HD sets in mind. Audio is supported via digital optical and analog (RCA connector) audio ports. The device connects to other computers either through an Ethernet connection or wirelessly through the standard IEEE 802.11b, g, and n wireless protocols. A USB port is also included on the device but is reserved for service and diagnostics.

Synchronization and Streaming

In sync mode, Apple TV works in a similar way to the iPod. It is paired with an iTunes library on a single computer and can then synchronize with that library, copying content to its own hard drive. After syncing, Apple TV is not required to remain connected to the network for the device to continue functioning. Sync modes include "automatic" for synchronizing all iTunes content to the hard drive (in a specific priority) and "selected content" to synchronize only specified content.

However, syncing iTunes content to Apple TV's hard drive is not required, and Apple TV can also function as a peer-to-peer digital media receiver, streaming content from iTunes libraries and playing the content over the network. Apple TV can stream content from up to five computers/iTunes libraries, and five Apple TVs can be linked to the same iTunes library.

With the Take 2 software update announced by Steve Jobs at Macworld 2008, Apple TV is capable of acting as a stand-alone device, no longer requiring a computer running iTunes on Mac OS X or Windows to stream or sync content to it. The update allows users to access the iTunes Music Store directly through Apple TV and purchase music, movies, and TV shows directly. In the same announcement, Apple unveiled movie rentals through iTunes, which can be streamed/synced from another computer running iTunes or downloaded directly.

Content Support

Apple TV supports video encoded with either the H.264 format for a maximum resolution of 720p (up to 1280 by 720 pixels) at 24 fps or the MPEG-4 video codec for a maximum resolution of 720 by 432 (432p) or 640 by 480 pixels at 30 fps. Audio can be encoded with AAC (16–320 Kbps), MP3 (16–320 Kbps, with VBR), Apple Lossless, AIFF, or WAV audio codecs. Apple TV also features support for files encrypted with the FairPlay digital rights management (DRM) technology. Attempts to sync unsupported content to Apple TV will result in iTunes error messages because iTunes supports more formats than Apple TV.

NOTE Most would opt for the 720p, if possible, but there is also a resolution of 960 by 540 at 30 fps, which is what Apple TV needs in order to play 30 fps at "Almost HD res."

Apple TV supports content purchased or rented from the iTunes store. A user can purchase iTunes store content from Apple TV itself or stream/sync purchased/rented content from a Mac or PC running the iTunes software client. Apple TV's audio chip supports 7.1 surround sound, and Apple says that some HD rentals from iTunes will be offered with Dolby Digital 5.1 surround sound. In 2007, the Apple TV officially supported only Dolby Pro Logic–simulated 5.1, though unofficially the full 5.1 surround sound digital discrete works if a 5.1-capable receiver is connected via the optical cable to Apple TV and the audio content is encoded as lossless.

Apple TVs come with either a 40 GB or 160 GB hard disk for storing downloaded or synced content.

Xbox 360

Xbox 360 (**Figure 9.2**) is a game console developed Microsoft as part of its popular Xbox product line. Xbox 360 is the successor to Xbox and competes with Sony's PlayStation 3 and Nintendo's Wii as part of the seventh generation of video game consoles.

Figure 9.2 Microsoft's Xbox 360 is a seventh-generation game console with a range of media support.

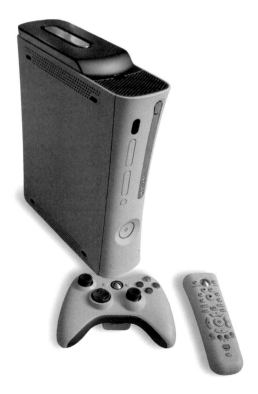

Multimedia

As you would suppose, Xbox 360 has excellent Windows Media/VC-1 support, but it doesn't stop there. Xbox 360 supports H.264, MPEG-4 (in several formats), and PlaysForSure WMV videos that have digital rights management (DRM).

Videos can be played from standard USB mass storage devices, Xbox 360 proprietary storage devices (such as memory cards or Xbox 360 hard drives), and servers or computers with Windows Media Center or Windows XP with Service Pack 2 or higher within the local-area network in streaming mode. This is possible with video files up to HD resolution and with several codecs (MPEG-2, MPEG-4, WMV) and container formats (WMV, MOV, TS). **Table 9.1** lists the details.

Table 9.1 Xbox-Supported Video

Format	Extensions	Video Profile	Video Bit Rate	Audio Profile	Audio Bit Rate
AVI	.avi, .divx	MPEG-4 Part 2 (Simple profile and Advanced Simple profile)	5 Mbps with resolutions of 1280x720 at 30 fps	Dolby Digital (2 channel and 5.1 channel), MP3	No Restrictions
H.264	.mp4, .m4v, mp4v, .mov, .avi	Baseline, main, and high (up to level 4.1)	10 Mbps with resolutions of 1920x1080 at 30 fps	AAC, 2-channel, low complexity	No Restrictions
MPEG-4 Part 2	.mp4, .m4v, mp4v, .mov, .avi	MPEG-4 Part 2 (Simple profile and Advanced Simple profile)	5 Mbps with resolutions of 1280x720 at 30 fps	AAC, 2-channel, low complexity	No Restrictions
WMV/VC-1	.wmv	WMV7 (WMV1), WMV8 (WMV2), WMV9 (WMV3), VC-1 (WVC1 or WMVA) in Simple, Main, and Advanced up to level 3	15 Mbps with resolutions of 1920x1080 at 30 fps	WMA7/8, WMA9 Pro (stereo and 5.1), WMA lossless	No Restrictions

In November 2006, Microsoft launched the Xbox Video Marketplace, a video store accessible exclusively through the Xbox console. The service allows users in the United States to download high-definition and standard-definition TV shows and movies onto an Xbox 360 console for viewing. Short clips may be streamed; however, most content is downloaded and then viewed. Movies are also available for rental. They expire in 14 days after download or at the end of the first 24 hours after the movie has begun playing, whichever comes first. TV episodes can be purchased to own and are transferable to an unlimited number of consoles. Downloaded files use 5.1 surround audio and are encoded using VC-1 for video at 720p, with a bit rate of 6.8 Mbps.

Xbox Marketplace Facts

An average HD movie download should be between 4 GB to 5 GB, and a two-hour SD movie should be 1.6 GB.

An average 44-minute (typical length of a one-hour TV program) HDTV download should be about 2.2 GB, and an average 22-minute (for a half-hour show) HDTV download should be about 1 GB.

A one-hour SDTV download should be about 600 MB, and a half-hour SDTV download should be about 300 MB.

Vudu

Although you definitely should have heard about the two devices just discussed, you could be forgiven for having not heard of Vudu. Vudu (**Figure 9.3**) is an interactive media device used to distribute full-length movies to any TV, using peer-to-peer (P2P) TV technology similar to BitTorrent. BitTorrent is a method of distributing large amounts of data widely without the original distributor incurring the entire costs of hardware, hosting, and bandwidth resources used to deliver the content. When data is distributed

Figure 9.3 Unlike Apple TV and Xbox, Vudu is designed to distribute content via P2P technology.

using the BitTorrent protocol, each recipient supplies pieces of the data to newer recipients, reducing the cost and burden on any given individual source, providing redundancy against system problems, and reducing dependence on the original distributor.

Movies are downloaded over a broadband Ethernet connection in MPEG-4 Part 2 format. SD movies are then upscaled to HD, and HD movies can be played back at 1080p. To ensure instant playback, the beginning of every movie in the catalog is loaded on the box. The rest of the movie begins to download while the user watches the first 30 seconds of the movie.

Given that Vudu is a proprietary box, it's unlikely you'll be creating content to send to Vudu anytime soon, but in the age of new-media start-ups, you never know. Vudu could easily change gears from a studio model and begin offering the ability for smaller distributors and content creators to provide content across its closed network.

Questions have arisen about Vudu's quality and the actual speeds at which it can provide content, but it is an interesting model regardless. The biggest concern for most is whether this young, unknown company can reliably provide content.

RECIPES FOR COMPRESSING VIDEO FOR STBS

If you have decided to create content for delivery to some sort of STB, I am going to assume you are targeting IP-based delivery, not broadcast. If you are really intending to broadcast your video, that probably means you work in the broadcast industry and know how to do it, or it could be that you are running some sort of crazy pirate TV station, and frankly I just can't get involved, because the FCC frowns on that type of stuff. Remember how much they hassled Christian Slater in *Pump Up the Volume*? If you really want to get the message out these days, you don't have to break the rules (I bet even Slater would just start a podcast these days). We already made Apple TV–targeted content with Compressor in Chapter 5, so let's look at some other easy ways to compress video meant for delivery to TVs and set-top boxes.

Ripping a DVD with HandBrake

DVDs are an incredibly popular way for feature-length films, event and corporate videos, and even home movies to be distributed. But if you have ever looked at the contents of a DVD on your computer, unless you know what you're looking for, nothing seems particularly familiar as a movie file per se. Well, that's because DVD players, of course, are looking for a particular file format and structure (see Chapter 6). And sure, you can use the DVD player software in your computer to play back that disc, but suppose you want to do more. Suppose you've been given a DVD with a movie you need to compress for sharing on the Web—can't be done, right? Wrong. It can be done, and it's not even particularly hard.

So before I go too far, let me just say this for the record: You shouldn't be ripping commercial DVDs for nefarious reasons (see the sidebar "Did I Just Say You Could Pirate Video?"), and you shouldn't really be using DVD as the source format for compression content. Yes, you can do it, and I'm going to show you how because eventually you will have to do it. But the compressionist in me (and probably several of you reading this) originally cringed at the idea.

MPEG-2 that has been encoded for a DVD isn't a great source. It is very easy to share, send, and even decode, but it puts a ceiling on the quality of any file you try to create with it. If the content you're making is meant for playback on broadcast TV or some similar way, you should *definitely* request a higher-quality source. However, if your files are meant for Web, mobile, or some other type of sub-SD resolution distribution, then you could technically get away with compressing video sourced from a DVD. Let me say it once more here: It's not going to be the best source material by any means, but you can use DVD material as your compression source if you must (and believe me, eventually you probably will). Whew!

Did I Just Say You Could Pirate Video?

No, no I most certainly did not. There are perfectly legal reasons to know why and how to extract and transcode your DVDs into some other format, such as if your clients have video to which they own the copyright that they want you to prepare for distribution in another medium and they have the content only in DVD format. Or you may have some private purpose in mind that marginally falls under the rubric of Fair Use (although the MPAA is pretty stringent on that count). That said, you absolutely should not try to sell or give away the commercially copyrighted material you rip. It doesn't really matter whether you agree or disagree with the copyright laws; the fact of that matter is that if you're caught sharing movies either by your ISP or a studio, you're going to be in a world of hurt. A cease-and-desist or takedown notice is the mildest slap on the wrist you'll get. Record labels are already tying up the courts with cases against those they claim have stolen from them by sharing music files, and the movie studios are taking careful notes about how to go about this. This could end up costing you lots of time and money and just isn't worth it in the end.

And before you think I'm an industry shill, I'm all for digital downloads of content—I love the fact that we've figured out how to remove the physical medium of content altogether. I wholeheartedly want distributors to adopt this and find a happy balance between protecting the content owners and giving us, the public, the types of files and formats we want.

So, for your own peace of mind (and mine) and in an effort to prevent you from getting busted for a fairly silly reason, please don't use what I've taught you here for movie piracy.

Well, now that we've had that awkward conversation, let's determine our scenario. Let's assume our source is a video our clients shot. This is the screener for a show they are creating, and they need a fairly nice-looking Apple TV version that will also play back on the computer so they can show it off at an upcoming festival. There is a DigiBeta tape of it, but you have no access to a deck and have to get this done before they hop on a flight (see, I told you this situation would arise).

 **NOTE** The video used in this recipe is provided courtesy of Scenarios USA, *www.scenariosusa.org*.

Fortunately, there is a copy of the DVD screener that was being sent out. Although the video is 16:9 resolution, it was letterboxed and turned into 4:3 when the DVD was authored. Starting with that and using HandBrake (see Chapter 2 for more on HandBrake), let's compress an MPEG-4 clip directly from DVD:

1. Insert your DVD. If your DVD player starts up automatically, quit it.

2. Launch HandBrake (I'm using version 0.9.1—different versions will offer slightly different workflows).

3. As the interface loads, a window will automatically appear for you to select your source content. Select the DVD volume, and click Open (**Figure 9.4**).

Figure 9.4 Selecting a DVD volume to rip in HandBrake.

NOTE Since there is only one movie clip on here and we need the whole thing, there is no need to change anything. However, if you needed a specific part of a movie, you could select that here.

4. HandBrake will quickly scan your DVD to identify any titles and chapters that may exist. Titles would be separate movies on the DVD; chapters are the different markers within a title.

5. In the File window, enter a name for the compressed video you are creating. If desired, click the Browse button and select a new save location. (**Figure 9.5**).

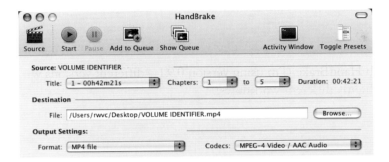

Figure 9.5 Choosing a destination file path for your ripped DVD content in HandBrake.

NOTE By default, HandBrake selects the desktop and the name of the DVD volume. If this is acceptable, you can skip step 5.

6. Make sure MP4 file is selected in Format and AVC/H.264 Video / AAC Audio is selected in the Codecs menu (**Figure 9.6**).

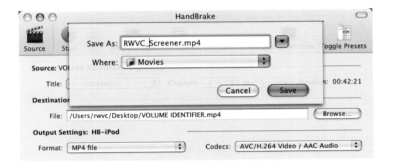

Figure 9.6 Selecting MP4 for the output format.

7. Keep the frame rate the same as the source (29.97), and select the x.264 (h.264 Main) encoder.

8. Set Average bit rate to 1500 kbps, and select the 2-pass encoding check box (**Figure 9.7**).

NOTE I'm choosing 1500 Kbps because this video doesn't have a lot of high-motion content. If there were more action sequences, I'd bump it up to as much as 2500 Kbps to compensate for the action.

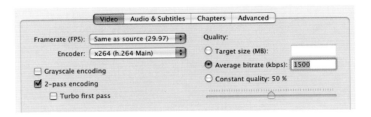

Figure 9.7 Setting our compression and encoding parameters.

9. Now click the Picture Settings button (shown earlier in Figure 9.4), and on the screen that comes up, choose none from the Anamorphic pop-up menu.

10. Since the source video is letterboxed, click Custom in the Crop section, and use the up and down arrows to create the following crop: Top 60, Bottom 62, Right 8, Left 0. You will see the image update in real time as you crop. Choose Slow in the Deinterlace pop-up menu and Weak from the options in Denoise. Click Close (**Figure 9.8**).

Figure 9.8 Because we're working with letterboxed video, we need to do a custom crop.

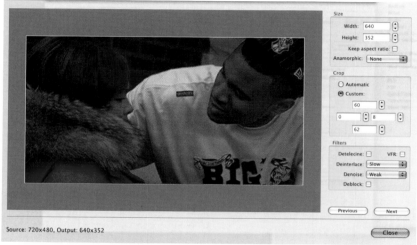

TIP Image settings are going to vary from video to video. At a minimum, you should deinterlace, but beyond that you could leave this untouched to avoid stepping on a land mine.

11. Now select the Audio & Subtitles tab (**Figure 9.9**). Change Sample rate (khz) to 48, and change Bitrate (kbps) to 160. Choose Stereo in the Track 1 Mix menu.

Figure 9.9 Setting audio parameters for our output file.

12. Select the Advanced tab. Technically you don't have to do anything here at all; however, if you want to tweak the H.264 encoder to try to get the best quality out of your video (even if it takes longer to encode), then try one of the following:

- Set the encoding parameters as I have in **Figure 9.10**.

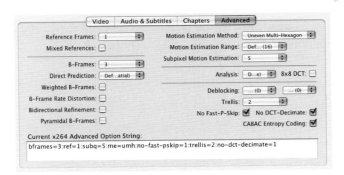

Figure 9.10 Here's where we tweak advanced encoding parameters, as shown, to optimize our encode.

- In the Current x264 Advanced Option String, type the following line (**Figure 9.11**):

```
keyint=300:keyint-min=30:bframes=6:ref=3:mixed-refs=1:
subq=5:me=umh: no-fast-pskip=1:trellis=0:no-dct-decimate=1:
vbv-maxrate=4900:vbv-bufsize=3000
```

Current x264 Advanced Option String:
```
keyint=300:keyint-min=30:bframes=6:ref=3:mixed-refs=1:subq=5:me=umh:
no-fast-pskip=1:trellis=0:no-dct-decimate=1:vbv-maxrate=4900:vbv-bufsize=3000
```

Figure 9.11 Current x264 Advanced Option String setting.

NOTE It is not necessary to set both of these advanced options—set only one. Both will apply advanced parameters to your encode. The Current x264 Advanced Option String setting applies some additional parameters not accessible through the GUI. If you're comfortable going this route, do so; otherwise, stick with the setting accessible in the GUI.

13. Click the Start icon in the menu bar to begin encoding your movie. A progress bar will appear at the bottom of the HandBrake interface (**Figure 9.12**) identifying what pass of the encode you are on, how many frames per second are being encoded, and an estimated time to completion.

Figure 9.12 This progress bar shows the status of your encode.

Encoding: task 1 of 2, 3.52 % (58.54 fps, avg 64.33 fps, ETA 00h04m30s)   1 pass in the queue

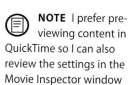

NOTE I prefer pre-viewing content in QuickTime so I can also review the settings in the Movie Inspector window (Command+I).

14. When the encode completes (HandBrake has a peculiar alert), you are ready to preview your clip. Verify that the clip plays in either iTunes or QuickTime.

15. Once it is loaded in an iTunes account synchronizing with Apple TV, the encoded file should sync automatically to the device and play back both on the computer and on Apple TV (**Figure 9.13**).

Figure 9.13 Syncing your movie for playback on your Mac and Apple TV.

Syncing "Beach's Shiny Toy"
Copying 1 of 1: RWVC_Screener

TIP Some would suggest increasing the resolution of the video to match the maximum that Apple TV supports, but remember, if you start with a lower-resolution source like SD DVD, then there is no benefit to adding pixels. It will just end up being a larger file size, not a better-looking video. Instead, just set your crop and make it the biggest resolution that fits the source specs. Then rely on the Apple TV to scale the video up appropriately.

Standard-Definition Video for Xbox

As discussed earlier in this chapter, Xbox will stream a variety of file formats and resolutions. Technically, since you can play so many file types, you could get away without optimizing your content for Xbox specifically. However, if it's your primary delivery platform, you might as well optimize your settings to provide the best possible playback experience. The files you create will have the added benefit of playing back quite nicely on computers as well, so the same files will work very well as portable content on a laptop (something I do often when traveling to avoid carrying a bunch of DVDs).

This recipe is meant to create SD-quality content for the Xbox, using the VC-1 codec (Advanced profile) and Expression Encoder. Our source material is anamorphic DV-NTSC video; therefore, as part of the settings, we'll need to adjust the resolution appropriately. The individual data rates and image settings could be tweaked based on your particular content.

1. To begin, click the Import button in the Media Content area of the Expression interface. Select the video intended for compression. Click OK to add the clip to Expression's interface (**Figure 9.14**).

Figure 9.14 Importing your clip into Expression.

2. Starting with the Video profile (**Figure 9.15**, top), in the Frame rate pop-up menu, select Source. Set the keyframe interval to 5 seconds, the profile to VC-1 Advanced Profile, and the mode to VBR peak constrained. Set the average bit rate to 1800 Kbps, the peak to 2500 Kbps, and the peak buffer to 5 seconds. Finally, set the resolution to 640 by 360.

3. On the Audio tab (**Figure 9.15**, bottom), deselect the Default Profile check box, and click the down arrow to expand the advanced audio settings options. Set Bitrate to 160 Kbps, Sample Rate to 44 kHz (if this is what your audio was recorded and edited at—otherwise select the appropriate rate), and Channels to Stereo.

Figure 9.15 Begin setting parameters in the Profile window.

4. In the Video Profile window (**Figure 9.16**), set Select Profile to the video size (640 by 360) you selected in step 2. Set Resize Mode to Stretch. From the Video Aspect pop-up, select Square Pixels. The aspect ratio should update to 16:9 automatically.

Figure 9.16 Choosing Video Profile settings.

5. Check the preview. Click the A/B split preview button to view a sample of the encoded video (**Figure 9.17**). This may take a few seconds to update, depending on your system.

Figure 9.17 A/B preview shows you the video before and after the encode.

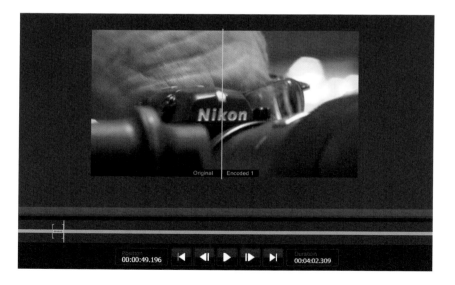

6. Click Encode to submit the video to the encoder. An audio and video progress bar will appear in the Media Content window (**Figure 9.18**).

Figure 9.18 Encoding in progress.

7. Upon completion, you can find the file on your desktop in a folder with a name like "ABEACH-LT 2-04-2008 12.43.17 PM," meaning "Computer Name – DATE – Time of batch encode." In the operating system, open this folder, and you will see the finished encode.

8. If you're satisfied with the results, transfer the file to the PC or Mac being used to share media with Xbox.

> **NOTE** Though it may seem like a PC-only thing, streaming video to Xbox 360 works on both the Mac and Windows platforms. Mac users need to purchase a small plug-in called Connect360 by Nullriver Software ($20 MSRP) to share their iTunes and iPhoto libraries with the TV via a networked Xbox 360. Connect360 supports WMV and VC-1 codecs, as well as audio and still images. Connect360 will even transcode incompatible formats to make them work.

Conclusion

Ironically, the television may see the most interesting technology changes over the next few years. We are in the very early days of a new wave of set-top boxes that mix traditional television transmission with IP video. As it becomes more commonplace, amateur productions are going to suddenly appear right along side your primetime schedule.

While the technology may grow and change, the fundamental aspect of creating video for it will probably remain similar to what I've laid out here. We will begin to focus more on making it easier for the end user to connect to the new distribution options. Just like podcasters had to learn new publishing techniques, content creators interested in hitting the set-top box will find themselves learning new ways to distribute their video as the technology changes.

Interview with a Compressionist

Gigi Cohen

Name: Andy Beach

Location: Raleigh, NC

Title/role: Director of Product Management and Video
Encoding Geek (the geek title is only honorary)

Company: Inlet Technologies

URL: *www.inlethd.com*

How did you get involved in video compression?

I was an AVID video editor and started getting hired for gigs more for my ability to do something other than go to tape with the project. I finally got hired in 2000 specifically to do compression by a design company in London and things just kind of snowballed from there.

What was your biggest project?

At my previous job (Magnet Media Films), I decided to update their archive by reencoding all six years of their library from the original Final Cut Pro sequences (which we still had). I exported uncompressed masters that went on a RAID 5 NAS; then I transcoded a fresh version in a variety of formats, mostly H.264 and Flash VP6, but some of the titles also got transcoded to VC-1. It was a total of 93 hours of source content, and after I finished the entire project, I had approximately 2.75 TB of encoded files! The whole process took about two months working on it in downtime and setting up encodes over weekends and evenings, but the hardest part of the whole job was getting some of the very old sequences (some from FCP 1.2) to relink with their media.

What was your favorite project?

As you can imagine, the one I just mentioned wasn't my favorite, just the biggest I've done in quite a while. My favorite is a toss-up. When I was living in the UK, I used to help stream live concerts regularly in 2000 from a venue in London. The first night I showed up, I was surprised to meet the manager who had been the band manager for the Pogues! Some of the shows were lame, but it was the first time I'd been involved with a multi-camera, multiformat, multi–bit rate, live streaming event.

The other favorite project (though it drove me nuts at the time) was working with a team at my old company to create a reusable interactive QuickTime skin for housing an archive of many videos. It combined a Flash interface and a Web back end to make it easy to upload and display a collection of videos in an organized way. A postproduction company used it as their Web site for a few years, and we had several internal versions we used, but it never caught on because at the time QuickTime just didn't have a large enough market share (this was 2002–2004).

What's your format of choice?

I guess I'd say H.264 meant for playback on multiple devices—Apple TV, iPod, PSP, and so on. I have a Pocket PC phone now as well, so I've been playing a lot with VC-1 Simple profile stuff.

What does your average workday look like?

I don't encode day to day anymore. I only consult on special projects and perform tests for the company I now work for. At least once a week, however, I encode at least a small batch of clips for work. I travel more than I used to, so I have been picking up seasons of TV shows I never watched and using HandBrake to get them on my iPod for convenient airplane watching.

What does your encoding hardware look like?

I have a 2.33 GHz MacBook Pro with 2 GB of RAM running Compressor, Episode Pro, HandBrake, and VisualHub. I have approximately 1.5 TB of storage split into three FireWire drives that acts as backup and workspace. I have a MiniDV and DVCAM camera at home but rarely capture from tape. When I do, I use Final Cut Pro.

I also have an HP xw8400 tower running Windows XP that has 2 GB of RAM and an internal 2 TB RAID. This system is primarily running Fathom (my company's software), but I also have Adobe Media Encoder on there as well. This is an eight-core machine, so it's got some serious encoding power! This system also has a capture card, so I can use it to do captures as well in Fathom (DVCAM, MiniDV, BetaSP, DigiBeta, DVCPRO HD, and D5 decks at work).

What's your encoding software of choice?

Cleaner was the tool of choice, but the third time it got sold, I promised myself I'd never let my heart get broken again. I'm agnostic now and will use just about anything to encode. On the Mac, I like Episode Pro and VisualHub the most. On the PC I like Fathom the most, but I'm totally biased on that one. When I see something I don't like, I just log it as a bug and ask someone to fix it.

What role does compression play in your work?

Compression is a big part of my life. It used to just be the thing I did after the project, but for the past seven years at least, it has been the primary reason I was involved in most of my projects.

What surprises you most about video compression today?

I am occasionally still surprised by the speed of the machines and the amount of encoding we can accomplish today. I can't imagine trying to do some of the work we used to do with G3s and G4s. And this isn't directly related to compression, but the size and price of hard drives still amaze me too. I have easily 3 TB of storage around my house in various places, and I regularly carry a 250 GB drive with me. My first hard drive for editing was a 2 GB SCSI for AVR17 work, and it cost me $450!

INDEX